THE GEORGE GUND FOUNDATION
IMPRINT IN AFRICAN AMERICAN STUDIES

The George Gund Foundation has endowed
this imprint to advance understanding of
the history, culture, and current issues
of African Americans.

The publisher gratefully acknowledges the generous support of the African American Studies Endowment Fund of the University of California Press Foundation, which was established by a major gift from the George Gund Foundation.

Black Elephants in the Room

Jorden,
Thanks for
supporting the
book!

Best,
Corey

Black Elephants in the Room

The Unexpected Politics of African American Republicans

Corey D. Fields

UNIVERSITY OF CALIFORNIA PRESS

University of California Press, one of the most distinguished university presses in the United States, enriches
lives around the world by advancing scholarship in the
humanities, social sciences, and natural sciences. Its
activities are supported by the UC Press Foundation and
by philanthropic contributions from individuals and
institutions. For more information, visit www.ucpress.edu.

University of California Press
Oakland, California

Library of Congress Cataloging-in-Publication Data

Names: Fields, Corey, author.
Title: Black elephants in the room : the unexpected
    politics of African American Republicans / Corey
    D. Fields.
Description: Oakland, California : University of
    California Press, [2016] | Includes bibliographical
    references and index.
Identifiers: LCCN 2016017310 (print) | LCCN 2016018317
    (ebook) | ISBN 9780520291898 (cloth : alk. paper) | ISBN
    9780520291904 (pbk. : alk. paper) | ISBN 9780520965508
    (ebook)
Subjects: LCSH: Republican Party (U.S. : 1854–)—
    Membership. | African Americans—Political
    activity—United States. | African Americans—
    Politics and government—21st century. | Identity
    politics—United States. | Allegiance—United States.
Classification: LCC JK2356 .F54 2016 (print) | LCC JK2356
    (ebook) | DDC 324.2734089/96073—dc23
LC record available at https://lccn.loc.gov/2016017310

Manufactured in the United States of America

25 24 23 22 21 20 19 18 17 16
10 9 8 7 6 5 4 3 2 1

CONTENTS

ACKNOWLEDGMENTS

I am indebted to the African American Republicans who agreed to participate in this study. This research was possible only because they allowed me into their lives and organizations. For many of them, that required a great deal of courage and did not come without risk. I appreciate their openness and honesty, and I am grateful they trusted me with their stories.

I began this project as a graduate student in the Northwestern University sociology department and completed the book while an assistant professor at Stanford University. Each institution has provided invaluable support, without which I would not have been able to complete this research. There are too many people to thank by name, but I appreciate the kindness and generosity of spirit that is the cornerstone of the intellectual communities in both institutions.

I have to thank Wendy Espeland for being a great mentor, adviser, colleague, and friend. This achievement would not have been possible without her help. Gary Alan Fine taught me the value of a quick mind, an observant eye, and thick skin. Together, they showed me that sometimes your toughest critics could also be your loudest cheerleaders. Wendy Griswold, Monica Prasad, and Reuel Rogers have provided invaluable feedback throughout the process of collecting data, data analysis, and writing. You all are my models for the kind of scholar I hope to become.

While at Northwestern, I not only met great scholars but also made great friends. Many people there demonstrated both sets of skills in providing feedback at various points throughout this project. I benefited greatly from the intelligence and insight of a large group of people: Elisabeth Anderson, Jean Beaman, Nicola Beisel, Ellen Berrey, Kieran Bezila, Japonica Brown-Saracino, Bruce Carruthers, Michaela DeSoucey, Kerry Dobransky, Gabrielle Ferrales, Jeremy Freese, Daniel Galvin, Murielle Harris, Steve Hoffmann, Marcus Hunter, Nina Johnson, Terence McDonnell, Mary Pattillo, Zandria Robinson, Brian Sargent, Heather Schoenfeld, Emily Shafer, Art Stinchcombe, Berit Vannebo, Celeste Watkins, and Harvey Young. The Culture Workshop and Ethnography Workshop at Northwestern helped incubate the project when it was in its infancy. The members of both workshops helped shape the final project in ways that made it better.

Since I arrived at Stanford, I have been welcomed into a vibrant intellectual community. My colleagues in the sociology department and at the Center for the Comparative Study of Race and Ethnicity provided enriching environments that grounded me as I refined the analysis and wrote this book. Whether through reading groups, hallway conversations, or formal presentations, I received valuable feedback from H. Samy Alim, Jennifer Brody, Al Camarillo, Lauren Davenport, Duana Fullwiley, Amir Goldberg, David Grusky, MarYam Hamedani, Allyson Hobbes, Tomás Jiménez, Ana Raquel Minian, Susan Olzak, Paolo Parigi, Vaughn Rasberry, Aliya Saperstein, Gary

Segura, C. Matthew Snipp, Sara Soule, Jesper Sørenson, Mitchell Stevens, Cristobal Young, and Patricia Young. The Institute for Research in the Social Sciences at Stanford hosted a manuscript workshop that was critical in rethinking important elements of this book. Discussions of this work (and all the other research presentations) at the Migration, Ethnicity, Race, and Nation Workshop in the Stanford sociology department never failed to make me think about this project in new and creative ways.

I also had the great fortune of having scholars from outside my home institutions comment on this research. I appreciate the thoughtful feedback provided by Amy Binder, Patrick J. Egan, Tyrone Forman, Cybelle Fox, Karen Trapenberg Frick, Alice Goffman, Arlie Russell Hochschild, Jennifer Johnson, Monica McDermott, Chris Parker, Vensa Rodic, Larry Rosenthal, Laura Stoker, and Amy Wilkins. Thanks, as well, to all the panelists and audience members who listened to parts of this work at conferences, seminars, and workshops over the years. Their comments, questions, and suggestions have improved this project in ways they probably could not have imagined.

Naomi Schneider at the University of California Press gave me the opportunity to turn a bunch of quirky ideas about an even quirkier group into a real book. Her insight was matched only by her patience. This book is better for having landed in her capable hands. I also owe a debt of gratitude to Letta Page. She slayed, and the book is better as a result. I would also like to thank the production staff at the press for all their help and diligence in getting the book published.

Michelle Jackson read (and improved) every version of this manuscript. She went above and beyond the call of duty and I'll be forever grateful. Writing this book would have been infinitely more difficult and lonely without her in the office next door. Koji Chavez and Marion Coddou came through with invaluable research assistance and mad trivia skills. I can only hope that I have been as helpful to all three of them as they were to me.

There were many people from my non-academic life who offered support and encouragement that sustained me throughout completing this project. The Wednesday Night Crew—Ashleigh, Annie, Carrie, Kate, and Nancy—kept me sane for years. Who knew pizza and reality television could be so critical to the development of sociological thinking? I am embarrassed to think about the number of sociology conversations Mark Gurley, Matthew Herrmann, Kim Kline, and Tezza Yujuico were forced to endure. Their patience in listening and responding infused this project with a measure of much-needed common sense. Brian Piech, Ed Gutierrez, Laura Deanovic, Paul Wade, and all my friends from 3rd Street kept me healthy and sane as I finished the book. Chrissy Stimmel has been a caring friend with words of wisdom that kept me grounded throughout this process.

I owe a special thanks to William Loney for the unyielding support and encouragement that pushed me over the finish line. Even when I was pretending like I didn't need it, it sustained me. Finally, for all their love and support, I would like to thank my family, particularly my mom, Rosalind Hill, and my sister, Ashley Eddins. You never stopped believing in me, and more importantly you wouldn't let me stop believing in myself. I could not ask for a more supportive and giving family. Without you, none of this would be possible. This book is dedicated to you.

Introduction

On March 4, 2016, in a speech at the Conservative Political Action Conference (CPAC), Dr. Ben Carson announced that he was suspending his presidential campaign. Only the most die-hard supporters of the former neurosurgeon could be surprised by the announcement. At the start of the campaign, he was polling among the top candidates, but as the race progressed, Carson saw his poll numbers drop precipitously. Lackluster debate performances and a poorly managed campaign were frequently cited as explanations for the campaign's failure. His qualifications to be president of the United States were questionable from the beginning, and his skills on the campaign trail failed to convince Republican primary voters or observers in the media that he was ready for prime time.

By the time Carson announced his decision to suspend his campaign, he had plenty of experience with the scrutiny that comes when you're in the spotlight. As a candidate, Carson never really gained traction with any particular policy agenda, and his campaign seemed adrift almost from the start. Few political analysts took his campaign seriously, and there was little in his life that was reserved from derision. He was mercilessly mocked throughout the campaign. Everything, it seemed—from his reserved demeanor to discrepancies about his childhood experiences—could become fodder for a biting blog post or a mean-spirited tweet. When a photo of a painting from his home—a portrait that depicted Carson sitting with an image of a black Jesus looking over his shoulder—was published as part of a profile in *The Guardian*, it was clear that his campaign had gone off the rails.[1] He could have survived the jokes if he were winning. But he was not winning. Carson failed to win any of the Republican primaries. He ended up with a fate similar to that of Herman Cain, the black Republican presidential candidate from the 2012 election cycle. Both initially generated a lot of media attention, but dramatically faded away as the primary ran its course. There was a lot of attention but not much to show for it.[2]

Carson has come to represent the almost comical status of contemporary African American Republicans.[3] However, before his political campaign, he was far from a laughingstock. In fact, he was something of a mythical figure among some African Americans. His hardscrabble upbringing in Detroit and later achievements as a pediatric neurosurgeon at Johns Hopkins Hospital had been presented in a television movie, and his political rise shared a similarly dramatic flair. Carson's rise on the Republican scene did not come out of nowhere. He had a long, if quiet, presence within politically conservative circles. He was even awarded the Presidential Medal of Freedom by George W. Bush. Thanks to an appearance at a National Prayer Breakfast, Carson went from low profile to conservative darling. He delivered a scathing speech that decried the moral decay and fiscal irresponsibility he thought were undermining the country and predicted that the United States would fall like the Roman Empire: "If you don't think that can happen to America, you get out your books and you start reading." Given that Barack Obama was also present at the breakfast, many read Carson's speech as an attack on the Obama presidency. Conservatives, particularly religious conservatives, soon rallied around Carson. The image of the quiet doctor taking on the Washington establishment resonated with the outsider rhetoric that has, of late, come to dominate Republican politics.

Ben Carson may have been 2016's black Republican of the moment, but he represents a broader insurgence by African American Republicans. The past decade has seen African American Republicans enjoying their highest profile since the Reconstruction era. In addition to the high-profile presidential campaigns of Cain and Carson, black Republicans have been elected or appointed to important positions that bring them ever closer to the center of power in U.S. politics. Condoleezza Rice and Colin Powell, both Republicans, each served as secretary of state in the administration of George W. Bush. Michael Steele was the chairman of the Republican National Committee from 2009 to 2011. African American Republicans have also made a splash in the legislative arena. The midterm elections in November 2010 saw a record number of black Republican congressional candidates.[4] Thirty-two made bids for office, and fourteen won their primaries. Only two, Allen West of Florida and Tim Scott of South Carolina, won, but they became the first African American Republicans in Congress since 2003. Scott is now one of two African Americans serving in the Senate, the first of this "rare breed" of black Republican senator since Edward Brooke in 1974. (Democrat Cory Booker from New Jersey is the other current African American senator.) Scott was one of three African

American Republicans elected to Congress in 2014, joining Mia Love and William Hurd. Like Clarence Thomas before them, this current group of black Republicans has captured the public imagination. African American Republicans have even broken beyond politics and infiltrated the world of rap music with the release of the Nas and Jay-Z single "Black Republican."

In a political climate where the Republican Party is not considered a hotbed of racial tolerance, this most recent crop of African American Republicans are often judged by how they respond to questions about race. The most recent Republican primary offers a nice illustration of this. Surprise front-runner Donald Trump brought all the subtlety and nuance we've come to associate with reality TV stars. Trump's campaign was blunt and direct, bursting with his characteristic bravado. In a pattern that would hold up throughout his campaign, Trump started his run with a controversy grounded in issues of race and racism. His campaign announcement was accompanied by claims that Mexican immigrants are "bringing drugs, they're bringing crime. They're rapists and some, I assume, are good people, but I speak to border guards and they're telling us what we're getting." Trump also called for the building of a wall between the United States and Mexico. Trump's inflamed rhetoric struck a chord with Republican primary voters, bringing to the foreground sentiments within the GOP that the party establishment usually attempts to downplay. Rather than denounce Trump, the other candidates downplayed many of his comments, or rushed to align themselves with his position. The circus-like atmosphere would have been comical if not for the racist nature of much of the campaigning. Even President Obama remarked on the unusual tone of the Republican primary campaign, telling journalists that "I was going to call it a carnival atmosphere, but that implies fun."

The inflamed rhetoric around immigration occurred as the country was also grappling with a series of police shootings of black men, and the corresponding protests. Though the Black Lives Matter movement has its origins in the social media response to the shooting death of Trayvon Martin, it became national news when protests developed in response to police shootings in 2014. By the time of the 2016 campaign, related activists were publicly challenging political candidates to state their positions vis-à-vis issues of racial profiling, police brutality, and inequality in the criminal justice system. Though the movement is decentralized, without any formal organizational structure, demonstrations attached to Black Lives Matter pushed issues of racial inequality and race relations more generally into the public discourse.

Against this backdrop, it was reasonable to think that the one black candidate in the presidential race might have something to say about issues of race and racism. Indeed, during the Republican Party's primary debates, Ben Carson was asked about racial divisions in the United States:

MEGYN KELLY: Dr. Carson, a question to you about God and his role, but also, one of the issues that the public was very interested in, and we touched on it earlier, is race relations in -this country, and how divided we seem right now. And what, if anything, you can do—you would do as the next president to help heal that divide.

CARSON: Well, I think the bully pulpit is a wonderful place to start healing that divide. You know, we have the purveyors of hatred who take every single incident between people of two races and try to make a race war out of it, and drive wedges into people. And this does not need to be done .... What we need to think about instead—you know, I was asked by an NPR reporter once, why don't I talk about race that often. I said it's because I'm a neurosurgeon. And she thought that was a strange response. And I said, you see, when I take someone to the operating room, I'm actually operating on the thing that makes them who they are. The skin doesn't make them who they are. The hair doesn't make them who they are. And it's time for us to move beyond that. Because our strength as a nation comes in our unity. We are the United States of America, not the divided states. And those who want to divide us are trying to divide us, and we shouldn't let them do it.

His response seemed calculated to appeal to racial conservatives. Carson's carefully crafted answer not only sidestepped claims about racial inequality, but positioned *conversations* about racial difference—not racial difference itself—as the problem. All that was missing from the response was concern about "black-on-black crime." Otherwise, Carson's comments hit all the key talking points from the hostile response conservative politicians had made regarding Black Lives Matter protests. Accordingly, the answer was praised in conservative news outlets. David French from *The National Review* wrote, "Here was one of the world's most brilliant doctors calling on his experience to tell a story that was fundamentally about the content of our character rather than the color of our skin." Carson's response was said to "enhance the conservative 'brand'" and "speak words of truth and virtue."[5]

Two consistent assumptions are present in this reaction and shape much of our thinking about African American Republicans like Carson: normally, racial identity motivates African American political behavior, and strong black identity is incompatible with Republican partisanship. Consequently, Carson is either positioned as a "brave" politician for pushing against expectation, or he is critiqued as a racial sellout. As the only serious black candidate in the race, Carson was thrust, perhaps unwillingly, into speaking to issues of racial division.[6] Throughout the course of his campaign, Carson's unwillingness to diverge from this color-blind narrative provided material for innumerable op-eds, Internet rants, and late-night monologues about what his candidacy symbolized about race and politics. However, Carson is but the latest black Republican to offer a message of color blindness on a public stage. Accounts of African American Republicans—both positive and negative—frequently position them as lacking racial identity or, at the very least, as willing to ignore their racial identity in service to partisan beliefs.[7] These assumptions taint African American Republicans whether they are famous or not.

This book challenges the image of African American Republicans as racial sellouts. Instead, I argue that some African American Republicans are deeply committed to black identity. Drawing on rich ethnographic observation and vivid first-person accounts of black Republican activists, I show the different ways black identity structures individuals' membership in the Republican Party. Moving past the talking points and outrageous statements associated with the African American Republicans we read about in the newspaper, this book exposes everyday people working to reconcile their commitment to black identity with their belief in Republican principles—a task routinely assumed impossible. Although the color-blind narrative invoked by politicians like Carson is present among the activists I studied, it exists alongside a narrative that places black identity at the center of black Republicans' politics. Indeed, tension between the race-blind and race-conscious approaches is the defining feature of African American Republican politics. Though they exist on the margins, the political machinations of black Republicans illustrate the importance of understanding both the meanings African Americans attach to racial identity and the political contexts in which those meanings are developed and expressed.

As I spent time with African American Republican activists, it became clear that it was not particularly useful to question whether or not they *have* black identity. Of course they do. Many rely on their black racial identity when accounting for their conservative beliefs and Republican partisanship. Participation in the GOP works to highlight the black identity of African American Republicans and, behind closed doors, these activists are often engaged in heated debates about what is "best for black people" and the appropriate way to conceptualize Republican approaches as the solution to the challenges that black people face in the post–civil rights era. Because considerations of black Republicans are obsessed with the legitimacy or authenticity of their blackness, less attention is given to how their racial identity informs the expression and reception of their Republican partisanship. This means that we treat African American Republicans as a monolithic group, which is unfortunate, because there are differences among them that are theoretically and empirically interesting. Throughout this book, I show how various, sometimes conflicting, sets of ideas, values, and commitments around black racial identity fundamentally structure the experiences of blacks in the Republican Party.

The experience of being African American and Republican unfolds within a political party that is unarguably dominated by whites. Consequently, African American Republicans must manage blackness in a predominantly white context. Their strategies for linking blackness with their partisanship raise questions about taken-for-granted assumptions regarding racial identity and black people's political behavior. How does racial identity get linked to particular political behaviors? How do political actors work to make political behaviors count as "black politics"? Heated rhetoric and endless talking points from all corners of the political realm obscure serious exploration of these questions. And that, quite simply, is the aim of this book: to illustrate how racial identity animates the political behavior and experiences of African Americans within the Republican Party.

Once black Republicans become famous, they all start to look alike. I expand on this idea throughout the book, but this reality necessitates paying attention to lesser-known black Republicans. So, rather than concentrate on the high-profile black Republicans who have already achieved a place of prominence within the GOP, my research details the more prosaic experiences of being black and Republican. The unknown activists I studied show how individuals manage an experience commonly considered oxymoronic, and without media attention or guaranteed party support. When you're not running for president, being black and Republican can mean rejection by friends and family and struggles for acceptance among fellow party members. In talking to nonelite African American Republican activists across multiple political contexts, differences in the beliefs, rhetoric, and political strategies emerge. Their understandings of how being black informs identity and experience diverge, and this divergence has consequences for how each connects their race and their politics. Observing the efforts of these activists, it becomes clear that the work of aligning black identity with Republican partisanship is not easy and that not all African American Republicans go about it in the same way. Enumerating those differences helps show how they are ultimately filtered out by selection into the Republican elite. More broadly, the case of African American Republicans shows the importance of attending to the variation in how black people understand their racial identity. The experiences of African American Republicans force consideration of the different ways that black people attach meaning to their racial identity and how those meanings inform political behavior.

THE UNEXPECTED POLITICS OF AFRICAN AMERICAN REPUBLICANS

Roland Scott[8] has been a Republican all his life—it never occurred to him to be anything else. He remembers childhood door-to-door campaigning with his mother for Eisenhower, even as he lived in a segregated neighborhood where Republicanism was in steep decline. In this regard, Roland's neighbors were like most blacks in the country. Still, the idea of a black family going door-to-door to campaign for a Republican president did not draw any particular notice. Roland recalls, "It wasn't strange like it is now. We were Republican, but it's not like anyone in the neighborhood had a problem with us." Roland speaks fondly: "It was a good place to grow up," and "people worked hard and took care of their families." But his attitude is only partly nostalgic. He sees similar behaviors in his neighbors today, even though he now lives far from where he grew up. "It's still the same way in the area I live in now. People working hard, trying to do the best for their families. It's harder today because everything is so expensive and stuff. But black folks still working hard and trying to get ahead." In general, Roland takes a very positive view toward "black folks." He speaks of a community guided by a strong work ethic and family values—guiding values that, he believes, make blacks a natural fit for the Republican Party. He's not blind to the problems of the black community, but he says that "we can't let a few bad apples spoil the bunch." The promotion of business and family, things Roland sees as central to the Republican agenda, are central to success for the black community, too. The fact that people are now surprised by his party affiliation is, in turn, a surprise to him.

Inez Smith is also unknown to most political observers, but she has a different perspective. She, too, grew up in a close-knit black neighborhood and speaks fondly of the days "when everybody in the neighborhood looked out for one another. You could be out any time of day or night and feel safe. And if you were acting up, you'd get one whooping from your neighbor and then another one from your momma when you got home!" Inez, however, is much less sanguine about the current state of the black community. She sees a community in despair and believes the values that once made the community strong are in short supply today. "It breaks my heart to see what is happening in the black community," Inez laments. "Just turn on the TV or read a newspaper. Crime. Drugs. Teen pregnancy. And all the while so-called black 'leaders' all have their hands out calling on the government to give black people something. What happened to the days when black people wanted to earn what we got?" Inez did not grow up Republican. She describes her family as "Democrats. Just like everybody else." Yet for her, it's the Republican Party that offers blacks a chance to embrace the moral order of the community she remembers. According to Inez, "Black people have fallen, and got to get back up by changing themselves and nobody can do that for them."

Despite their shared political obscurity, Roland and Inez bring their racial and political identities together in conflicting ways. Roland sees conservative social policy as amplifying values inherent to the black community; Inez sees Republican policy as an opportunity to save the black community from itself. Roland and Inez also report very different experiences within the Republican Party. Both are active members of their state party associations, and each has been engaged in work to encourage more African American participation within the GOP. Yet their different approaches to linking blackness and conservatism affect their ability to work with each other and with their white Republican counterparts. Inez finds that white Republicans embrace her perspective and encourage her efforts to reform the black community through the spread of Republican principles. Roland, in contrast, complains that he is marginalized by white Republicans uninterested in hearing how the party needs to reform itself to capitalize on the latent conservatism he sees untapped in the black community.

Roland and Inez are pretty far removed from public notice. They are both African American and both identify as politically conservative Republicans, but they are not what comes to mind when you hear about black Republicans. They are not full-time politicians. Their political engagement happens in between work and family obligations. But compared to more (in)famous African American Republicans, they, perhaps, provide more insight into the real experience of being black within the Republican Party. The African American Republicans who win congressional elections, dot the landscape of cable news, and advise presidents are anomalies. In reality, very few are famous. They do not run for office. They are not providing television commentary on the Republican primaries. Instead, like most voters of all stripes, these two go about their politics in relative obscurity. They are certainly politically engaged, but they—like most of the other activists I met doing this research—are pretty regular. And that itself is a surprise.

No one expects a "regular" black person to be Republican, and with good reason. Since the 1930s, African Americans have been withdrawing their support from the Republican Party. Figure 1 graphs black support for the party since 1936, and the decline is clear (in chapter 1 we'll revisit this evolution of black partisanship in greater detail). In the 2012 presidential election, only about 5 percent of blacks cast votes for the Republican candidate, Mitt Romney.[9] That was consistent with the election in 2008. Single-digit percentages are not that uncommon. The Republican presidential nominee has not garnered more than 10 percent of the black vote since 1976.

Public opinion surveys generally find about 7–10 percent of blacks identifying themselves as Republicans. Even though significant numbers of African Americans would define their political ideology as conservative or express conservative social values, that conservatism rarely translates into Republican partisanship. As a consequence, very few blacks are Republicans. The inverse is also true: very few Republicans are black. Some estimates put the number as low as 2 percent.[10] Thus, African American Republicans are minorities within both the black and the Republican communities.

Today, the idea of a black Republican is not just anachronistic, it's oxymoronic. However, these numbers mark a total reversal of fortunes. At the Republican Party's inception, black voters were an important aspect of their electoral coalition. Furthermore, abolition provided a moral center to the Republican Party. Given the realities of contemporary party demographics, it seems hard to believe that the founders of the Republican Party were keen on including blacks in their voter coalition. Currently, the party makes little room for the moderating, centrist conservatism that made it more hospitable to African American voters.[11]

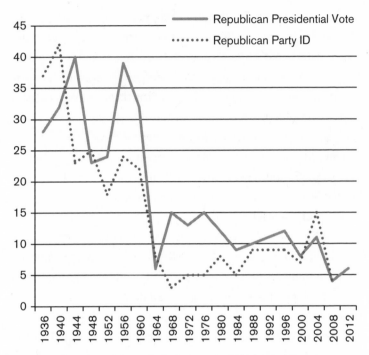

Figure 1. Black Republican presidential vote and black Republican party identification.

sources: *Blacks & the 2012 Republican Convention,* Joint Center for Political and Economic Studies, citing 1936–56 data from Everett Carll Ladd, Jr., and Charles D. Hadley, *Transformations of the American Party System;* 1960–80 partisan identification data from Paul R. Abramson, John H. Aldrich, and David W. Rohde, *Change and Continuity in the 1984 Elections;* 1960–80 presidential preference data from Gallup Opinion Index 1980; 1984 presidential preference data from CBS/New York Times exit poll, November 1986; 1988 presidential preference data from ABC News/Capital Cities; 1988 party identification data from JCPES Gallup survey; 1992 party identification data from Home Box Office (HBO)/Joint Center Survey; 1992 presidential preference data from Voter Research and Surveys; 1996 vote data from Voter News Service; 1996 party identification data from 1996 JCPES National Opinion Poll; 2000 vote data from Voter News Service; 2000 party identification data from 2000 JCPES National Opinion Poll; 2004 vote data from Edison/Mitofsky National Exit Poll; 2004 party identification data from 2004 JCPES National Opinion Poll; 2008 voter data from National Exit Poll; 2008 party identification data from 2008 JCPES National Opinion Poll; 2012 presidential preference data from CNN.

So, despite some high-profile exceptions, African American Republicans are few and far between. Indeed, one could argue that the attention famous black Republicans garner is disproportionate to their numbers. However, people like Roland and Inez are interesting, in part, because of the perception that they are engaging in *unexpected politics*—political behavior that is inconsistent with the cultural expectations associated with a social identity. To call African American Republicans' politics unexpected is in no way to make a normative claim about "good" or "bad" partisan choices. Rather, it is an acknowledgment that they have made an unconventional partisan choice, one that runs counter to most others who share their racial status. However, the sources of that inconsistency are not a function of any inherent incompatibility between "black interests" and the Republican Party, but of the way both black interests and conservative social policy are constructed. In their attempts to resolve this incongruence, African American Republicans like Roland and Inez illuminate the processes through which identity politics are made.

The concept of "unexpected politics" naturally assumes an "expected politics."[12] This expectation is grounded in presumptions about the collective interests of blacks as a group and how those interests are served by Republican policies. Accordingly, not all groups are subject to "expected politics." For instance, while the political leanings of white men and white women follow some empirical trends, when it comes to politics there is no strong cultural expectation for them to behave in a particular way. Although an argument could be made about acting counter to their "rational" interests, no one is surprised when a white woman is a Republican or when a white man is a Democrat. But for African Americans, Republican partisanship is incongruent with expectations of what black people are "supposed" to care about.

A major source of the unexpectedness of their politics is the Republican Party itself, specifically the way it has addressed issues of race. A cursory look at the news shows a party that could reasonably be considered hostile to racial minorities. As the 2016 primary vividly illustrated, Republicans are more than willing to deploy racially hostile rhetoric to stir up the concerns and fears of white voters. Despite the fact that three of the candidates could be classified as racial or ethnic minorities, inclusion was not a central theme of the campaign. Attacks on women, immigrants, and racial minorities dominated the narrative through the Republican convention. Under these conditions, it makes intuitive sense to express surprise that a black person would be a Republican (let alone campaign to lead the party). How could a black person support a party that offers up as its nominee a man who calls for restricting the ability of racial and ethnic minorities to enter the country? Juxtaposed against an understanding of the Republican Party as the current political home for extreme racial views and explicit race baiting, the idea of a black person supporting the GOP *is* noteworthy.

While there are good reasons to be surprised by African American Republicans, it is important not to obscure the similarities between them and other African Americans. Across many demographic characteristics, Republican do *not* differ from their Democratic counterparts. Data from the American National Election Survey provide some insight into the similarities between blacks who are Republican and those who are not.[13] On the whole, African American Republicans look a lot like other black people. This is consistent with the activists I talked to, who stressed their similarities to other black people.

As one of my respondents put it, "I think more blacks would be Republicans if it didn't have such a bad reputation in our communities. I think there are a lot of closet black Republicans out there." Another put it more ominously: "We walk among you!" In general, African American Republicans do not have significantly higher incomes or go to church more.[14] Indeed, depending on the data used, they are just slightly statistically more likely to *never* attend church. Interestingly, the characteristics associated with Republican partisanship among whites are not strongly associated with Republican partisanship among blacks. Still, it is important to remember the difficulty of getting a grasp on the demographics of black Republicans because there are so few of them.

Given our reliance on demographic categorization to slice and dice political constituencies, the lack of obvious differences between black Republicans and Democrats is a little unsatisfying. It would be nice, and consistent with popular opinion, if African American Republicans were all very affluent. We could easily say they support conservative politics to further their class interests. Or, if they were particularly religious, we might understand how they could be enticed by the GOP's conservative social issues. In fact, many of the activists I spent time with were both affluent and socially conservative. However, on the basis of multiple sources of survey data, it just doesn't seem to be the case that African American Republicans are any more affluent or religious than any other black groups. And while the lack of differences might be surprising, it is worth noting that this finding is consistent with research that fails to find significant gender or class schisms within African American public opinion.[15]

Despite the demographic similarities, African American Republicans are forced to wrestle with issues that their black

Democratic counterparts do not have to deal with. Similarly, despite shared policy preferences, the unexpected nature of their partisanship makes their experience of the GOP different from that of their white Republican compatriots. Because their existence is so unexpected, African American Republicans are often engaged in an explicit project of linking identity and politics. They are forced to make themselves legible to a range of audiences—family, friends, white Republicans, other blacks. A central part of this legibility project is making it seem "natural" that black and Republican go together.

IDENTITY AND POLITICS

While the belief that social identities—like race, gender, class, or sexuality—drive behavior is present across a range of domains, it is especially prominent in the political arena. Around election time, speculation starts about who will vote for whom. Each demographic becomes the subject of debate. Will soccer moms vote for the Republican? Can the Democratic candidate secure the support of the NASCAR dads? Who will win the Latino vote? Depending on your perspective, these questions enliven the political landscape or pervert the political process. But whatever your take on the infotainment nature of the election cycle, an underlying assumption is that the groups we belong to shape our political behavior. Social categories act as cleavages that divide the electorate, and they are central to how we make sense of political actions.[16]

This is especially true in relation to African American political behavior. African Americans' racial group membership is thought to be a defining identity that organizes political attitudes and behaviors.[17] Race operates as a master status that provides an explanation for black political behavior. Partly this is driven by the consistency in African American partisanship. The vast majority of blacks cast ballots for Democratic candidates, and there is clear and consistent support among the black electorate for more liberal policy issues. Consequently, the African American vote is rarely in doubt. In presidential elections, black voters are an important constituency for Democratic candidates to woo in the primaries. But in the general election, their politics are considered a lock. So while campaigns are busy decoding the identities of soccer moms and NASCAR dads, the workings of black racial identity and political behavior are treated as a given.

This contributes to a strong sense that black racial identity is associated with particular political behaviors. But why would sharing the same racial identity lead to similar political behaviors? One explanation is that people in the same racial group share similar structural positions within the political system. Because they are segregated residentially and socially, African Americans develop distinct patterns of political behavior.[18] Alternatively, we can think of group membership operating through social-psychological mechanisms. In this approach, black people feel connected to one another and they can substitute the group interests for their individual interests. Political scientist Michael Dawson has shown that attachment to other members of their racial group is central to African Americans' political actions, and he argues that this racial identification is key to explaining the more liberal policy attitudes of African Americans.[19] Racial identification, as an idea, captures whether an individual feels their life chances are tied to the racial group as a whole. For Dawson, it provides African Americans with an easy way to determine their interests in a "rational" way using the status of the group. Because of the power of racial status in shaping life chances, group interests efficiently replace individual interests. Dawson, along with other researchers who come out of the "linked fate" tradition, offers a more complex take that relies on the subjective sense of group attachment, not just shared structural location. Still, the general model of political behavior in this scheme is similar to research from the structural approaches and research on cleavages. It's a relatively straightforward model of action wherein black identity drives political behavior, end of story.

And it's true that when racial identification is high, African Americans generally support left-leaning candidates and policies. This finding holds across socioeconomic divisions, as "perceptions of linked fate act as a liberal counterbalance to the greater conservatism of the more affluent."[20] Other researchers report similar findings. When examining preferences for racial redistricting, Katherine Tate finds that blacks who reflect concern for fellow blacks are more likely to be strong advocates for increased numerical representation of minorities in Congress and to favor election-rule changes to achieve that goal.[21] Tate demonstrates that "ample research on blacks has established that having strong racial identity, measured as the perception that one's fate is tied to the fate of the race, corresponds to liberal policy positions."[22]

The public perception of African American Republicans certainly corresponds to this identity model of political behavior. People respond to black Republicans in strong and polarizing ways. Their white counterparts hold them up to illustrate the diversity of the GOP, while ironically *also* pointing to them to affirm a colorblind politics that downplays the significance of race. Those on the political left regard them as marginal to the African American community, and their partisan affiliation is maligned as racially inauthentic. Some see African American Republicans as saviors who refuse to stay beholden to shallow identity politics. Others see them as self-interested sellouts or jokes. Across these responses, there is the assumption that, for most black people, racial identity is central to political behavior.

African American Republicans themselves make it tough to figure out how their black identity relates to their partisan choice. The famous ones are notoriously cagey around issues of race, often attempting to maintain a delicate balance by expressly downplaying racial identity and holding themselves up as rejecting unthinking identity politics, but also willingly offering up their blackness as a marker of authenticity and insight. So, while Ben Carson downplayed the importance of race in the 2016 Republican debates, he also attempted to deploy race on his behalf during the campaign. In an interview with Glenn Thrush from the website Politico, Carson was less circumspect about discussing race and his own black identity.[23] He declared that he understood the experiences of "real racism," and dismissed contemporary concerns about racial discrimination within the Republican Party. When asked if he felt pride at Barack Obama's election, Carson took an opportunity to assert his black identity by juxtaposing his experiences against Obama's childhood.

> CARSON: Like most Americans I was proud that we broke the color barrier when he was elected but I also recognize that his experience and my experience are night and day different. He didn't grow up like I grew up by any stretch of the imagination.
> THRUSH: That's right.
> CARSON: Not even close.
> THRUSH: He is an *African* American as opposed to an African-American.
> CARSON: He's an *African* American. He was, you know, raised white. Many of his formative years were spent in Indonesia so

for him to claim that he identifies with the experience of black Americans is a bit of a stretch.

This selective embrace of black identity is not unique to Carson. It seems as if it is common among African American Republicans who enter the national spotlight. Herman Cain also illustrated this duality throughout the 2012 Republican primary campaign. Cain especially tried to have it both ways when dismissing concerns about racist rhetoric directed at the president while also presenting himself as more authentically black than Obama. At a conservative convention, Cain emboldened the crowd, saying, "You will get called racist simply because you happen to disagree with a president who happens to be black. You are not racists! You are patriots because you are willing to stand up for what you believe in!" In different contexts, Cain was eager to invoke his black identity, describing himself as "an American. Black. Conservative." In the same interview, he rejected the term *African American* because "I'm American, I'm black and I'm conservative. I don't like people trying to label me. African-American is socially acceptable for some people, but I am not some people." Despite his concerns about labels, he was happy to tag Obama as "more of an international ... I think he's out of the mainstream and always has been. Look, he was raised in Kenya, his mother was white from Kansas and her family had an influence on him, it's true, but his dad was Kenyan, and when he was going to school he got a lot of fellowships, scholarships, he stayed in the academic environment for a long time. He spent most of his career as an intellectual."[24] For Cain, like many black Republican politicians, race does not matter—until it does.

The underlying approach of the identity model animates both popular and academic thinking about politics. There is a certain straightforward elegance to it, and it maps onto what we see in political behavior. Studies consistently find differences between blacks' and whites' political behavior. So, knowing whether or not someone is black is useful in understanding that person's political behavior. Despite the consistent effects of racial identity on political behavior, though, the mechanisms of its effects are less well specified. Identities can be linked to a range of political behaviors. By focusing too much attention on documenting the empirical link between an identity and a behavior, we lose sight of how identity politics are the result of a process. This leads to taking certain connections for granted—being black and voting Democrat, for example. But that's too easy. It takes *work* to link any identity to a specific set of political actions. Without attending to that work, we are left with confirmation that "race matters" but little certainty about *how* race matters in political behaviors.

REEVALUATING THE LINK BETWEEN IDENTITY AND POLITICS

In our analyses of political behavior, we tend to think of race as a static, unchanging characteristic—something that is either "present" or "absent." You are black or you're not black. Then, we imbue that characteristic with causal power. By employing this "identity" approach, we restrict our understanding of—and effectively squash possible other ideas about—how race can influence political behavior.

Racial identification is important in understanding African Americans' political behavior, but it is only one way in which attachment to an identity group manifests itself.[25] For one thing, the presence of an identity is no indication of its importance. For instance, someone might identify as a Minnesotan, but that identity has no bearing on how they make decisions. Similarly, a voter may identify as black but not see their racial identity as having any implications for their political behavior. Variations in the political behavior of blacks from African or Caribbean countries illustrate this point. Though they share the identity "black," their political behavior is not always aligned with that of American-born blacks.[26] In the case of blacks of African or Caribbean descent, the presence of a "black identity" provides only a partial explanation of political behavior. Consequently, relying solely on a measure of identification produces a limited account of the relationship between an attachment and a political behavior.[27] What scholars call a *salient* identity "is conceptualized (and operationalized) as the likelihood that the identity will be invoked in diverse situations."[28] So a person's level of attachment to any of their identities can vary across identification and salience measures. For African Americans, the centrality of race is distinct from the presence or absence of identification with a racial group.[29]

While acknowledging that race is an axis of identity, I will argue that race is *more* than identity. It is also a set of ideas and beliefs about who black people are. African American Republicans all identify as black, but there are very different ideas circulating among them about what it means to be black. Differing ideas about black people divide African American Republicans, and these ideas influence multiple aspects of their political behavior. Race isn't just a marker of identity *for* black people, it's also a set of ideas *about* black people. Conflicting answers to the question "Who are black people?" shape the experience of being African American and Republican. Although a plethora of research identifies distinctions in how African Americans conceptualize themselves, rarely are these differences used to account for variation in black political behavior.[30] As I will show, African American Republicans are often engaged in a heated debate about what is best for black people and about the appropriate way to conceptualize Republican partisanship as a solution to the challenges that black people face in the post–civil rights era.

Another argument that plays out in this book revolves around how political context influences individual and collective understandings of race. We often assume that race drives political behavior, and there is a great deal of convincing research that supports this position. My own findings lend support to the idea that a range of race-related processes have implications for how politics looks among African American Republicans. However, my findings also demonstrate the importance of understanding how the political context in which they are embedded shapes the way individuals understand race and how they can express their racial identity. Black individuals' success within the Republican Party is contingent on very particular understandings and expressions of racial identity, racial ideas, and racial performances. So, I argue that the relationship between race and political behavior is reciprocal: just as race drives politics, politics drives how race is understood and deployed.

Despite their small numbers, African American Republicans provide a useful context in which to examine the ways that social identities like race are linked to political behavior. Black identity is used to account for differences in rates of political participation, policy attitudes, and ideological cohesion among African Americans. Treating African American Republicans as if they lack authentic black identities illustrates how our discussions of race and politics are tied to a static, causal model that treats black people's racial identity as the driver of political attitudes and behaviors. Yet the realities of Roland, Inez, and the others in this book force us to explore how black identity can be commandeered on behalf of a wide range of political action. As the people I studied show, black Republicans are connected to other blacks. Though there are serious and consequential differences in how they feel about that connection, of course they understand themselves as embedded in black communities. Treating them as if their Republican partisanship reflected a "lack" of black identity would inadequately capture their political experiences. Instead, their black identity—and the meanings they attach to it—is a defining feature of their experiences within the Republican Party.

OUTLINE OF THE BOOK

This book is intended to open a door into the lives of African American Republican activists, to show how race structures how they understand themselves as well as their membership in the Republican Party. In the process, the book gives readers a theoretical framework for disentangling the increasingly complicated dynamics of race and politics in the contemporary United States. However, before summarizing what this book will cover, it is worth briefly explaining what it will not do.

In the process of examining the experiences of African American Republicans, I will examine some of the forces that drew them to the GOP. However, this research does not attempt to detail the process through which African Americans become Republicans. It does not definitively answer the question "What makes black people join the Republican Party?" Rather, it focuses on the experience of being African American *within* the Republican Party. While I certainly think that understanding what it's like to be black and Republican sheds light on why more African Americans do not choose that pathway, to fully address the question requires examination of black Democrats. This book does not do that. Rather, I explore variations in the experiences of African American Republicans to see how different meanings are attached and expressed within the racially conservative context of the GOP. Furthermore, I take an agnostic approach to any specific policy issues discussed in the course of this analysis. Throughout the course of the book, I will detail how African Americans believe that Republican policies will benefit or harm black citizens. In my analysis, I refrain from adjudicating the merits of their assessment of black people's interests or the quality of their proposed political program. Such judgments are well beyond my expertise and, fundamentally, are not relevant to the broader arguments presented throughout the book.

The book follows a fairly straightforward outline. Chapter 1 offers a big-picture overview of the historical relationship between African Americans and the Republican Party. In contrast to their current unexpected status, it used to be common for blacks to support the party. Abolition was at the center of the party's creation, and African Americans were a critical constituency. Only in the 1930s did the majority of African Americans start supporting Democratic candidates in presidential elections. While shifts in how each party handled economic issues precipitated black voters' exodus to the Democratic Party, it was the Republican Party's response to the civil rights movement and demands for racial equality that produced its antagonistic relationship with blacks. In tracing this history, it becomes clear that black political behavior develops in concert with shifts in the broader political context. In the case of partisanship, black political behavior can only be understood in the context of strategic choices the Republican and Democratic parties made in response to a shifting electoral calculus.

Chapter 2 turns to contemporary African American Republicans and examines their reputation with two important constituencies: other black people and white Republicans. Though they manifest this in different ways, black Republicans fear that their partisanship causes both groups to question their racial authenticity. Among other blacks, this questioning coalesces into a "sellout critique" that frames African American Republicans as operating counter to their black identity. African American Republicans report being held in a "skeptical embrace" by white Republicans who worry that African American Republicans will not be able to subordinate their racial identity to their Republican partisanship. Both the sellout critique and the skeptical embrace are grounded in a perceived incongruence between black racial identity and Republican partisanship. Yet African American Republicans themselves articulate strong identification with black identity and Republican partisanship. As a consequence, they are challenged with linking their racial identity and their partisanship in a way that removes unexpectedness.

The next chapters take up the ways that African American Republicans meet that challenge. They are not a monolithic group, and their divisions are critical in understanding how black identity is linked to conservative politics. Chapter 3 is about African American Republicans whom I label "color-blind" because their strategy for linking black identity to Republican politics involves de-emphasizing the role of race in black people's lives. They see themselves as linked to a broader black community, but they reject identity politics as the pathway to racial uplift. They endorse Republican social policy as part of a commitment to an abstract notion of conservative politics, not because the policies are good for black people. For race-blind African American Republicans, the best thing for blacks is to abandon race-based identity politics. Chapter 4 examines an opposing strategy used by race-conscious African American Republicans. For this group, race is central to their personal and political motivations. Black identity provides the motivation for joining the Republican Party. They also use black identity to inform how they discuss the merits of conservative social policy. In contrast to their race-blind counterparts, this group supports Republican policies because of their perceived benefits to blacks. Both chapters chart the meanings that each group of Republicans attaches to racial identity and how those meanings inform the framing of Republican policies. More specifically, each chapter shows how different ideas about black people and their interests drive the two different approaches to making being an African American Republican seem uncontroversial.

In chapter 5, we see how these two strategies—with their competing ideas about black people and their political interests—are difficult to sustain within a single organization. Given their small absolute numbers, similar experiences of unexpectedness, and general agreement on most policy issues, one might imagine that African American Republicans would have little trouble organizing. However, the opposite is the case. This chapter shows how differences in their approaches to thinking about race and their framing of conservative social policy prevent African American Republicans from forming stable, long-term organizations. It is difficult for African American Republicans to organize because of intense interpersonal conflicts and political disagreements, both of which are actually manifestations of competing beliefs about the role of black racial identity in the political arena. Multiple cases of organizational failure demonstrate how internal conflict inhibits basic organizational tasks like defining audiences, developing organizational missions, and determining tactics. These fights simultaneously expose the personal and political fault lines among African American Republicans.

While the tensions between the different factions of African American Republicans can be heated and deeply personal, their infighting also has implications for relations with the Republican establishment. Chapter 6 addresses how these tensions structure relations with white Republicans. White Republicans provide the platform upon which black Republicans gain election, notoriety, and resources. The relationship is symmetrically beneficial since black Republicans provide tangible proof of racial diversity within the GOP. The GOP has been vocal in calling for increased diversity among both the leadership and the rank and file of the party. For the most part, these efforts have not been very successful, and this chapter uses the experiences of African American Republican activists to partly illustrate why. To maintain support among white Republicans, African Americans must talk about black identity in a way that is consistent with what white Republicans want to hear. When African-Americans call on white Republicans to speak to black interests specifically and treat conservative social policy as a basis for black advancement, relations with white Republicans are contentious and adversarial. As a consequence, a very specific kind of African American Republican rises to prominence within the GOP. African American Republicans' relations with their white counterparts illustrate how the political context and institutional demands shape the way they think and talk about their racial identity.

The book concludes by exploring the broader lessons that can be taken from the case of African American Republicans. While most people will pay lip service to the belief that there is not a monolithic black experience, political analysts spend very little time exploring how differences among black people shape their political behaviors. Throughout this book, I show how variations in the perceived importance of race structure ideas about black interests and affect African Americans' experiences of Republican partisanship. Through the stories of people like Roland and Inez, we also see how meanings are central in understanding how African Americans express support for the Republican Party, as well as how that support will manifest itself in actions. This research also demonstrates the importance of understanding how the political context in which African American Republicans are embedded shapes the way they understand race and how they can express their racial identity. Rather than being only about how race drives political behavior, the experience of African American Republicans is animated by a reciprocal relationship between race and politics. These findings call attention to the multiple ways in which race works in the political arena, but they also provide guidance for how we might think about the ways that other social identities inform political behavior. Although the voices within this book are primarily African American and Republican, the lessons I draw from them are relevant to broader conversations about the relationship between identity and politics.

CHAPTER ONE

From Many to Few

In one of my first conversations during this research, Walter expressed excitement that someone was seriously studying African American Republicans. Walter and I initially connected because of his involvement with a local libertarian group, but he had a long history of involvement with both African American community groups and Republican political organizations. After our first meeting, he insisted on taking me out to a fancy lunch at the restaurant in a private club. As we chatted over impressive club sandwiches and enjoyed an even more impressive view, he told me that he loved the idea that someone was taking him and other black Republicans seriously. Still, participation in my research was bittersweet. He hoped the project would counter negative portrayals of African American Republicans, but the idea that they were worth studying *because of* their race and politics struck him as a problem. He couldn't help but feel that my project was, on some level, confirmation of his outsider status in the public imagination. He asked flatly, "Why is it that nobody talks about black Democrats?"

Walter's question is a penetrating one. It calls attention to the way we automatically associate Democratic partisanship with African Americans and regard any aberrations with raised eyebrows. In his own way, Walter hints at a central issue of this research: What has to happen to make a combination of identity and politics noteworthy? Of course we talk about black Democrats. But where there are debates about what role blacks should play in Democratic leadership, no one spends much time remarking on the strangeness of a black person supporting the Democratic Party. Black voters are a prominent and reliable part of the Democratic coalition. So, in Walter's parlance, no one talks about black Democrats because the Democratic Party is seen as the natural place to fulfill the political interests associated with black racial identity. I suspect that Walter recognized this, and his question was posed to push me to examine the expectations that surround black racial identity and political behavior. We talk about black Republicans because they are not what we expect. They don't fit in with our ideas about how racial identity and partisanship should go together. But this has not always been the case.

The surprise that meets contemporary African American Republicans would surely confuse an observer of nineteenth-century politics, because the current lack of support for the Republican Party among black voters marks a striking realignment. At the party's origins, African Americans were a central component of the GOP's electoral coalition. Yet today it feels like a noteworthy achievement when a Republican can manage to secure double-digit support from black voters in a presidential election. A number of forces—within the black community and within the Republican Party—aligned to fundamentally reorient black partisanship in the United States. Certainly, some of the shift in black partisanship flows from changes in what black voters want in a political party. However, the political parties have altered the landscape within which black voters make their decisions. In other words, changes in black partisanship have been heavily influenced by changes in the consideration set—the choices available to those black voters. This chapter traces the history between black voters and the Republican Party and outlines the shifts in the composition of the GOP and its policy positions that have made it an unlikely home for African American interests.

Over time, the political parties have fundamentally altered their relations to race-related issues and black voters. Where the Republican Party was once perceived as the "natural" home for black interests, the Democratic Party is now perceived as the political party most likely to help African Americans. As a consequence, the actions of GOP leaders have large implications for the way that we view African American Republicans. There are, perhaps, even larger implications for how African American Republicans themselves connect their blackness to their partisanship. The shift in status of the African American Republican—the move from standard to unexpected political actor—highlights how perceptions are a function of the wider political context.

The African American Republican activists I spoke with were quick to remind me that the current state of relations between blacks and the Republican Party represents a stark departure from the GOP's historical origins. For those outside of the party who question their politics, they present Republican history as proof that Republican politics can be compatible with black identity. For those within the party, history is used by today's black Republicans to make claims on material and symbolic resources by recalling a time when blacks were a key constituency and the party was committed to having blacks as full-fledged participants in charting the direction of the GOP. Empirically, knowledge of the realignment of black voters away from the Republican Party is important because today's African American Republicans draw on this history when making claims to legitimacy, both within and outside the party.

The evolution of black voters' relationship to the Republican Party also sheds light on broader questions about the expressions of black political behavior more generally. African Americans' partisan choices, though often organized around "black interests" (however they are defined), can only be understood within the framework of broader changes in each political party's ideologies and electoral coalitions. A broad sweep of African American partisanship must, admittedly, only provide general trends. Yet, to understand the image, attitudes, and experiences of contemporary African American Republicans, it is important to situate them within the broader historical patterns.[1]

Today African Americans' estrangement from the Republican Party feels long-standing and, often, intractable. Upon closer reflection, it becomes clear that the estrangement that makes contemporary African American Republicans so unique is largely a function of an electoral calculus that has shifted the party away from them. We soon see the utility of political scientist Hanes Walton's insistence that "black political behavior is best understood as the result of individual, community, systemic, and structural factors, which over the years have all acted together in a complex, changing fashion."[2]

REPUBLICAN ROOTS

Any discussion of black partisanship has to begin with slavery. As a group, African Americans held very little electoral power;

the overwhelming majority were enslaved and denied the vote. However, there were pockets of black enfranchisement. Most of these were located in the North, but there were other spaces in the country where enforcement of black disenfranchisement was lax and blacks participated in local elections.[3] For free blacks in the North, political engagement focused on efforts to achieve legal equality, a theme present throughout the course of black political engagement in the United States.[4] Consequently, free blacks evaluated their partisan choices through the lens of abolition. On this account, initial relations with the Republican Party were tentative.

Abolition was central to the origins of the Republican Party, founded in 1854. Many of the original Republicans were anti-slavery advocates and members of explicit abolitionist parties, and the leadership of the new party was eager to expand its potential coalition of voters. Given its abolitionist roots, Republican leaders thought that free blacks were likely to be an easy and immediate source of support additional support.[5] Initial Republican appeals to the black electorate were grounded in opposition to slavery and played on frustration with the limited existing political options. Central to this strategy was positioning the new party as the best of the available options for blacks. Yet black opinion leaders and politicians were slow to return the Republican embrace.

The Republican Party presented a platform that called for preventing the expansion of slavery in new U.S. territories, while leaving the institution intact where it already existed. Frederick Douglass, arguably the most prominent black political figure of the time, found this hedged stance on slavery unacceptable. Writing in his widely read newspaper, *Frederick Douglass' Paper,* he argued that "the Black community couldn't accept the abolitionists' invitation to join the Republican Party because, due to its position on slavery, it does not go far enough in the right direction."[6] Instead, the new party must, if it were to claim black men's allegiance, "take a higher position, make no concessions to the slave power, strike at slavery everywhere in the country."[7] Douglass was joined by other black political leaders in his skepticism about the party's partial commitment to abolition, but the Republican position on the slavery issue was much closer to that of free blacks than the Democratic alternative. Blacks offered tentative support for the Republican Party in the 1856 presidential election and more substantial support of Lincoln in 1860. Walton describes the pre–Civil War political environment and the constraints facing black voters:

> Although there was some Black criticism and denunciation of the Republican party, Blacks formed Republican clubs and strongly supported the party in 1860. Black Republicanism before the Civil War was largely the result of a lack of effective alternatives in the existing political system.... The emergence of Black Republicanism was firmly rooted, in the final analysis, in the desire of Blacks to destroy the slavery institution, and a large factor was the lack of verbal commitment or actions toward this goal among other political parties.[8]

From the start of the Civil War through Reconstruction, black support for the Republican Party shifted in numbers and intensity. The war, and the enfranchisement that followed, created a sizable new voting constituency. Black support for the Republican Party solidified after Lincoln's assassination—it was seen, by blacks, as a tribute to Lincoln. More consequentially, Republicans were the only party to make any concession to black interests or to open their party leadership to black politicians. The Republican Party endorsed a range of symbolic and substantive positions designed to satisfy black voters, and four black delegates were included in the 1868 Republican National Convention (a first for any party's convention). The Republican Party went on to vigorously support legislative acts and three constitutional amendments (the thirteenth, fourteenth, and fifteenth) that were interpreted as substantive instances of the Republican Party attending to black interests.

So the foundation of black support for the Republican Party lay in the humanitarian policies it supported through 1870. Support for pro-black policies was driven by political expediency and ideological commitment. While these policies certainly empowered the oppressed, they also worked to secure a solid voting bloc and to undermine Democratic opponents. Democratic intransigence, too, strengthened black support for Republicans. When contemporary African American Republicans talk about the GOP's positive history with black voters, this is the period they most often reference. Democrats are cast as the party of racism, firmly rooted in the Ku Klux Klan and other domestic terrorist groups intent on disenfranchising black voters after the Civil War. By contrast, the "Party of Lincoln" narrative presents Republicans as the party rooted in black civil rights. This account, to be sure, ignores the half-hearted nature of even early Republican support for abolition *and* the fact that any mutually beneficial relationship between blacks and the party during the Civil War and Reconstruction was short-lived.

Much of Republicans' ability to engage in pro-black legislating was contingent on their national dominance and the relative weakness of the postwar Democratic Party.[9] After a failed secession, white southerners were politically weak, and the absence of political competition freed Republicans to address concerns of black voters. Once the political environment became competitive again, the relationship between black voters and the Republican

Party became strained. By then, blacks represented just one component of an unstable electoral coalition.

By 1870 the southern Republican coalition consisted of three groups: Scalawags, Carpetbaggers, and Black and Tans, a group consisting of black Republicans and their allies. It was a fragile coalition, with key elements committed to anti-black positions. Ultimately, the coalition fractured as key elements of the party played to anti-black sentiment in an effort to remain competitive in southern states.[10] However, with voting restrictions on southern white men lifted, Democrats—drawing on support from white southern politicians—reclaimed control over political and governing institutions at the state level. Black and Tan Republicans faced a particularly difficult political context after Reconstruction. Blacks were systematically terrorized and removed from the voter rolls. This left the Black and Tans without a voting constituency and, as the Democratic Party regained strength in the South, the Republican Party was marginalized on the local and state levels.

Though the post-Reconstruction political environment was not amenable to issues of racial justice, different factions within the party hurled charges of racism and made claims to black support. These had little bearing on elections. The reinfranchisement of southern white men coupled with the disenfranchisement of black men meant that Republicans were practically powerless in local and state politics. The various factions of the party vied for control over Republican state conventions, lobbying to be the southern representatives for the national presidential nominating convention. Because southern Republicans were most able to exert their influence in presidential nominating politics, the party's factions needed to marshal support. In this context, all the factions of the Republican Party wanted at least the appearance of black support.

V.O. Key argues that, at this point, southern Republicans focused their efforts on exerting influence at the national level.[11] Recognizing they had no realistic hope of securing state offices, national party players took advantage of the situation and played the splintered southern Republican Party's factions against each other. With black voters disenfranchised, they gained little, if anything, from the bargaining, vote buying, and alliance building prompted by the nominating conventions. Some black politicians were able to leverage personal political and material gains, given that all the southern factions desired the symbolic representation of all possible political constituencies.[12] However, by the election of Herbert Hoover in 1928, even the minor spoils of patronage were unavailable to Black and Tan Republicans and, by extension, to the black Republican leaders who made up a sizable portion of that faction's constituency: "Lily-whiteism not only depleted what few followers the Republicans had in the Black community; it also made it difficult for younger Blacks to join. The result is that in nearly every southern state today, there are very few Blacks in the Republican party."[13]

Despite its start as a relatively pro-black party in the South, disenfranchisement after Reconstruction all but eliminated the black voter from participation in Republican politics. The machinations of Republican presidential politics further marginalized black political leaders. As Walton notes of the Republican Party's origins, "In the beginning it had Black support in the South, then deliberately subordinated those supporters and finally eliminated them."[14] Where blacks could vote, they still supported the Republican Party in national elections. Republicans could be cynical and manipulative on racial issues, and, often, black voters saw very little material benefit flowing from their support of Republican candidates. Indeed, outside of some small spoils of political patronage and the occasional position as a party functionary, blacks—particularly southern blacks—saw very few benefits from their post-Reconstruction support.[15] Yet, given the available options, the Republican Party was more amenable to black interests than the Democratic Party for most of the time between the Civil War and the early 1900s. With the New Deal, black leaders and voters saw potential allies in the Democrats, and their allegiance to the Party of Lincoln began to erode.

A STEADY SHIFT

By the early 1900s, black participation in the party had been marginalized as Republicans were focused on trying to secure white votes in the South. Their efforts bore little fruit: the Democratic Party had a stranglehold on southern politics, and Republican outreach to whites resulted in few positive results. Instead, the party sacrificed its black voting base and any southern sway, while retaining national-level power. Deep loyalty to the legacy of Lincoln and a lack of partisan alternatives led black voters and political leaders to align themselves with the GOP well into the twentieth century. By the 1920s, both of these factors would lose force in black political behavior.

While Democrats and Republicans in the South engaged in competitive race-baiting, northern Democrats tentatively reached out to African American voters. Shifting demographic trends and the need to build winning electoral coalitions, rather than any particularly progressive stance on race-related issues, were the big drivers of northern Democrats' interest in black votes.[16] As millions of blacks began migrating from the South, their presence altered the political dynamics of eastern and midwestern cities.[17] While they were not yet a particularly potent political constituency, African Americans' relative loyalty to the Republican Party threatened to embolden Republican politicians in northern Democratic strongholds.

Simultaneously, the deep economic crisis of the Great Depression upset the political status quo across the country. As Michael Fauntroy notes:

> The Depression disproportionately damaged African Americans. Black unemployment, already higher than any other group in the country, became, in many cities, two- to fourfold their black population proportions. Nearly one-third of black Baltimoreans were unemployed in March 1931, almost twice the black proportion of the city's population. According to the Urban League, by 1931, one-third of southern urban blacks were jobless; a year later, that figure grew to more than one-half.[18]

Nancy Weiss describes the situation for African Americans during the depression in similar terms. Although the general picture of black employment, with blacks concentrated in semiskilled, laboring, and servant jobs, had always been somewhat bleak,

> What was new in the early 1930's was the crushing impact of the Depression on this already depressed economic structure. Blacks in the rural South bore the heaviest burden.... In the cities, those blacks who managed to hold on to their jobs suffered a crippling decline in wages.... Wages aside, employment of any sort for blacks in the cities was increasingly hard to come by. Fierce competition from whites meant that even the most menial jobs were no longer reserved for Negroes.... [Unemployment] was the most prominent index of black misery, but it had broader implications: overcrowded housing, the erosion of savings, the loss of homes and household possessions, the disruption of family life.[19]

Economic suffering made black voters amenable to Democratic outreach efforts.[20] At the state and local levels, African Americans were incorporated into the northern Democratic machines. Through a mix of patronage politics and limited participation in party leadership, Democrats were able to secure black support in eastern and midwestern urban centers. This incorporation would set the stage for the later rise of black leadership of urban centers, but full incorporation into the Democratic coalition was elusive.

Franklin Roosevelt and the Democratic leadership were not particularly interested in race issues and, at times, worked aggressively to distance themselves from black constituencies. The national party was sensitive to alienating southern Democrats by being perceived as racially progressive. Roosevelt refused to meet with the National Association for the Advancement of Colored People, and the Democrats offered only the most cursory attention to racial equality in their national platforms. Even the programs of the New Deal, critical to drawing blacks away from the Republican Party, suffered from the Democrats' lax attitude toward racial equality. At the start of the Roosevelt administration, "most of the programs demonstrated the limits to New Deal assistance for blacks rather than its reach."[21] There were wide racial disparities across a range of programs, and blacks saw little benefit from programs like the Civilian Conservation Corps, the Agricultural Adjustment Administration, the National Recovery Administration, and the Federal Emergency Relief Administration. The local management of New Deal programs ensured that the institutional denial of black equality in the South would be reflected in the administration of program benefits. While there were exceptions, the administration of New Deal programs was inflected with the same discriminatory attitudes and practices that were prevalent throughout the United States.[22]

So why was the Democratic Party—or any establishment party—appealing to blacks in the New Deal era? First, because average blacks had little expectation of or hope for true change on racial issues; and second, because economics, rather than race, drove most black electoral behavior (perhaps most electoral behavior at all) during the Great Depression. Although black leaders in the 1930s were vocal in calling for racial equality, the threshold of racial animation was so low that even the most cursory of attention by the Democratic Party would pass muster. Furthermore, the "rising tide of all boats" brought about by New Deal programs was particularly good for blacks. Even though the administration of the programs was guided by racial inequality, something was better than nothing during the Depression. And the Democratic Party at least gave a little something. The Depression provided a context in which African American politics was oriented toward shoring up a fragile economic position.

While race and class are most certainly linked, in the context of New Deal politics the increased salience of economic uncertainty provided an opening for the Democratic Party to make inroads among black voters without having to make large concessions on issues of racial equality. Although Republicans were still competitive among black voters, the New Deal would signal the start of the serious erosion of black support for the Republican Party. That erosion would not culminate until after the civil rights era.

The shift in African American partisanship continued with each successive presidential election. In 1948, under Harry Truman's cautious expansion of Roosevelt's limited civil rights agenda, the majority of blacks identified as Democrats. Truman set up the President's Committee on Civil Rights (CCR), calling for equal voting rights and employment opportunity for African Americans. Though the CCR had a limited impact, the move signaled at least a rhetorical commitment to black equality and marked "the first time since Reconstruction that an official federal government organ made such a statement."[23] Truman also desegregated the armed forces with Executive Order 9981. These small policy concessions to the cause of civil rights furthered the Democratic encroachment into the black electorate and continued to build on gains made by the New Deal policies, providing a viable partisan alternative to black voters without going so far as to alienate southern Democrats.

The two major parties curried favor with black voters through limited and often symbolic gestures, neither wanting to risk being viewed as "too progressive" on black issues. Furthermore, international policy dominated the national agenda as the country entered World War II. Blacks were increasingly leaning Democratic, mainly drawn in by economic policies, and this was reflected in presidential voting between 1936 and 1956.[24]

Republicans did make some efforts to attract African American voters by offering tentative appeals grounded in the language of equality and civil rights. The Civil Rights Act of 1957 was passed with support from Republican President Dwight Eisenhower. Initial versions of the act would have established equal voting rights for African Americans, and some versions sought to create a Justice Department section to monitor voting-rights violations. It was eventually watered down in an effort by Democrats to prevent schisms within their party over issues of race. Still, black voters continued to migrate to the Democratic Party.

As black political protests gained steam in the 1950s and with the passage of civil rights legislation in the 1960s, the Republican

Party's neutral attitude toward racial issues turned hostile. As an electoral strategy, it would pay dividends, but it would also trigger a fundamental reorienting of black partisanship and virtually eliminate African American support for the Republican Party.

CIVIL RIGHTS—ERA POLITICS

Throughout U.S. history, much of black political organizing was fomented outside the traditional realm of political activities like voting and party organizing. So while the protest politics of the civil rights movement often drew popular attention, the sort of politics that animated the movement had been a feature of black political behavior since the end of slavery.[25] However, the protests of the civil rights movement were crucial for setting up the contemporary relationship between African Americans and the major political parties. Particularly, both parties responded to the rise and success of the civil rights movement in ways that shaped black partisanship for at least half a century.

By 1960, the civil rights movement was in full swing, and African Americans had been engaged in marching, protesting, and other acts of civil disobedience to agitate for more racially progressive policies in housing, education, and voting.[26] In response, both parties moved hesitantly toward civil rights for blacks, but northern Democrats were faster to recognize the potential of the black electorate growing in urban centers in the North. President Kennedy made symbolic gestures to Dr. Martin Luther King, Jr., as the Democrats painted themselves as the more progressive party. Indeed, blacks were more and more a part of the northern Democratic machine and, since 1948, southern Democrats had proved themselves a volatile part of the Democratic coalition.

White northerners' public opinion was shifting in favor of civil rights, and international pressure mounted for the United States to address issues of racial equality.[27] After Kennedy's assassination in 1963 and Democrats' assertion of dominance over the political landscape, the stage was set for a big legislative move on civil rights. As Paul Frymer describes,

> Kennedy's death, the civil rights movement's ability to galvanize public opinion and place pressure on the national government, and fears of foreign policy officials that the communist and potentially communist world was watching helped provide the necessary incentives for the Democratic-controlled government to finally pass a number of significant pieces of legislation in the mid-1960's. Most prominent among these were the 1964 Civil Rights Act, the Voting Rights Act in 1965, and the Fair Housing Act in 1968.[28]

This legislation passed with bipartisan support,[29] but the Republican embrace of civil rights would be short lived.

Their retreat was hastened by the incorporation into the Republican Party of southern Democrats who opposed civil rights. Indeed, Barry Goldwater, the Republican presidential candidate in 1964, ran almost solely on an anti–Civil Rights Act platform. The campaign strategy used civil rights as a wedge to make inroads into the traditionally Democratic and anti-black stronghold of the South. While the strategy did not pay dividends in 1964, Republicans saw gains in southern districts at the congressional level. More importantly, the Goldwater campaign laid the foundation for more successful outreach efforts by sparking a conservative revival in the party.[30] It cemented African Americans' departure, as the Goldwater campaign symbolically linked the Democratic Party to African American political interests, completing the partisan reversal that began with the New Deal. Over 90 percent of black voters cast votes for Johnson.

Later, Richard Nixon successfully leveraged this "Southern Strategy"—that is, "Republicans' efforts to win conservative white support by distancing themselves from progressive and moderate position on racial issues of importance to African Americans"—in the 1968 election.[31] Against the backdrop of urban unrest, white voters in the North and the South were hesitant about the implementation of civil rights policy (bipartisan as it had once been), and Nixon capitalized on that reticence.

African Americans within the Republican Party did not sit idly by while their party adopted such an aggressive stance against civil rights. Indeed, they did quite the opposite, mounting a vociferous and organized resistance to the anti-black sentiment they felt was coming to dominate the GOP. At the nominating convention for Goldwater, black Republicans denounced the nominee and his supporters. African Americans within the party organized in hopes of making racial equality a concern within the party. These efforts often put them at odds with their white counterparts in party leadership, but they demonstrate that, even when animosity toward racial equality was the official party position, African American Republicans worked to align their commitments to both partisan and racial identities. As historian Leah Wright Rigueur notes, "With the exception of a select few, the party's black members had watched the rise of Goldwater Republicans with anger and dismay. African American loyalists were disheartened by the party's apparent inability to support civil rights, a position that reinforced Black Republicans' already marginal position within the GOP."[32]

African Americans were also still willing to support Republican candidates at the state and local levels. Liberal and moderate elements within the Republican Party were able to garner black support in a number of elections. When Republican candidates made appeals for their votes, African Americans signaled that they would support Republican candidates under certain conditions. In New York, the majority of African Americans supported Republicans in New York City's 1965 mayoral election and in the 1966 governor's race. In 1967, Edward Brooke was elected as a U.S. senator in Massachusetts—the first black Republican senator since Reconstruction. Brooke skillfully balanced Republican partisanship with policy positions that resonated with black voters.[33] This often put him at odds with GOP leadership. As the Republican Party continued to thin its ranks of liberals and moderates, and as racially conservative southern Democrats shifted their partisan allegiance, the influence of African American Republicans like Brooke would wane.[34] And African American voters cemented their general understanding of the GOP as inhospitable to their interests.[35]

THE "NEW" BLACK CONSERVATIVES

Although the GOP never made inroads into the black electorate after the 1964 Goldwater campaign, the rightward shift in the political mood did not leave all African Americans outside the sphere of Republican political influence. In fact, the late 1970s saw the emergence of a small, but influential, network of African American conservative scholars, pundits, and political operatives. Previous strands of political conservatism in black communities had been seen as "organic," growing out of grassroots organizing. By contrast, this wave of black conservatives was perceived as "inorganic," because most of its ideological and material support was provided by white patrons. Influential conservative politicians and think tanks began buttressing the efforts of black political conservatives. Bracey writes:

Black neoconservatives received little or no backing from the black community, a fact corroborated by the labels "outcast" and "dissenter" that black conservatives affixed upon themselves. Black neoconservatives found themselves in a position not unlike that of George Schuyler late in his career—a voice for black empowerment without an organic, black community base from which to operate. Although black neoconservatives had declared an urgent need to break with the reigning black civil rights leadership, it was quite clear that no black neoconservative enjoyed a mandate from the people to make that call. Indeed, one might argue that whoever made that call must be devoid of any authentic contact with [the] African American community, as there was little reason to think that mass black support for liberal Democratic policy and the civil rights leadership was open to debate.[36]

Even while black voters continued to overwhelmingly reject the increasing political conservatism of the Republican Party, a cadre of key African American intellectuals who embraced conservative ideology emerged. The 1980 Black Alternatives Conference, informally called the Fairmont Conference after the San Francisco hotel where it was held, served as a "coming out" party for these new black conservatives. It gathered leading black conservative thinkers under the auspices of finding "new ideas and approaches to black and other minority problems."[37] The conference also gave Ronald Reagan a space within which to find leading black conservatives to join his administration. In many ways, the Fairmont Conference's star players and ideas would become the public face of African American Republicans for the next thirty years. For most of those in attendance, the embrace of the Republican Party and its ideological and policy positions was grounded in a commitment to free-market principles and "traditional" social values.

A central theme of the conference had been the need for African Americans to move beyond understanding their political interests as grounded in their racial status. This theme would play well with white conservatives, but it failed to resonate with blacks in any meaningful way. And while it was not uncommon for African American conservative thinkers in the 1980s to frame their conservative beliefs as a pathway for black advancement, these pols staked their reputation on repudiating identity politics, claiming they were a perversion of the goals of the civil rights movement of the 1950s and 1960s.[38]

Outside this minority of minority politicos, African Americans consistently rejected the ideological offerings of white political conservatives and their African American colleagues. Black conservative thinkers were (and remain) charged with "simply insert[ing] themselves into a predominantly white discourse on race, a move for which they have been duly compensated by various forms of patronage; they are nothing more than the black face of the white Right."[39]

When the center of Republican politics shifted to the right in the late twentieth century, racial conservatism was a central driver. Fauntroy defines racial conservatism as "an ideological philosophy held by whites that seeks to shape the racial status quo to their benefit and resist any changes in the social, political, and economic status quo that benefit minorities."[40] We can see it embodied in the post-1964 "Southern Strategy," which played on the dissatisfaction of southern white voters. But Republicans have long argued that the shift was ideologically, not racially, driven. The GOP centered its messaging behind fewer constraints on business, lower taxes, and decreased intervention by the federal government—the latter frequently falling under the banner of "states' rights." African Americans, for the most part, rejected these hedges and saw the Republican Party as more racist.[41]

Republican electoral strategies in the 1980s only further increased tensions. Much of the rhetoric around states' rights, low taxes, welfare reform, and tough-on-crime measures was racially coded, if not explicitly directed.[42] Still, GOP politicians engaged in efforts to secure black votes. Partly, they hoped to break apart a solid and reliable Democratic constituency; even small inroads into that base could pose huge electoral problems for Democratic presidential candidates. Republicans also saw an alignment with the socially conservative beliefs of many African Americans and thought that genuine, good-faith efforts could secure more of their votes.

It is important to note that some Republican candidates were more palatable than others. At the state and local levels, Republican outreach efforts saw some success. A strategy designed by the African American political consulting firm Wright-McNeill saw some positive results in state and local elections in 1980, for instance.[43] Those numbers never translated to presidential elections, but Republican presidents like George H. W. Bush garnered high job-approval ratings among African Americans.[44] Bush's numbers led some Republican strategists to suggest that, in a reelection run, he might get as much as 20 percent of the African American vote, even though his campaign had been responsible for the infamous "Willie Horton ad"—accused of playing on the worst of racial "predator" stereotypes—deployed to attack his Democratic opponent, Michael Dukakis, in 1988.[45]

The "compassionate conservatism" of George W. Bush represents a more recent attempt to bring racial minorities under the GOP's "big tent." President Bush appointed several high-profile African American cabinet officials but never received a significant portion of the black vote.[46] Today, the discourse around race and conservative politics has become highly charged. The election of Democrat Barack Obama as the nation's first African American president and the Republican Party's uneasy embrace of the Tea Party and its racially questionable rhetoric have combined to further alienate African Americans from the Republican Party. No matter how many black spokesmen and commentators the Republican Party can muster, the strong pulls from the political right, tugging the party ever further away from its once centrist rhetoric, leave few African Americans convinced that they are constituents, rather than merely votes, for conservatives.

Historically, the relationship between the Republican Party and African Americans has included moments of productive support and instances of sustained acrimony.[47] The movement of African Americans from Republican partisanship into stalwarts of the Democratic coalition shows the malleability of the links between race and partisanship. Though partisanship is often understood to function at the individual decision-making level, the experience of African American partisanship is uniquely tied to the collective experience of blacks and the organizational responses of the major political parties to their demands for recognition, equality, and opportunity. Partisan choice, though enacted at the individual level, is mediated through meso-level organizational processes grounded in particular historical contexts. The strong empirical association between black social status and Democratic partisanship is a function of the processes of distancing and embracing that both parties have engaged in to secure electoral majorities, not any inherent link between Democratic Party ideals and African American interests. The shifts in Republican policy positions, particularly on race issues, worked to alienate black voters and send them into the Democratic camp. Once African American support was solidified within the Democratic Party, Republican leadership was able to make electoral inroads by counterposing the GOP to the (perceived) blackening of the Democratic Party and thus produced a context in which black support for the GOP became unlikely. Frymer has described the situation for black voters as one of "electoral capture," where Democrats can do little to advance black interests because Republicans are doing even less to garner their votes.[48] However, as the idea of a unified set of "black interests" has come under attack—both within and outside of black communities—the Republican Party has deployed a series of strategic, if sometimes symbolic, outreach efforts to generate a conservative thinking class and thrust African American Republicans into the spotlight as markers of GOP diversity.

This chapter opened with a question from one of my interviewees: Why don't people talk about black Democrats? The commonplace does not generate a lot of attention, so when 96 percent of black voters go for the Democratic candidate, it won't make headlines. The unexpected politics of African American Republicans, however, makes for good news. The historical record suggests that one of the reasons for the novelty ascribed to black conservatives is the strategic choices in the history of the Republican Party that have positioned it as antithetical to anything that could be conceivably framed as "pro-black." Correspondingly, this perception taints anyone engaged in Republican politics. For much of their history in U.S. politics, African American political interests have been dominated by efforts to gain political and economic equality. While neither party has a particularly stellar history of addressing those concerns, the past few decades have seen the Republican Party moving explicitly away from them.[49]

For a party that originated with abolition as a central plank of its platform, the whiteness of today's Republican Party is quite the achievement. And the move from being embracing to hostile to black interests is rightly understood as an achievement. It is the result of a series of considered choices by GOP leadership throughout time. These choices have placed contemporary African American Republicans in an unenviable position. To make the case for their own partisanship, African American Republicans often rely on history, and any argument that wants to position blacks as supported by the GOP and central to its success requires delving into the history of the party. Yet such mining of history does little to convince anyone doubtful of African American Republicans. The unexpected nature of their politics often means that they themselves are subject to debate: Are they Republican enough if they're black? And are they black enough if they're Republican? It's little wonder that my respondents, far from championing their party's race-neutral rhetoric, instead had ready answers for how they could be both black and Republican—like Walter, they'd had to answer those questions often.

CHAPTER TWO

Beyond Uncle Tom

At twenty-four, Eric was a relative newcomer to political debate, but, by his account, he had heard all the possible criticisms and insults of African American Republicans. He didn't take it personally anymore, and, in fact, he seemed to delight in recounting the epithets hurled at him as a black Republican: Uncle Tom, sellout, traitor to the race, house nigger, and "the white man's bitch." The last, his personal favorite, came during a particularly heated online exchange. Eric told me the site, a forum for discussing black politics, ran a story about a particularly egregious instance of a white Republican politician suggesting that blacks were intellectually inferior. Eric agreed with the overwhelming majority of commenters: the statement was clearly racist. But another theme emerged in the comments—this anti-black attitude is part and parcel of Republican partisanship, and racist beliefs are endemic to the Republican Party. Preparing himself for the "flame war," Eric commented.

In his comments, Eric was unsparing in his criticism of the politician, but he stressed that individual racist attitudes were present on both the left and the right. The actions of one person did not always represent the group. Soon a fellow commenter suggested that Eric sounded like "one of those black Republicans," and when Eric confirmed that he was, he was told that he'd "willingly made himself into the white man's bitch" and that it would be hard for anyone to take Eric's views seriously. Eric told this story with relish. A great storyteller who had polished this one to perfection, he smiled and practically jumped out of his seat when he delivered the climactic insult. Still, he was economical in the details—not quite vague, but, claiming he didn't want to "out" his online persona, he left out specifics about which website he was using or which politician was being debated. Because the story felt a little too rehearsed and the insult too on-the-nose, I admit I wasn't entirely convinced of the veracity of this particular story. That said, I had certainly seen plenty of similar online conversations in my research, and even if Eric was lying, it was telling that he chose to present himself as an object of derision, fundamentally misunderstood on the issue of his racial identity. For Eric, the point of the story was not about the racism of one politician or even the racism in the Republican Party. Rather, the well-executed punchline was meant to call attention to the public perception of African American Republicans.

Across my interviews and observations, black Republicans reported insults that often came from other African Americans, though many also mentioned frustration with the "mainstream media" for saying things about African American Republicans they would never dare say about any other black person. For some, it stung. For others, like Eric, the needling just made for some good stories. And for still others, the questioning of their race, their political allegiances, and implications that they were too dumb to see that they were pawns was just a part of the larger bullying culture of "identity politics." Regardless of their attitude toward these comments, African American Republicans felt that their political partisanship made them vulnerable to attacks on their racial authenticity; every single black Republican I spoke with recounted an experience of having their racial loyalty disparaged.

In contrast to the almost universal negative responses from other blacks, African American Republicans found white Republicans fairly supportive of their unexpected partisanship. Yet even that support came with a certain degree of discomfort. The loyalty concerns of white Republicans inverted the challenges from other African Americans. Eric provided a useful illustration, telling me that, in general, he considered whites very encouraging of his participation in Republican politics. He was regularly sought out for speaking engagements and consulted on outreach efforts to black voters in his already solidly Republican state. He had even been encouraged to seek a leadership position in a young Republican group. While other blacks vilified his partisanship, his white counterparts prized his participation in the GOP. "When I'm going to a party function and my friends know about it, I kind of feel like they might throw shit at my car as I drive away," Eric joked. "But at the same time, it's like the white folks celebrate when I drive up!" Still, he was sure that the whites' adoration was contingent on him being seen as more committed to ideological principles than to black identity.

Thus, Eric found his conservative beliefs and loyalty to the GOP called into question, and he consistently felt that his presence at Republican events was greeted with skepticism until he could establish his "conservative bona fides." "White Republicans," he said, "have this really divided reaction" to African

American Republicans. On the one hand, there was an eager embrace of minorities. GOP leaders have long been vocal about wanting to make the Republican Party racially inclusive.[1] On the other hand, white Republicans were aware of the strong link between black voters and the Democratic Party. The perceived unexpectedness of African American Republican partisanship raises questions about the divided loyalty. To whom are African American Republicans most loyal—the GOP or other blacks? And just as Eric was not alone in his experiences with African Americans' derision, my other respondents confided that they, too, had encountered conflicted responses from white Republicans.

.   .   .

Despite, or perhaps because of, their small numbers, African American Republicans generate a great deal of attention and are a group that people talk a lot about, often in very polarized ways. They draw sharp responses from friends and enemies alike. Because African American Republicans are aware of the attention that their unexpected politics draw, many use that attention as a platform for spreading their beliefs about the virtues of conservative social policy and Republican partisanship. Some even take a certain amount of pleasure in going against the grain. For many, their pride is bolstered by a belief that their unexpected politics comes with special insight. Many of my informants were quick to note their "unique" partisan choice and how it makes them stand out from other blacks. Like many people engaged in unexpected behaviors, they prize this specialness because it makes them different.[2] One told me: "I find that a lot of the times blacks just look to see what other blacks are doing and go do that. Look, we've been raised together regardless of socioeconomic background because of racial segregation. So some people are still socialized that way and they say black people vote Democrat, I'm going to vote Democrat. Black people support Obama, so I'm going to support Obama."

A similar attitude was reflected in relation to white Republicans. When discussing demographic changes in the United States and the corresponding need to target minority voters, one activist said, "Anybody can see you can't just have white folks dominating the party anymore.... It's like the world is changing but they [GOP leaders] don't wanna see it. They just aren't coming at it from the same perspective as me." African American Republicans believe they know something no one else does. They see things that black liberals cannot and they have a perspective that white Republicans lack. They see themselves as special. Believing that you know something everyone else doesn't naturally brings some excitement.

But unexpectedness cuts both ways. Though African American Republicans themselves think that being situated between two seemingly incompatible political worlds gives them unique insight, they are concerned about what others make of their unexpected political location. While the intersection of their race and partisanship may create opportunities that a black Democrat or a white Republican could never access, black Republicans rarely see themselves as the beneficiaries of opportunity. Rather, they consistently understand themselves as articles of wonder, kept under scrutiny, their motives called into question by all sides. They find themselves getting criticism from one group and qualified praise from the other. The criticisms, mostly from other blacks (and occasionally their white liberal allies), are grounded in an assessment of how Republican policies will affect blacks. The criticisms also reveal a particular understanding of how race relates to politics, in which racial identity is *supposed* to shape an individual's understanding of their political interests and structure their political choices. The praise, generally from white Republicans, is often qualified for much the same reason. *Shouldn't* this "black elephant" in their midst really be somewhere else? *Isn't* the Democratic Party the "natural" home for black voters?

The activists in this study feel that other blacks and white Republicans operate with a similar assumption: African American Republicans have attenuated racial identification. Put simply, that means black Republicans do not attach to a primary identity as a black person. In fact, many accuse African American Republicans of operating in direct opposition to the interests of black people or, more benignly, looking "beyond race" to make political decisions. Either way, the very idea of conservative blacks paints them as somehow "less black" because of their partisanship. I found quite the opposite.

THE SELLOUT CRITIQUE

African American Republicans feel that their harshest criticisms come from other African Americans. They are positioned as marginal to the African American community, and their political beliefs are maligned as racially inauthentic. So the black political right has been described as part of a group of "new accommodationists" who serve as proxies for white hegemony, having "bought wholesale into the racist, capitalist American system, refusing to see that racism is not an aberration but rather an intricate part of that system."[3] Essentially, African American Republicans are perceived as working counter to the interests of African Americans as a group and contributing to a legacy of ingrained, taken-for-granted white supremacy in the United States. As the father of former Congressman J. C. Watts (an African American Republican) famously put it, a black person supporting the Republican Party is like "a chicken supporting Colonel Sanders."[4]

This "sellout" critique takes multiple forms. It can attack the racial loyalty of African American Republicans; it can position them as dupes exploited by the Republican Party; it can accuse them of selfishly following individual material interests to the exclusion of group uplift; and it can suggest that African American Republicans are just plain dumb. In truth, African Americans deploy these criticisms against any Republican: many African American voters think that all Republicans are anti-black, greedy, and dumb. It's the racial tone of these criticisms that is specific to African American conservatives.[5]

All the threads of the sellout critique are summed up nicely by a commenter at *The Root,* a website reporting on issues related to African American politics and culture. Commenting on an article about a record number of black Republicans running in primary races in 2010, "leart2" writes:

> I think most of these Black Republicans are grossly naive about their inclusion in the Republican Party. The Party want[s] to try and use them in what ever way they can while not supporting anything Black or anything related to the Black Community. Back in the day it was understood that Blacks became Republicans because the "Line" was shorter for Black Patronage. Maybe that is what's going on now, because I can't understand why a Black would go through the trouble of trying to identify themselves as a Republican with all of their Racist Warts.[6]

On another *Root* article, a commenter attempts to explain why there are not more African American Republicans in black communities, distinguishing conservative (framed as reasonable) from Republican (framed as unreasonable):

> You probably don't see many Black Republicans in the hood because people in the hood tend to know who is and who isn't their friend. There are PLENTY Black Conservatives. There are FEW Black Republicans. As long as the Republican Party remains the "good ol' boys" club and treat Blacks like dust on their shoe (unless Black folks do things like deny racism exists or throw other Blacks under the bus) then there will continue to be few Black Republicans. Michael Steele is not enough. It takes a mindset change among the party.[7]

It's worth noting that this response is not entirely ideological. There *is* a distinct strain of conservatism organic to black politics, and experimental research shows that, under certain conditions, African Americans can be convinced to support an individual conservative candidate.[8] The disparagement, then, is distinctly partisan, grounded in beliefs about the Republican Party—both what it stands for and its relationship to African American voters. Across media, from Internet comment threads to political talk shows, the sellout critique is explicitly and implicitly deployed, reinforcing the notion that a black Republican deserves a double take.

In this critique, *sellout* is "a disparaging term that refers to blacks who knowingly or with gross negligence act against the interests of blacks as a whole.... [and it] is a messy, volatile, contested term about which disagreement is rife, especially when it comes to applying the label to specific persons or conduct."[9] Using "sellout" allows people to police the boundaries of group membership, outlining appropriate and inappropriate behaviors for African Americans in the political sphere and constraining the "acceptable" choices available to members of the group.

As a result of their unexpected partisan choice, the activists I interviewed are positioned as classic examples of the sellout. Certainly, the public face of African American Republicans shapes this image, and many high-profile black political conservatives are known for their eviscerating critiques of black culture and black political leaders. These critics from "within the community" draw media attention broadly, but the sellout critique may be at its most stinging on the individual level. Like Eric, the people I spoke with all offered stories about how their racial authenticity or partisan loyalty has been questioned. Many felt they were seen as working against the interests of black people. Mark, a thirty-seven-year-old lawyer, articulated a litany of accusations that African American Republicans like him encounter: "'Everybody knows black Republicans are Uncle Toms selling out other black folks.' 'They don't care about black people.' 'They want to be white.' 'They desperate for white folks to love them.' [laughs] I've heard it all. And most of it from black people." Mark laughed and made light of the attacks but was quick to clarify: "Seriously, though, I'm nobody's Uncle Tom."

Elwood, who at the time of our conversation was a recent college graduate in a southern red state, experienced similar challenges to his racial loyalty and saw them as the main difficulty of Republican partisanship for African Americans: "It's really frustrating. People think just because you are black, you can't be a Republican.... I get people all the time telling me I'm acting white. Like somehow I'm less of a black person because I voted for Bush." Confronted with the idea that identity drives politics, yet embracing a politics that the overwhelming majority of people who share their racial identity reject, African American Republicans feel judged as operating outside the bounds of appropriate black behavior.

The awareness of their image as sellouts emerged in one-on-one interviews, but it was also present in more public settings. It was rare to attend a meeting, presentation, or talk where an African American Republican speaker did not acknowledge their "rarity." Just as African American Republicans invoked humor in individual interviews, in public settings they made jokes to downplay the negative associations they attract. In a panel discussion about conservative influences on contemporary black politics, one speaker called himself "one of that strange and rare specimen: the black Republican." He got a good laugh. At a different panel discussion, a congressional candidate began his talk by declaring that black Republicans are more rare than unicorns—but while people love unicorns, they hate African American Republicans. The analogy might be a bit convoluted, but the mostly white audience ate it up. Humor appeared to be a part of every African American Republican speaker's repertoire, as if they recognized that everyone in the room was aware of the discordance of being both black and Republican, so the best way to break the ice was to address that "uniqueness" head-on.

Because black Republicans expect to be seen as sellouts, it comes as no surprise when they are attacked as sellouts in the media, but the private questioning of their connection and commitment to other African Americans is disconcerting. Among my respondents, Republican partisanship was extremely rare in their families, especially among extended family. Some had spouses who shared their conservative policy leanings and socially conservative values, but very few had other family members who would identify themselves as Republicans. This could make for awkward family gatherings.

Edward grew up in a staunchly Democratic household in the Midwest. When his family gets together, he told me, politics is always on the table: "I like talking politics. My dad likes talking politics. My momma, she tries to pretend like she doesn't care about politics, but she knows every little thing that's going on in the news." Despite the shared interest, the subject of partisanship produces deep, often unspoken, rifts between Edward and his parents.

> What's so crazy about it is that we probably agree on like ninety percent of issues. But I don't think they can get their head around me being a Republican. Me and my dad, we can go at it sometimes. And he's never come out and called me a sellout or anything. But he has made it known that, in his mind, no black man should be supporting the Republican Party. I just keep trying to show him you can be a good black man and support the Republican Party.

When I asked how he demonstrates that, he said, "That's what's so crazy. I'm just doing all the stuff they brought me up to do. You know. Work hard. Be a good Christian. Stay true to family and friends. Trying to be a good representative of my people. Trying to show there's no limit to what a black man in America can do." This was a key irony for Edward: the very things that comprise being a "good black man" are also the things that, he feels, draw him to the Republican Party. But his partisan affiliation creates a distance—if a surmountable one—within his family. Now Edward simply knows to expect that he'll be on the defensive at the dinner table.

The perception that racial identity drives partisan choice leaves African American Republicans on the wrong side of racial identity politics. The charges of selling out are something African American Republicans expect, and they arm themselves with prepackaged responses (see chapters 3 and 4). Yet, despite their comfort with addressing these charges, they are frustrated. They see themselves as tightly bound to black communities, if always on the defensive. As a response, many, like Edward, try to find common ground among family and friends, often by focusing on a shared concern for African Americans as a group. Indeed, many of them position their engagement in Republican politics as motivated by a deep and unyielding concern for black people. Gwen, a red-state Republican in her fifties, told me: "People think if you have affiliated with the Republican Party, you don't like black people. And that is entirely wrong from my standpoint. I affiliate with the Black Party, I mean, the Republican Party, because I love black people and I see what is happening to us."

Roland, a political organizer, stressed his firm identification with and commitment to black communities: "I've been involved in the [black] community, for all my life, at a lower level enough for people to see that first of all I'm concerned about the least of all. I mean, they want to make Republicans sound like they all big shots and they're bourgeoisie and everything. But I've always worked in the black community. I've always preferred working at the community level."

Hunter, a twenty-six-year-old who once thought of himself as "liberal" but had fully embraced conservative politics and Republican partisanship, reported:

> It's almost because I was black that I started to embrace conservatism. All of the values that my parents passed down to us—get married before you have kids, send your kids to private school, speak good English—were Republican values. It was strange that all these other aspects of our lives were telling us we were supporting other ideologies that we were against. We go to Catholic church, but we support abortion. We don't take handouts, but we support an unfettered welfare state.... I started looking at the things that were hurting the black community and pretty much it boiled down to liberalism.

For Hunter, it was all about striking the right balance: "The level of responsibility you feel for other blacks is different than it was in the sixties. Though I acknowledge that if it weren't for other people who felt a stronger need for helping other black people, we wouldn't be at this point to begin with. So that's, again, what I'm talking about. We do need both, look out for each other and look out for yourself." Conscious of his own success, Hunter grapples with balancing personal advancement against a responsibility to the broader community of blacks.

The charge that they are "less black," then, is inconsistent with how African American Republicans see themselves. It is also out of line with how they describe the circumstances in which they grew up, as well as the people and historical moments with which they identify. African American Republicans talk in ways that suggest they see themselves as connected to a broader black community. Unfailingly, activists refer to "us," "we," and "our community" when referencing black people. They link themselves to a broader black collectivity by identifying with important black historical moments, black physical spaces, and black public figures.[10]

Intriguingly, it was also common for African American Republicans to both share racial identity and express dismay with their association to other blacks. The connection to other African Americans is not just rhetorical. Most interviewees lived in predominantly black communities, and those who didn't spent significant time in black neighborhoods visiting family and friends. African American Republicans remained embedded in familial networks—immediate and extended—that provided a link to broader networks of African Americans.

Many were also involved in "Black Republican" organizations that stress the intersection of their racial and partisan identities. Their unique political location actually served to encourage strong racial identification, since a central part of their authority among non-black Republicans is grounded in their ability to speak to what happens in black communities. In this regard, they have a vested interest in identification with other blacks. They are also expected to take the lead in discussions about race, whether in regard to outreach efforts or when white Republicans want a general sense of what is "going on" with black people.

Hunter, the former liberal, described how his blackness was highlighted through increased conversations about race now that he was a Republican. "I talk more about race as a Republican than I did as a liberal. I just talk differently about race. A lot more honestly and openly." Hunter, like many of the people I interviewed, stands at the intersection between racial *middlemen,* who try to build bridges between Republicans and the black community, and *tokens* prized because of the symbolic value of their racial identity.[11] Put another way, it's hard to forget that you're black when surrounded by white people. In this way, an unexpected political location heightens racial identity.

Randall Kennedy argues that, despite its dangerous aspects, sellout accusations are inherent in any collective enterprise and often serve a useful role.[12] When you're on the receiving end of the charge of selling out, it's hard to see it as anything other than negative. African American Republicans are resentful about their suspect status, and this can manifest itself in anger at the weight of expectations that accompany what blacks are "supposed to do." Those African American Republicans who were more established in their local conservative political communities were more vocal about their frustrations. Some said they often courted the anger of other African Americans, making intentionally provocative comments about the black community's relationship to the Democratic Party and denigrating the political savvy of the average black voter, implying that it was the unthinking black Democratic voter who was a racial traitor: voting the way you're "supposed to" isn't, they implied, being a responsible voter at all.

James, who in his forties had recently become more active in Republican politics in his state, was angered by attacks on his racial credibility. We met at a conservative conference in Washington, D.C., where we were seated at a table with three other African American Republicans. To that point, the conversation had consisted of general small talk and introductions. When I explained that I was studying African American Republicans for a research project, the subject quickly turned to how African American Republicans were, in James's words, "misunderstood." For him, the crux of the misunderstanding was the perception that African American Republicans endorsed a political party that was racist—both in terms of its membership and in its policy positions toward blacks. But rather than trying to articulate how his being Republican was consistent with a strong sense of racial identity, he attacked his attackers by questioning the racial implications of *their* politics: "It doesn't bother me when they call me Uncle Tom. They're the ones with the slave mentality living on the Democratic Party's plantation.... The so-called civil rights leaders are the poverty pimps selling out the black community." His language echoed racially coded terms I would hear many times in my research. Describing the relationship between African Americans and the Democratic Party as "plantation politics" meant that black politicians and voters were nothing more than slaves on a Democratic plantation, doing what they were told. Nor was he the only African American Republican who referred to primarily Democratic black political leaders as "poverty pimps," with their livelihoods depending on black economic inequality. These responses attempt to co-opt the charge of race traitor and use it to validate Republican partisanship, even while reifying the idea that identity drives political behavior. In this inversion of the "sellout" charge, though, it's Democrats who engage in politics that are detrimental to blacks as a group.[13]

Attacking the political sophistication of their accusers is a way of arguing that people who would classify Republican partisanship as the marker of a sellout are ignorant of political history and unthinking about contemporary politics. George captured both:

> We [black people] bought the lie that Republicans don't like black people and Democrats support black people. Part of that is the Republicans' fault because they ignored the black vote. Many blacks don't know that Republicans pushed the Voting Rights Act through. But blacks think Republicans don't care about us, so they leave the party.... But the real history is that it was Democrats who were the party of lynching. Black folks don't know that. And its Democratic policies that are killing the black family. It was Democrats who supported welfare policies that kicked black men out of the home.... Asking a black to call yourself Democrat is like asking a Jew to call himself a Nazi.

This sort of response is not aimed at allaying the fears that other blacks might have about the Republican Party. Rather, it presents a historical argument about the Democratic Party's crimes against the black community and suggests that Republican partisanship is as an indicator of political savvy and historical knowledge among African Americans. The argument strips specific facts from broader historical context, and it's gained very little traction among non-Republican African Americans.

Neither responding to the sellout critique with their own charges of selling out nor attacking the political knowledge of their attackers is a tactic original to the African American Republicans in this study. Attacks on the "civil rights establishment" and black political leaders are consistent with arguments deployed by high-profile African American conservatives.[14] Even though these kinds of responses to the sellout charge attack rather than appease, they also attempt to align Republican partisanship within a tradition of black politics. This suggests that African American Republicans are all too aware of their connection to other blacks and are quite sensitive to the perception that their politics make them racially inauthentic.

THE SKEPTICAL EMBRACE

In contrast to their chilly reception within the African American community, the Republicans I interviewed felt much more accepted and encouraged by their white counterparts in the party. Still, while grateful for the support, they noted how often it's accompanied by skepticism. From the stories African American Republicans tell, two concerns drive the mixed response they receive from whites in the GOP: the party's desire for diverse representation and its concern that racial loyalty will trump partisan affiliation. The first is consistent with a broader push for diversity in U.S. institutions, since the perception of racial discrimination often undermines moral legitimacy. However, this first concern is tempered by the second, grounded in anxiety about balancing outreach efforts to black voters with a principled stand against what white Republicans consider "identity politics." The tension between the concerns is behind Republicans' skeptical embrace of blacks within their ranks.

In white Republicans' framing, African Americans in their party are presented as taking a principled stand against an overwhelming tide of politically liberal ideology and Democratic partisanship in black communities. One local Republican Party official in an extremely Democratic city told me, "It takes real bravery for these guys to stand up and say they are Republican. You have everyone in their community supporting Democrats, and here they are going against the popular opinion. I wish more African Americans would display the courage of their convictions like this." After a thoughtful pause, he chuckled and added, "I wish white people in this city would stand up to act on their beliefs like this. If they did, we'd see a lot more Republicans in this town." African American counterparts, for Republicans like this, are models not only for other blacks, but also for political conservatives more generally.

The framing of African Americans as outspoken and courageous is, fundamentally, grounded in a belief in the strength of racial solidarity. African American Republicans are "brave" only if one believes in a strong sense of cohesiveness among blacks, a cohesiveness based on shared racial identity that makes speaking out an indicator of courage. But white Republicans' belief in the strength of racial solidarity also makes them question African American Republicans' partisan loyalty. It's a double-edged sword.

A well-documented instance involved Colin Powell's endorsement of Barack Obama in the 2008 presidential election. After Powell's endorsement, Republicans were quick to suggest that racial loyalty, not policy, drove his decision. The endorsement was held up as proof of African Americans' willingness to prioritize race over the party line, and criticism was fast and vocal. Key conservative figures offered explicit race-based critiques of

Powell's support that reflected anxiety about where the loyalties of African American Republicans actually lay. An October 2008 article on the website Politico quoted an email sent to reporters by Republican commentator Rush Limbaugh:

> "Secretary Powell says his endorsement is not about race," Limbaugh wrote in e-mail. "OK, fine. I am now researching his past endorsements to see if I can find all the inexperienced, very liberal, white candidates he has endorsed. I'll let you know what I come up with.
>
> "I was also unaware of his dislike for John Roberts, Clarence Thomas, Samuel Alito, Anthony Kennedy and Antonin Scalia. I guess he also regrets Reagan and Bush making *him* a four-star and secretary of state and appointing his son to head the FCC. Yes, let's hear it for transformational figures."[15]

Joining the chorus was Pat Buchanan, a former senior presidential advisor and conservative media figure, on *Meet the Press*. Buchanan suggested that political analysts *must* question the role racial loyalty played in Powell's decision: "Alright, we gotta ask a question, look—would Colin Powell be endorsing Obama if he were a white liberal Democrat?"

The African American Republicans I spoke with talked about the weight of this concern. They felt they were required to prove their allegiance to the party and its ideology in a way their white counterparts were not. The most benign interpretation is that it makes political sense, given African Americans' high levels of support for the Democratic Party. Bennet, a thirty-six-year-old activist in a liberal state, blamed the lack of Republican outreach to blacks on party officials' concerns that they couldn't be a reliable constituency: "I think there's a lack of trust on both sides. Black folks don't trust Republicans. But you can't really blame them [Republicans], honestly. With most of us voting for Democrats, they don't really have any reason to think we would support them. It's race first for most black folks. That's why leadership in the party doesn't think it would make sense to come after the black vote."

In a more humorous vein, Jeffrey, a twenty-seven-year-old auditor from a blue state, discussed what he saw as the defining and legitimating issue for African American Republicans: affirmative action. In describing his experience as one of the few African Americans at a statewide Republican convention, he told me about how he never quite felt like he was fully embraced by his white conservative counterparts, even when their views overlapped on policy positions:

> I can talk with a white Republican for like forty-five minutes to an hour. And the whole time we're vibing and feeling each other on all kinds of issues. But you can see it in the back of their eyes. It's like they've been holding back waiting to ask about the one issue they want to know your opinion about ... affirmative action [laughs]. I swear, you can talk to a white Republican all day but until you pass the affirmative action test they gone always be looking at you sideways.

This was a common feeling. Many thought affirmative action served as a test to gauge their relative commitments to the GOP and to their fellow African Americans, particularly since the issue could easily be framed as putting race and partisanship in direct opposition.[16] Affirmative action was often invoked in unrelated policy discussions, the activists told me, so that white Republicans could take their measure:

> Everybody wants to know what you think of affirmative action. When it comes up, all the heads in the room turn and look at you. It's really an issue you can't win with. Come out against it, black people think you're a sellout. Come out for it, Republicans will say,

"See. I told you they all stick together." Personally, I think there has to be a middle ground on this issue. I mean, even Colin Powell and Condoleezza Rice support some form of affirmative action, but let me try that here. They'd run me out of the party!

By the end of the discussion, Jeffrey was laughing about the prospect of being "run out of the party," but the humor was displacing serious concern around the charge of being an ideological sellout, or a Republican in Name Only (RINO) in party parlance. Even African American Republicans who oppose affirmative action recognize the importance of it for testing the commitment of blacks in the Republican Party. Robert, staunchly opposed to *any* social policy that considers race and any framing of social policy as beneficial for a particular race, acknowledged this, saying, "I know it upsets them [other African American Republicans] when people always want to know what they think about affirmative action." He explained why he thought white Republicans were interested in the affirmative action issue:

> But that's because they're trying to see which side are you on. Are you stuck in the same old identity politics? Or are you willing to truly stand up for conservative, Republican values? I choose my values not my race because at the end of the day values are more important. So I don't mind when they ask. I look 'em straight in the eye and tell them I hate affirmative action more than they do!

Affirmative action is not the only issue on which Republicans wrestle with the appropriateness of demanding ideological consistency. Across a number of issues, the GOP struggles to strike the appropriate balance between party unity and encouraging healthy debate.[17] Similarly, Democrats juggle a broad range of issues and positions in their efforts to build governing coalitions. However, African American Republicans contend that they face a particularly high burden of proof to establish their conservative credentials.

It might not be surprising that African American Republicans in liberal areas feel that their white counterparts are suspicious of their loyalties. The GOP is weaker there and has less to offer activists in terms of patronage rewards. However, this feeling was present even among activists in conservative states where the Republican Party was strong and performed well. Elwood, the young, enthusiastic organizer and champion of the party in a red state, expressed similar concerns about his loyalties, though it was unclear how frustrated he was by those concerns. "On some level I do have to prove myself. I mean, since most blacks are in the Democrat [*sic*] Party they don't expect someone like me to be committed to the Republican cause. So I work twice as hard. But you know, brothers like you and me, we've always been told that we have to work twice as hard to get half as much."

African American Republicans' response to white Republicans is much more muted than their reaction to their perceived rejection by other African Americans, and it is shaped, primarily, by their relationship to the larger GOP structure. Those who are actively engaged in "mainstream" Republican groups and the state party structure take a more measured response. Like Robert, Jeffrey, and Bennet, they can understand white skepticism—but understanding is not the same as endorsing or encouraging. Rather, African American Republicans who regularly interact with white Republicans resign themselves to the mixture of praise and skepticism. Some even use it to their advantage. Like the candidate who played up the maverick nature of his politics, they see an opportunity to leverage the perceived rarity of being an African American Republican for personal gain. To quell concerns about loyalty, these African American Republicans are vocal about their conservative beliefs and extol the importance of placing ideology before identity.

More privately, they express resistance to the expectation of lockstep agreement with their GOP counterparts. One former political candidate talked about how labels are too restricting:

> We get forced into this label mentality.... Now, the problem is some people very narrowly define those. When in fact, with each label, I bet you can find a broad range of people who fit that description. I tell people that just because I ran as a Republican doesn't mean I'm a Kool-Aid drinking Republican where I believe everything that they say and all of that and on and on and on. *Au contraire!* Maybe seventy percent of what they are supposed to ... seventy percent of what the Republican ideology is supposed to be, I agree with. But yet I am viewed as a black Republican.... My point being, you take "black Republican," some people want to narrowly define it for their purposes.... [L]abels are used as an accommodation for a lot of people who are trying to put their spin on something or are trying to justify their argument or trying to sell their idea or whatever the case may be. And so this whole label game in the media is especially bad at trying to put everybody in a category because of their sound-bite industry. It's all about the sound-bite. It's never about the full story or the information.

However, for the vast majority of African American Republicans I spoke with, concerns about white Republicans are more remote. To the extent that white Republicans showed little regard for any "pro-black" brand of Republicanism, most African American Republicans in this study had little consistent interaction with them. Later chapters detail how the racialized politics of some African American Republicans strained institutional relations with their white counterparts. So although ideological litmus testing may not be experienced as a profound attack on their identity in the way that the sellout critique is, it has important implications for how African American Republicans fare within the broader context of GOP institutions. For now, it is enough to say that concern about white Republicans is partly a function of how embedded African American Republicans are in mainstream GOP institutions. Although it's experienced as a very real thing, ideological litmus testing is a lot less top-of-mind compared to the sellout critique.

African American Republicans understand that their political location—at the margins of both black and Republican politics—means that people across the political spectrum question their loyalties. From their perspective, this questioning centers primarily on the issue of racial identity—they are convinced that others doubt the possibility of being fully committed to both black identity and Republican partisanship. Among fellow blacks, this manifests itself in a sellout critique that questions their racial authenticity. White Republicans' questions produce a skeptical embrace that also places ideological loyalty in competition with racial identity. Though they come from very different audiences, both responses are grounded in a similar assumption. Black identity is thought to be at odds with Republican partisanship, and this structures how everyone responds to black Republicans.

Occasionally, African American Republicans take this questioning as proof that they have staked out the correct political stance. Caught between rejection from blacks and distrust from other Republicans, African American Republicans can use their alienation as a source of political legitimacy. As one respondent put it, "When both sides don't know what to make of you, you are probably doing something right." But for most, this questioning is not so easy to brush off. Indeed, constantly being questioned produces what the editors of *Black and Right,* a collection of essays from black political conservatives, call an "existential predicament." They argue:

> The existential predicament of the black conservative in America is a profound one. On the one hand, when he expresses his sincerely held views, other black people often dismiss these positions as the disgusting cloying of an "Uncle Tom." On the other hand, white conservatives, unfamiliar with the realities of black life in America and the tremendous courage required for a black person to openly express conservative politics, underestimate the significance of his expression and so manifest a certain passivity and indifference to the black conservative's dilemma.[18]

The African American Republicans in this study did assume that others believed they were not strongly racially identified, or they wouldn't be Republicans. And they felt that white Republicans were suspicious that they could "move beyond race," but, after being tested on "litmus" issues like affirmative action, they found whites very supportive. Neither perspective can capture how African American Republicans talk about their own sense of racial identity and their connection to other blacks.

Among the African American Republicans in this study, it's fair to say there's a consistently high level of racial identification. They see themselves as embedded in African American communities, and they often frame their participation in Republican politics as motivated by concern for other blacks. They are also deeply committed to the principles of the Republican Party, even when they feel that party leaders act in ways that are contrary to those principles. For them, the incongruence between racial identity and partisanship is an artifact of perception, not reality.

While my respondents expressed a wide-ranging connection to specific black people, including family members and an abstract black community, other research on black political behavior has drawn on more specific measures of racial identification. One of those is a survey measure of "linked fate."[19] Linked fate captures the extent to which respondents feel a sense of connection to blacks as a collective. The measure is often based in a single item: "Do you think what happens generally to black people in this country will have something to do with what happens in your life?" In surveys of black voters, the majority of Republican respondents agree with this statement. Drawing from two samples of voters from the 2008 and 2012 American National Election Survey, among black respondents, 53 percent of Republicans agreed, and 25 percent of those who agreed felt "a lot" of linked fate. Given the tiny number of black Republicans in national survey samples, it's wise not to make too much of this finding.[20] But the response is consistent with the way my respondents talked about their connection to black communities: African American Republicans generally seem to express a connection to blacks as a group.

African American Republicans' professed sense of racial identification defies their public image and the expectations of other blacks and white Republicans. In this regard, their identification with blackness is empirically interesting. It suggests that, as a group, they might not be as ridiculous as observers have assumed. However, their commitment to black identity also complicates the assumed relationship of black identity to political behavior. African American Republicans demonstrate that the presence of black identity cannot be automatically aligned with any particular type of political behavior. In many ways, this should not be surprising.

Despite observers'—black and white—obsession with whether or not African American Republicans express a black identity, identification provides a very vague assessment of their commitment to racial solidarity. Claiming black identity captures whether or not individual blacks see themselves as part of a larger collective of "black people," but it tells us very little about the valence or salience of that connection. The feeling of group connectivity could be experienced as positive and empowering, but black identity might be perceived as a constraint that limits individual expression. It is also possible that the experience of linked fate can vary by context. In some situations, feeling connected to other black people might be empowering. In other contexts, the link to other blacks might be experienced as constraining.

Additionally, identification alone provides little insight into the significance placed on racial identity by individuals. Black people are not just black. They have other social categories with which they could, and do, express identification. Research suggests that it's important to be aware of how other social identities intersect with race. Analyses that account for this "intersectionality" show that the impact of identities varies. In some situations racial identity "trumps" other identities, but in other instances identities besides race might dominate decision-making processes.[21] Focusing on the presence of racial identification reveals little about how individuals juggle multiple, and occasionally conflicting, social identities. Consequently, political observers must pay more attention to the meaning and centrality of racial identity when examining black political behavior.[22]

Furthermore, relying solely on a measure of identification produces a limited account of the relationship between racial attachment and black political behavior. We cannot assume that the presence of a strong racial identity directs political behavior in any particular partisan direction. Knowing that blacks are connected to one another sheds little light on how that connection is enacted in the realm of politics. While commitment to black identity is normally strongly connected with Democratic partisanship, intervening mechanisms are required to cement this association. As such, research must be attuned to the possibility that identification with blackness can support a variety of political outcomes. Pushing beyond whether or not actors identify with a racial group also leaves open the possibility that racial identification can be channeled into a broad range of political actions and strategies, as well as how racial identity is perceived in relation to other collective identities or individual characteristics.

By explaining black political behavior through racial identification, both the sellout critique and the skeptical embrace are consistent with accounts in scholarly literature and popular political discourse, and both also share the limitations of an "identity model" of political behavior. Neither is fully equipped to account for the subjects in this study, who express high levels of racial identification yet engage in partisan choices that diverge from most African Americans. For African American Republicans, a strong sense of racial identity does not necessarily run counter to Republican partisanship. Accordingly, the question isn't whether or not African American Republicans identify as black. Rather, a more useful inquiry would explore how race is linked to the conservative politics of the Republican Party.

Given the prominence of the sellout critique and the skeptical embrace, making this link is important for personal and political reasons. Personally, resolving this tension is important if black Republicans want to feel a part of both a broader black community and their own families. African American Republicans feel marginalized by other blacks, and that's distressing. Politically, they must also account to white Republicans. White Republicans are critical to the political success of black Republicans; because blacks have thoroughly rejected the Republican Party and most of their emissaries, African American Republicans mostly gain institutional traction through the patronage of white Republicans. So if a black Republican wants to find political success, it must be in conjunction with the support of white Republicans. For example, when African American Republicans are elected to Congress, they come from predominantly white districts.[23] Consequently, African American Republicans have to manage the identity concerns of other blacks and of white conservatives.[24]

African American Republicans are frustrated. They identify with black people and black things. By extension, they also try to link Republican partisanship to a broader tradition of racial-uplift politics within the black community. While they didn't use the term *linked fate*, my respondents universally spoke in a way that suggested they saw their own fate as tied to the rest of black Americans. This connection can be perceived as a positive or a negative—either way, the connection to other blacks remains. This leaves African American Republicans with the challenge of aligning their commitment to black identity with their conservative political ideology and Republican partisanship. This linking of "blackness" to "Republican-ness" is key to negotiating relationships with other blacks and with white conservatives. Chapters 3 and 4 address how African American Republicans work to align their partisan affiliation with their racial identity. I divide African American Republicans into two camps: color-blind and race-conscious. Race bears on their political choices in different ways.

CHAPTER THREE

Race Doesn't Matter

The New Connections conference was dedicated to applying the philosophy and logic of Booker T. Washington to the problems of contemporary blacks. This black conservative organization was the brainchild of Walter, the activist who asked why no one was questioning black Democrats' allegiances, and the Libertarian Institute provided much of the event's funding. The Libertarian Institute would probably rather be described on the basis of its political philosophy and not the race of its members, but it is worth noting that, at the time, the organization's leadership was all white. Materials at the conference described the relationship between the Libertarian Institute and the New Connections as "a unique and very productive partnership whereby the Institute's work gets a better hearing in the black community while the New Connections' work benefits from our professional staff and access to resources."

Throughout the weekend, the conference combined the language of racial uplift and the spirit of a church revival. If not for the bland conference furniture and fluorescent lighting, you might have thought you were actually at a church service. Older women wore big hats and bright skirt suits that managed to strike a balance between reserve and ostentation. Audience members peppered the talks with an encouraging "amen" every so often, and the occasional baritone voice would encourage the speaker to "preach" after a particularly salient point was made. After days of breakout sessions that explored contemporary political, social, and economic challenges facing the black community, the final event was a panel discussion featuring academics, politicians, and political organizers. There were about forty people in the audience, and the crowd was racially mixed, about half white and half black. Everyone seemed to know one another. As a technician finalized the audiovisual setup, people leaned over the seats to talk with one another and express excitement about the panel.

One of the panelists, Adam Nelson, had a long history of working with Republican organizations, and his clothes were as conservative as his politics: blue blazer, khaki slacks, blue button-down shirt, and a bowtie. Nelson was an older black man who spoke with a distinct, almost over-enunciated diction and cadence. A charitable reading would describe his voice as precise, but it could be taken as a pseudo-British affectation. His bearing was prim, practiced, and verged on the comical. It was as if Carlton Banks from *The Fresh Prince of Bel-Air* had grown up and taken the stage. Nelson began his talk by suggesting that the failures of Richard Nixon and Martin Luther King, Jr., prevented increased black support for the Republican Party. With regard to King, Nelson argued that the leader had made black grievances the basis of his platform, leading directly to what he described as the black community's current inability to "rise above victimhood." Nelson said he would have preferred King to center his claims on the broader American promise, not just black victimhood and oppression. While the facts of his assessment were debatable, it garnered a positive response from the small audience.

Then Nelson transitioned to a critique of Nixon's support for affirmative action programs, which he described as wedding the victim mentality to an affirmative action mentality. This was a mistake, in his estimation, because blacks need to focus on the "promise of the American Constitution." With a flourish, he declared that "We are nothing better than America promises to become." Nelson closed by saying that the "race" question is subordinate to the "human" question: blacks should not have to, or want to, ask for help from anyone, because "wealth is infinite, because it is created by human beings." While aspects of Nelson's talk were opaque (what exactly does it mean to say that "wealth is infinite," and what is the "human" question?), the general tone was quite clear. The Republican Party, and its conservative politics, could provide blacks with a pathway to move beyond the victimhood associated with identity politics.

· · ·

In chapter 2, I showed that African American Republicans wrestle with negative perceptions from other blacks and from white Republicans. In response, they often invoke the strength of their connection to blackness. Yet that only partially addresses the problem. A key element of both the sellout critique and the skeptical embrace is the perception that blackness and Republican partisanship are incongruent—that a professed black identity cannot be squared with the politically conservative social policies of the Republican Party. In order to address the authenticity concerns of other blacks and the loyalty concerns of white

Republicans, they must align blackness with Republican-ness. In effect, they must make their unexpected politics expected.

Among the activists I studied, two strategies were used to link racial identity and politics. One draws on a color-blind worldview, while the other centers black identity and black interests in a race-conscious worldview. Linking race to Republican politics requires calibrating multiple sets of meanings, and I observed three among African American Republicans: (1) the meanings they attach to race in their own lives, (2) the meanings they attach to being black, and (3) the meanings they attach to being a Republican. Accordingly, the color-blind and race-conscious approaches to linking blackness to Republican partisanship are correlated with differences in pathways into the Republican Party, definitions of "black people," and framing of Republican policy preferences. This chapter focuses on color-blind African American Republicans, and the next chapter will address their racial-uplift counterparts.

In his talk at the New Connections conference, Adam Nelson embodied color-blind African American Republicans' efforts to claim a black identity while simultaneously downplaying its importance. The color-blind strategy resolves the perceived disconnect between black racial identity and Republican partisanship by downplaying the role of race in the lives of black people. Being black and Republican becomes consistent to this group because race is not central to how they make political decisions—when race is not the orienting frame, Republican partisanship is not necessarily inconsistent with being black. Indeed, depending on what social characteristics one prioritizes, Republican partisanship might make complete sense.

Color-blind African American Republicans acknowledge that being black is a part of who they are, but their racial identity is not central to how they see themselves. Race is just one of many characteristics that define who they are. This allows for the foregrounding of other identities that make for a smoother fit with Republican partisanship. So while not abandoning racial identification, the color-blind strategy allows race to be weighted against other characteristics. The color blindness is grounded in the idea that black people rely too much on race as both the cause and solution to the problems that face their communities. In this respect it reflects a central tenet of "color-blind racism" as identified by sociologist Eduardo Bonilla-Silva: a minimization of racism "that suggests that discrimination is no longer a central factor affecting minorities' life chances."[1]

PATHWAY INTO THE REPUBLICAN PARTY

Color-blind African American Republicans tell similar stories about their entry into the Republican Party. Like most African American Republicans, their partisanship is explored through narratives of conversion. Rarely did they grow up in Republican families. In their accounts, they were Democrats because that was all that they had known. It wasn't until they became more thoughtful and engaged that they realized they supported the wrong political party. More than their race-conscious counterparts, color-blind African American Republicans center their stories on an "aha moment" when they realized the alignment between their worldview and the conservative principles and policy promoted by the Republican Party. Across interview subjects, the contours of the story were quite similar: after a long period of passively accepting the political attitudes of family and friends (generally assumed Democratic loyalties), he or she began to examine which values were most important personally.

Around the same time, they had contact with someone involved in Republican politics—rarely an official outreach effort—and, through repeated discussions, realized that their own values and beliefs were aligned with those of the Republican Party. Many times these stories follow a "once was blind, but now I see" formulation. Over lunch, Jesse told me of what he called his "coming out" story.[2] From my field notes:

> He describes how growing up everyone he knew was a Democrat. He didn't give much consideration to his own partisanship. He just went along with the flow without doing much political questioning. From his description, he was pretty apolitical.... When he started his own business a few years ago he found himself giving serious consideration to his own political beliefs. He describes it as part of a process of taking himself more seriously in general. He also found himself being much more concerned with tax policy and "overregulation" by the government. He describes this clarifying of his own political thoughts as part of his own "growing up." When he began to articulate his beliefs to himself, he realized that he had always been conservative. At that point, he found himself paying more attention to candidate platforms and agreeing with the fiscal policies of Republicans who were running for office in his state. (June 2008)

Identification with racial identity, while placing a low priority on that identification, suggests that the color-blind African American Republicans were drawn to the party because of shared beliefs, but it also illustrates how the realization that Republican affiliation was an *option* did not occur to them until they had political discussions with friends and acquaintances from outside of the black communities in which they grew up. Whether it was having a white roommate in college or a politically active white coworker, color-blind African American Republicans report coming to their partisanship partly through informal exposure to white conservatives.

Further, they took pains to express that they had become open, not to a new set of beliefs or ideas, but to a new partisan affiliation. They saw themselves as aligning their politics with their beliefs and values. This made them virtuous, and unwilling to espouse beliefs for political expediency. Tim explained: "One of the things about being a Republican is the conservative values. You are honoring your integrity. You stand for something. You are not changing who you are just to fit into a situation." For Tim, this integrity is what distinguishes Republicans from Democrats. He went on to liken his commitment to the GOP to black historical figures who "were Republicans because in a way it coincided with how they lived their lives and the rules. The things that they would judge or the laws that would be created, the bills they would create that would be turned into laws. That's not so with the Democratic Party. Again, their whole ideology is we're liberal. We're vast.... But in the Democratic Party it's whatever goes." Democrats, according to Tim, are motivated by political expedience, not principle.

The shift in perspective is not always the direct result of being "converted" by a Republican proselytizer. Sometimes a changing life situation causes a realignment of values and partisanship. For one color-blind African American Republican, it was business ownership:

> When I began to think about myself as a business person, I looked at how I saw free enterprise and being able to be in a situation where I get to work hard and make a difference in my life and other people's lives without a lot of governmental red tape. Those were the kinds of things that began going through my mind. Subsequent to that there have just been other situations that have helped me to see.

It is difficult, perhaps impossible, to deduce whether or not being introduced into Republican networks lowered the racial consciousness of this type of African American Republican or if lower racial consciousness facilitated their introduction into politically conservative networks. Realistically, the relationship is probably recursive.

However the process unfolded, color-blind African American Republicans tended to view their partisan affiliation as a marker of enlightenment, a sign that they knew something that other black people didn't know: the pitfalls of letting their racial status define them or set expectations around what they can achieve. For the African American Republicans I spoke with, the policy prescriptions offered by the GOP were consistent with their ideological beliefs. But equally important was the fact that Republican affiliation allowed them to downplay the importance of their racial identity—their partisanship demonstrated their commitment to avoiding the collective thinking they saw as stifling black people.

THE PERSONAL MEANINGS OF RACIAL IDENTITY

African American Republicans, in general, express strong connections to other black people (see chapter 2). They see themselves as linked to other blacks in public perceptions and in interpersonal relationships. However, color-blind African American Republicans put very little stock in these connections. For them, race is just one factor among many that define them. When trying to make sense of their own life situations or the situation of other blacks, they insist that they don't look to race as an explanation.

As Inez, introduced at the start of the book, put it: "I'm a black woman. I can't hide from that. I don't want to. But I'm more than just a black woman. I'm also a professional, a taxpayer, a wife—among other things." Inez carries multiple identities, and the salience of any given identity is contextual. Although she expresses a connection to her race-mates, Inez's comments suggest that race is one among many social identities and is not always relevant in every aspect of her life. Using similar language, Derrick described prioritizing other attachments over his racial identity: "My relationship with God is first and foremost. My relationship with my kids is next. Then my work. Then my blackness as a black man. My feeling is that in our community we push the blackness over here [signals to the front] and it becomes more than our faith. And I say that's out of order. Our relationship with God is more important than my being black." Throughout our conversation, Derrick stressed that it was his religious, not racial, consciousness that shaped his political beliefs.[3] Similarly, Hunter, the former liberal quoted in chapter 2, talked about deprioritizing racial identity without abandoning it: "As a liberal, [I was] seeing myself as black before a great number of other things. Now, I don't socialize myself first as being black. I'm a man before I'm black. I'm an American before I'm black. I'm still black, though."

Color-blind African American Republicans do not suggest that race is irrelevant to all aspects of their lives. Rather, they are firm in their conviction that race is just less relevant in structuring their political beliefs and actions than other factors in their lives. When asked how his racial identity influences his politics, John, a twenty-four-year-old from a southern red state, told me how he divorces his racial identity from his political beliefs: "Honestly, I don't think that much about how race impacts my politics. Mainly because I don't think it does. I mean, it's not like I'm not black or anything. I know that! It's just that I don't think politics is about black and white. It's about doing the right thing and that has nothing to do with race." John felt that his de-emphasizing of race was consistent with the black struggles to have all races treated equally, in effect making his approach to politics the culmination of the civil rights movement. For John, his political stance is a matter of doing the "right" thing for all people, quite apart from its impact on black people specifically.

So racial identity produces a connection and concern for other blacks, but it doesn't orient how John and others like him think about the causes or appropriate policy responses to issues in black communities. For them, too much attention to race is itself an impediment for blacks, especially when the focus is on blacks as the victims of racial discrimination. All African American Republicans react negatively to the notion of blacks being defined by this history, but those deploying a color-blind worldview took a particularly virulent objection to any suggestion that victimhood is the marker of the black experience in America. Many interviewees expressed dismay at the "victim" mindset they saw motivating black politics. When discussing civil rights organizations' focus on racial discrimination, Derrick called for a shift: "We've got to start rethinking this [focus on racial discrimination]. I like how the Urban League is doing. How they've restructured their organization to think about economic empowerment. They've moved away from the whole social justice thing to economic empowerment. And I say bravo! It's about time."

A key component of this color blindness requires downplaying black racial identity and connection to other blacks, but there are exceptions to this color blindness. Importantly, racial identity is thought to be a reasonable basis on which to make family or cultural decisions. Blackness has personal salience, but not a political salience. For instance, many respondents I classify as color-blind politically talked about preferring to attend black churches. They thought black churches better represented how they wanted to worship and provided an experience that, in their opinion, could not be replicated in non-black worship services. School choice presented another example: color-blind African American Republicans were very attuned to the racial demographics of the schools their children attended. They held equal concern that a school could be "too black" and that their child might be the only black student in a class. Across all my interviews, respondents expressed similar sentiments. But among the color-blind African American Republicans, this position was a little surprising. Given their emphasis on race as only one of many identities and their pointed critiques of race-based identity politics, their selective attention to race is counterintuitive. Even with their strong disavowal of "race politics," respondents in this group did not embrace a de-racialized worldview in all contexts. I soon realized that it was part of their division of personal and public life. When it comes to black identity, the personal is most definitely *not* political for these color-blind black Republicans.

Racial identity was less salient when they thought about arenas like work or politics. In the political arena, African American Republicans shy away from racial distinction. The alternative lenses they employ are varied, but religion and ideology are two of the more prominent in guiding their thinking about politics. This runs counter to the assumption, present in both scholarship and the popular imagination, that the meanings and importance of racial identity are constant across African Americans. Color-blind African American Republicans' relationship to racial identity is fluid and shifting, with relevance ebbing and flowing depending on context. Racial identity is not a master status directing all manner of behavior for these people. Its importance varies across context, relevant personally but not politically. Though it certainly seems politically naive to suggest that race doesn't matter politically, race-blind black Republicans talk about "black interests" in such a way that de-centering racial identity makes sense. Part of the reason color-blind African American Republicans are ambivalent about centering race in their political worldview is that they perceive race as distracting from "real" problems black people face. Consequently, it's important to attend to not just the presence or absence of their racial identity, but also to how these black political actors construct the political needs of blacks as a group.

"BLACK PEOPLE" AS PATHOLOGICAL: CONSTRUCTING A BLACK POLITICAL SUBJECT

> There was a time when black folks had to scrimp and scrape just to get by. We had to make it happen by hook or by crook . . . but those days are in the past and black folks are still holding on to that "just to get by" mentality. We got to want better before we can do better.

With his focus on blacks' responsibility to "want better," Jason, a thirty-seven-year-old from a blue state, articulates one of the central premises of color-blind African American Republicans' account of black people. In effect, he is creating a *black political subject* that works as a stand-in for the person being served by particular social policies. Among African American Republicans, the black political subject is used to motivate black interests. Behind any construction of policy interests rests unspoken ideas about the political subject who benefits (or loses) from social policy. The black political subject is distinctly political in that it is a representation of black people that undergirds attitudes and opinions (as well as motivates action) in the political arena. In other words, the black political subject doesn't necessarily represent the totality of black people. So African American Republicans will often invoke one set of narratives in relation to politics and another set of narratives in relation to other social arenas—like family, popular culture, or religion. However, the political and nonpolitical arenas are not totally distinct, and personal experience often informs how African American Republicans think about blacks as political actors. Often this concept is implicit, never overtly discussed. The black political subject is certainly not articulated among my respondents as "these ideas I have about black people that motivate my discussion of conservative political positions." Nevertheless, they certainly have particular ideas in mind when they discuss black people as a collective.

The color-blind account of the black political subject is fairly pathological, presenting blacks as operating within a value system that leads to worse life outcomes compared to other racial and ethnic groups in the United States. Blacks, they believe, fail to embrace "traditional" values of family, work ethic, and personal responsibility and attach to a pattern of dependency on government programs and on racism and discrimination as "excuses" for black failures. For them, the current state of black America is a departure from an idealized past in which blacks, even under the crushing force of legalized discrimination, embraced a commitment to work and family and relied on close personal and neighborhood networks in times of need. Fundamentally, blacks—and, by extension, what passes for black culture—are regarded as morally suspect. This vision is reminiscent of the "culture of poverty" arguments that periodically crop up in policy arenas and situate blacks in a culture of poverty that prevents them from finding material success and broader cultural acceptance. Thus, blacks are framed as subscribing to a pathological value system, at odds with the rest of American society, and as making individual choices that lead to negative life outcomes. African American Republicans who endorse this pathological account lament the ways in which blacks have internalized and reified what they called "ghetto culture."

Decidedly urban, this vision of black people is embodied by the local street thug. Often when talking about the problems blacks face, the specter of black men hanging out on the corner is omnipresent among African American Republicans' rhetoric, invoked as representative of today's lamentable black youth and deployed across a range of contexts. From education to political engagement, when representing the problems of the black community, the color-blind discourse is accompanied by an imagined black subject who is male, urban, and unmotivated. "In our community we don't got science stars," one interviewee stated while discussing the state of urban schools. "If we're lucky we got basketball stars. But mostly we've just got a bunch of guys standing on the corner doing nothing." Discussing the future direction of black voters' political engagement, another respondent referred to the song "The Greatest Love of All," asking, "Remember that Whitney Houston song, 'I believe the children are our future'? Well, she needs to look around. Our future is lil' hoodlums hanging on the corner, pants falling all down." This sentiment was also elicited when asked about their personal life goals. In distancing himself from the negative image of blacks, one interviewee asserted, "I'm not trying to be like all those other black men standing on the corner letting life pass me by.

I'm trying to do something." Each of these comments came from a different interviewee in conversations about very different topics, yet each illustrates how the "corner" and the perception of the activities that occur there are used to demonstrate black people's deviation from "mainstream" American values.

African American Republicans who echo this portrayal of black men also point to the naturalization of what they feel are pathological cultural values. These skewed values, they believe, get passed down from generation to generation, creating a cycle of deviance. George, who lives in a big city in a solidly blue state, calls this an identity crisis. "We have an identity crisis among ourselves. A lot of black men will not openly admit their faults ... but we have them." With regard to his own transformation, George envisioned himself as a role model for those in the community who were still caught up in making bad life choices:

> I'll be able to reach out.... I'll be able to minister to these people. They look at me and they'll be like, "Man, George is looking pretty good. What did he do? He stopped drinking. He stopped cursing. He stopped whoremongering and he's focused on his family. He's focusing in on his family. He's focusing in on his community." Now when I say that we don't have no black leaders, I'm including myself in that because for a long time I'd sit back and talk about the problem but do nothing about it. I've now taken my vision and put it into action.

However, the challenge in black communities is larger than individuals changing their behavior. It requires community-wide change. Responsibility and blame extend beyond any individual black person who might fit the negative stereotypes associated with cultural pathology. Even nondeviant blacks are complicit in the decay in black communities, either too afraid to intervene or with personal value systems so corrupted that they don't feel any sense of personal responsibility. George sees this attitude in his relatives' response to neighborhood violence and enacts a hypothetical conversation:

> "Don't get involved. Don't talk to the police. Don't talk to the government. Just keep your mouth shut." I speak to my aunts, my wife's aunts, and it's like, "Umm uh. Something happens on the block and the police come, I'm not talking to them." Why not? "They here to put somebody in jail." The boy kills somebody and you saw it. Where does he belong? "Oh. He just needs Jesus." Naw, he need ... okay fine. If he needs Jesus, are you going out there to talk to him? "I can't talk to that boy." Why not? "He crazy." Take him off the street then!

The fact that this is a hypothetical conversation provides insight into what George thinks of his relatives and, by extension, the black community they represent. And what they represent is a distinct lack of courage: "We don't have enough black men with courage. We lack the courage to stand on that corner and say, 'Hey, why are you here? What's wrong in your life that you feel you need to be standing on this corner and selling drugs?'.... Get active in your community. Catch that kid walking down the street or into a store." George's frustrations are aimed at individual wrongdoers, as well as a broader community he sees as sanctioning bad behavior.

Also central to the color-blind vision is the notion of dependence. According to these African American Republicans, blacks too often look to external sources for support, and economic independence and self-sufficiency are lost characteristics among black people. As Jeremiah, an entrepreneur in his mid-forties, explained:

> We believe that Uncle Sam should be taking care of every little thing we do. And that's not what a lot of our civil rights leaders were thinking. They were fighting for self-efficiency. And yet, you know, somehow down the line we've lost that. We've become a cul-

ture of dependency. We're dependent on the government to help us with our mortgage. We're dependent on the government to help with Medicare and Medicaid. We're dependent on the government for our retirement plan.

This is a common perception, but Jeremiah was also articulating a position on government dependence that many Republicans of all races share. Indeed, *most* Republicans decry government dependence. The difference here is that this dependence is specifically linked to one racial group. Government dependence is not just an abstractly bad thing, as Republican ideology suggests, but a pathology of the black political subject that represents a departure for black people who have historically been fiercely independent. More disturbingly, the color-blind adherents imply, this sort of dependence erodes the work ethic among blacks.

It is no surprise that African American Republicans invoke government dependence to frame black people. With the propagation of the "welfare queen" as the face of welfare reform, Americans of all stripes came to associate government dependence with black people.[4] A familiar trope during the 1980s assault on social welfare programs, the welfare queen was said to game the welfare systems by taking a check rather than working. Talking with Donna and Belinda, two African American women (one self-identified as Republican and the other as Democrat) who lived in a consistently Republican state, Donna said of welfare reform: "We don't need welfare reform. We need black reform. These girls out here getting pregnant by any-old-body. They just think a baby is a way to get a check." Belinda jumped in and they began a heated, though seemingly well-worn conversation: "D. C'mon now. You know that ain't everybody. Sometimes people make mistakes."

DONNA: Yeah, people make mistakes. But when you make a mistake, and your momma made the same mistake, and your grandmomma too, it stops being a mistake and starts being a pattern.

BELINDA: You talking like that's everybody though.

DONNA: 'Cause it is! [Smacking the table laughing.]

BELINDA: You gone have him thinking you worse than these white folks around here.

DONNA: I don't care what he thinks. And I for sure don't care about these white folks. [Laughs] For real though, this is not even about white folks. This is about *us* needing to get ourselves together and stop having babies you can't take care of and stop expecting other folks to do something for you. Do something for yourself.

Their conversation illustrates how African American Republicans face contestation when they invoke the image of blacks as morally loose and dependent, but it also shows how a Republican can locate the problems of black people squarely within the black community. By Donna's logic, black people's problems exist outside the purview of white people. And though she claims to not care what "white folks" think, her color-blind construction of black people and their problems sits easily with ideas about black people that motivate politically conservative social-welfare policy.

The black man on the corner and the welfare queen are stand-ins for black people when Republicans articulate their ideas about black Americans as a whole. Far from being bound by racism and discrimination, the vision of the black subject positions black people as *overly* concerned with racial distinctions. African American Republicans support this position by arguing that blacks, as a group, have wandered from the principles of equality, community, and personal responsibility that made the civil rights movement so morally and politically salient. Racism is treated as an excuse for individual failings, not as a systemic problem that constrains black social actors. To be sure, African American Republicans who subscribe to this view don't deny that racism exists. Some are actually quite pessimistic about the possibility of ending racism. But this reality is held up as the primary reason for not focusing on racism. The logic is that if racism is not going away, it doesn't do much good for black people to focus on it. Victor, an African American Republican from a very competitive swing state, suggests:

> When it comes to opportunities out there, there are opportunities that black people aren't taking advantage of. It's perpetuated that "the white man is against me and I can't do it." Okay, this happened in the past, and there may still be some out there, but you don't see other minorities who come over here.... You don't see the Pakistanis or the Arabs or the Mexicans, for that matter, allowing what somebody else thinks about them to stop them from doing what they need to be doing. They go around them. They go over them. We need to take that same mentality. Nobody is going to stop me from my dream.

Here again, blacks are hiding behind racism, using it as an excuse for a failure of self-motivation or commitment.

This construction of the black people borrows from common tropes and is very much consistent with what sociologist Joe Feagin calls the "white racial frame," particularly the component of that frame that focuses on how stereotypes are constructed and maintained.[5] However, because they often draw on their own personal experiences, African American Republicans who invoke these negative stereotypes about blacks do not really experience them as stereotypes. To them, these attitudes are accurate reflections of the reality of contemporary black life. Yet drawing from "real life" poses a problem: how do they account for themselves? Since they don't reject black identity, they are forced to manage their personal relationship to an image of black people that *they* propagate.

Despite their professed connection to and concern for other blacks, African American Republicans who positioned blacks as morally suspect kept the socially imagined group called "blacks" at arm's length. Though they accepted that their fate was linked to blacks as a group, this reality proved frustrating. My color-blind respondents often had fairly negative attitudes about black people and their potential for collective political action. As a consequence, they thought of themselves as different from other blacks in important ways. They saw themselves as having special insight into the problems of black people, standing outside the "groupthink" that plagues black communities, and seeing things from a unique and uniquely informed perspective. Often this outsider status runs counter to "insider" claims invoked to legiti-mate their political solutions to the problems of black people.

The maintenance of this rhetorical distance should not be confused with a disavowal of black people. Even if they wanted to, these African American Republicans couldn't escape the linked fate of African Americans. Rather than draw strength from this connection, they focus their efforts on cultivating their individuality. Racial identity, particularly in the political arena, is experienced as constraining. While most African American Republicans experience racial identity as constrain-ing in the context of Republican politics, those in the color-blind group believe they are constrained by the behavior of other blacks,[6] that they are *tainted* by the stigmas generated by other blacks. In response, they stress how their personal and political commitment to individuality and self-determination allows them to escape the fate they attribute to blacks as a group. If most blacks are bogged down by collective racial identity, their own individuality liberates them from the strictures of identity. They "tell it like it is" and argue that the problems of black people will not be overcome if their counterparts do not speak out openly and honestly. It often felt, in my interviews, that the vehemence of color-blind black Republicans' beliefs about black people are partly a function of their inability to be separated from them.

Ultimately, this vision deploys some of the worst stereotypes about blacks and is far more negative than the views expressed by any white Republicans I talked with over the course of my research. However, as I will discuss later, white Republicans explicitly endorse this vision of blacks by providing a forum for African American Republicans to present their conception of blacks and their problems to white audiences. This vision also informs a range of political action open to color-blind African American Republicans.

WHAT DOES IT MEAN TO BE REPUBLICAN?

In discussions about politics, African American Republican activists—of both the color-blind and the racial-uplift variety—rarely focused on the nitty-gritty details of policy implementation. They were not policy wonks by any stretch. Instead, they spoke generally about the tenor of policies that they supported, and that support was consistent with the GOP policy position on almost all issues. Color-blind African American Republicans are actually much more committed to the "party line" than their counterparts with higher racial consciousness. Although (as I demonstrate later) there is a great deal of overlap in policy support, the two groups of African American Republicans invoke very different framings and justifications for their policy positions. Not surprisingly, color-blind African American Republicans de-emphasize race as a criterion for judging social policy, and instead focus on the broader ideological and moral appeal of conservative policies.

This policy framing is consistent with color-blind African American Republicans' belief that blacks are overly concerned with racial discrimination. Their color-blind framing de-emphasizes the importance of race in both the causes and solutions to the social issues that black people face. Accordingly, the color-blind framing aims to obscure the weight of race in the political arena. Instead of creating targeted policies for black people or speaking to race-specific benefits of a policy, the color-blind framing attempts to eliminate race from policy consideration. This approach is built around the idea that the prevention of legal discrimination brought about by the civil rights movement has eliminated the need for social policy built around racial difference. For African American Republicans who embrace color blindness, social policy that betrays any consciousness of racial distinction is as bad as Jim Crow–era segregation laws, in that both acknowledge and promote a racial distinction.

The color-blind approach takes social policies and frames them as good for all social groups. Their broad applicability is key to their appeal. Consistent with Republican policy preferences, African American Republicans support low taxes and policies that favor stimulation of markets over extensive social supports. However, the way these polices are framed depends on how they are oriented toward seeing race in the political arena. For the color-blind activists who work to de-emphasize an explicit focus on race in their politics, the framing of Republican ideological positions draws most heavily on abstract ideas about the "goodness" of policy. Any policy's specific effect on black people is secondary. If it has a positive effect on black people, that's good, but the effect on blacks is not the reason for supporting the policy. If it has a negative effect on blacks, that's unfortunate, but that effect is not a function of those affected being black, because the policy is promoted on a color-blind basis. Even when a policy's effects have disparate racial impacts, those who championed the policy are absolved; intent and motivation take precedence over outcome in the color-blind logic embraced by color-blind African American Republicans.

Kevin, a small-business owner, embodies this attitude. He prides himself on being a model for other blacks in his neighborhood, and he is very upfront about the importance of staying networked among other young, black business professionals. But these commitments exist alongside an equally strong conviction that, for all the importance he places on race in his personal life, it does not guide much of his political thinking. In his words, "I just feel like we, as black people, have to stop seeing everything in black and white. You find what you want to see. You keep looking for racism and you'll find it soon enough. I just try to do my own thing and let my success speak for itself." Kevin stands by his aversion to "black and white" thinking when it comes to social policy. It stands to reason that part of this is pure self-interest. Kevin has no problem with the race-based ties of black professional groups when they help his business. But a similar race consciousness is less directly beneficial for him when it comes to politics. Instead, the value of conservative policy is that it is, to him, based on "principles that benefit everybody," not just narrow interest groups. This position is reflected in his desire for lower taxes:

I know that some of these policies will help my people. You learn how to use your money wisely and invest it.... And I think that once black people start making money, they see the benefits of having money.... And what it [tax reform] does is keep us from the death tax [inheritance tax].... You know, the government takes fifty percent or something ridiculous like that. You know what that does? That keeps us from being able to transfer to our children stuff that we want to pass down to them.... I think it's a money issue period. And people try to make it into a black issue, and it's actually a class warfare issue between the haves and the have-nots.

Kevin is adamant that social policies are best when they are applied equally to everyone. Consistent with this color-blind approach, he sees low taxes and pro-business policies from a race-neutral, ideological perspective. When he does invoke social categories, he draws on a class-based framing. In his mind, fiscally conservative policies are good for everyone.

Taking up a similar color-blind perspective on economic policy, another African American Republican said, "Yeah, I think Republican politics is good for people period. And black people just need to realize that. Certain monetary policies, they're color-blind. They are. If the dollar goes up or the dollar goes down, it has nothing to do with black people." Color-blind African American Republicans see economic policies as one arena where race is less salient. However, they take a similar approach to issues that can be more directly linked to black people. Even on these issues, African American Republicans argue that race—and its individual failings—should not be enshrined in social policy solutions that will affect everyone.

This lack of consciousness is manifested across a broad range of issues. Robert, a fifty-six-year-old in a southern red state, adopts a color-blind perspective when discussing "black issues":

"When people start talking to me about certain black issues, I ask, 'What do you mean? What are black issues?' There are some in which we are disproportionately targeted. Criminal justice system is one.... But you know if you are out committing crimes and there are more black people committing crimes, there's going to be more black people in jail." Robert bristles at the idea of "black issues," while disparities in arrest rates are explained by the perceived individual choices of black criminals, not systemic racism and a legacy of the social control of minorities. He also calls on individual choices when accounting for health disparities between blacks and whites: "You're not going to change disparity in life span with a silver bullet, with a single piece of legislation. Those are health issues. Those are life choice issues." Robert was unenthusiastic about the prospect of health equality, not because health inequalities are produced and reproduced in a racist social world, but because black people make poorer decisions about their health.

Across issues, color-blind African American Republicans deploy a framing of Republican policies that resists attending to race (either in regard to the motivations behind the policies or to the implications of their outcomes). Similar to his perspectives on criminal justice and health disparities, Robert invokes the power of market-based reform when discussing school vouchers—he says they "force schools to compete. Once you give people choices and schools can't count on that money, they'll get their acts together or they'll close." Kevin, quoted above on tax policy, takes a similarly color-blind approach when discussing education policy. For him, just as the idea of any race-based benefit in lower taxes is irrelevant and beside the point, race awareness in social policy is precisely what the civil rights movement was fighting *against*.

COREY: What did you think about No Child Left Behind's impact on black school districts?

KEVIN: That one kind of annoyed me. I support the policy, but I think it got all caught up in politics.

COREY: What annoyed you about it?

KEVIN: No Child Left Behind is about raising standards for all kids. If you support better schools, you just support better schools. That's not a white issue or black issue. That's just a good schools issue. People want their kids to go to good schools. I don't care if you live in Robert Taylor or in Wilmette. We can't ask for equality and then try to see everything just by how it affects us.

Kevin's color-blind framing is consistent with a later claim that "black folks spend too much time talking about what 'the man' did to them and not enough time getting their own shit together." This confirms his desire to move beyond identity politics based on race, and it allows him to take the moral high ground, distinguishing himself from other blacks so caught up in racial discrimination that they cannot take responsibility for their own actions. While his framing is somewhat different from Robert's free-market approach, both draw on race-neutral justifications for education-reform ideas.

Faith-based initiatives present one policy context in which a seemingly race-neutral social policy is framed as being especially beneficial for black communities. Officially established under the George W. Bush administration in 2001, the Office of Faith-Based and Community Initiatives (now renamed Office of Faith-Based and Neighborhood Partnerships) was central to the "compassionate conservatism" promoted by the administration and designed to allow faith-based and community groups to provide federally funded social services. In 2005 the *Los Angeles*

Times noted that "When the president cites the initiative's emphasis on funding small and independent church organizations that have never received government funds before, the message has a special resonance with black congregations."[7] Faith-based initiatives have been held out as an opportunity for the Republican Party to make inroads with African American voters, and, at the national level, GOP leadership attempted to leverage the program with black leaders and voters. After the 2004 presidential election, many thought the program was partially responsible for a slight rise in black support in critical swing states. However, among the African American Republicans I spoke with, reaction to the program was mixed, particularly among the color-blind group.

Moses is a minister in the suburbs of a large city in a midwestern blue state. With his conservative political beliefs and religious connections, he seemed like the kind of person who would have a lot to gain from the expansion of faith-based initiatives. However, he was not at all enthusiastic about the policy's prospects. He felt that he had the appropriate mindset to properly enforce the goals of the program, but he was skeptical about how well it would work in most black churches. According to him, "You can't just give money to most of these churches. The problems in the community start from the ground up, but they are in every aspect. The black church is in the pocket of the Democrat *[sic]* Party.... If the church elders have the same values as the members, how is funneling money into them going to change anything?" For Moses, faith-based initiatives are suspect, because the churches that will be running them are riddled with the same distorted values as the people they serve.

Not surprisingly, affirmative action is another issue where color-blind policy framing is particularly charged. Moses provides a nice illustration of the color-blind position on this issue as well. In short, color-blind African American Republicans argue that affirmative action is discriminatory. They say that using race as a criterion for distribution of resources is always unfair, even if it is done on behalf of blacks and other historically marginalized groups. Affirmative action programs are presented as antithetical to the historical struggle for civil rights, and the goals of the movement are often invoked in opposition to affirmative action policy. Moses's skepticism about faith-based initiatives extends to affirmative action. Just as he was concerned about the values of churches that might benefit from faith-based initiatives, he worried that affirmative action would give jobs to people who don't deserve them. He offered that his position might be "unpopular," but for him, "it's a matter of qualification.... If you have folks who don't deserve it getting jobs just because they are black, it is going to ruin it for the qualified black folks." When I counter that, to the contrary, his position is quite popular in the Republican Party, he clarifies that "Mostly, it's not popular to other black people. But, you know, you aren't gonna have everybody be your friend when you don't toe the party line." Presumably, the "party line" here refers to African American support for affirmative action, but Moses was not alone among race-blind black Republicans in rejecting affirmative action. For him, and for African American Republicans like him, the perception of preferential treatment undermined black claims toward equality.

Opposition to affirmative action was often couched in relation to white perceptions. It's bad policy because it makes blacks look hypocritical to white observers. While hypocrisy was used to justify opposition to affirmative action, it was not the only justification. Not only is preferential treatment by race morally and ideologically wrong, but color-blind African Americans also contend that such policies ultimately have negative consequences for blacks. This is a strain of argument that black conservatives and nonconservatives alike have deployed for years. For instance, Yale Law Professor Stephen Carter argued that affirmative action policies have negative consequences for African Americans, who can come to feel they are defined by their racial identity and not their professional achievements.[8] Clarence Thomas, a current Supreme Court justice, has invoked a similar refrain in relation to his experiences at Yale Law School.[9] In writing about his time at Yale, Thomas expresses his dismay when he "realized that those blacks who benefited from it [affirmative action] were being judged by a double standard. As much as it stung to be told that I'd done well in the seminary *despite* my race, it was far worse to feel I was now at Yale *because* of it."[10] These lines of argumentation around affirmative action are not particularly novel and are well-worn from general debate about the issue. However, color-blind African American Republicans' responses to this issue do illustrate how these arguments are reliant on a particular construction of black people and the challenges they face.

The timing of the American real estate crisis provided color-blind African American Republicans with a fruitful illustration of the perils of affirmative action. They called into question policies designed to encourage lenders to give loans to black homebuyers in the subprime market. Aaron shared:

These housing programs went in and gave loans to all these folks who wanted more house than they could afford. And it was mostly black folks getting too much house. People didn't do it like they were supposed to.... You need to be renting and saving your little money until you can actually afford a house. These folks were just taking advantage of a government program that forced banks to make loans to black people who can't afford them.

When I suggested that loan programs might be necessary to close the wealth gap between blacks and whites, he was unconvinced. "The laws are on our side now. You can buy any house you want if you have the money. You don't get wealth from a handout. You get wealth from saving." It was clear that the subprime crisis was a perfect storm for color-blind black Republicans: individual moral failing combined with misguided government policy to the detriment of black people. People's greed and irresponsibility drove them to get bad loans, but Aaron reserved his strongest critique for the *policies* that encouraged lenders to invest in black buyers.

In many ways, color-blind African American Republicans are the embodiment of the extreme caricatures associated with the sellout critique. They say terrible things about black people that invoke the worst stereotypes. They think about policy in a color-blind way that is, at best, ambivalent about the impact social policy has on blacks. They agreeably spout the party platform on pretty much every issue. They confirm the suspicion that African American Republicans are the sellouts everyone thinks they are. However, to dismiss these African American Republicans solely as sellouts risks ignoring the complex relation to racial identity and ideas about black people that animate their politics—and the power of those politics in action.

Color-blind African American Republicans illustrate how debates about the relationship between race and politics are becoming increasingly complex in ways that our analyses— both scholarly and lay—have yet to acknowledge. The issue is not about whether "race matters"—even the most color-blind African American Republicans will agree that there are racist individuals and that racism exists—but whether race and racism have any role to play in creating social policy and political action.

Overall, color-blind African American Republicans are drawn to the GOP by a perceived alignment of values and policy, but also because it serves as a tangible marker of their rejection of the perceived groupthink among black political actors. Given their resistance to prioritizing race in politics, it is not surprising that these African American Republicans articulate a fairly negative and unsympathetic view of black people as a group and, since they carry a vision of black people as encumbered by an obsessive concern with racial discrimination, *ignoring* race is seen as the best route to ensuring that blacks are assimilated into mainstream American culture. "Seeing race," they believe, has been historically bad for black people.

While the validity of this logic is certainly questionable, the motivations and ideas that animate it illustrate the importance of the meaning and weight that actors attach to their racial identity in the political arena. And while there are important similarities between color-blind and race-conscious African American Republicans, their differences illustrate the multiple meanings that African Americans can attribute to racial identity and their consequences for political outcomes. With this in mind, let's turn to the race-conscious perspective.

CHAPTER FOUR

Black Power through Conservative Principles

Another panelist at the New Connections conference, Caleb Jones, was as concerned as Nelson with developing plans for black advancement. Both linked that advancement to conservative social policies, yet Jones and Nelson clearly thought about black advancement in very different ways. Where Nelson saw blacks needing to abandon a victim mentality, Jones saw them needing to harness economic opportunity. Broadly, where Nelson made cultural arguments, Jones talked about structure.

A central theme of Jones's talk was that both political parties had ownership of particular issues. He argued that the left had moved toward politics built around identity and social issues and away from class issues. Since the political right, including Republicans, embraced pro-business issues, he considered the modern Republican Party best suited for black advancement. Jones drew on Booker T. Washington's biography as an example of black commitment to economic development and suggested that blacks have always been—and still are—concerned with economic issues like jobs, loans, housing, and mortgages. As a consequence, black people's assumed support of the political left has gradually become a misalignment of values.

A bit abruptly, Jones shifted his talk. Success, he said, would mean not only setting the right economic conditions for blacks to succeed—black people must also fight racism. Noting that he had no desire to talk about "individual bad white people," Jones told the crowd that racism is a system-wide problem. He cited sociologist Devah Pager's work on ex-felons' attempts to get employment and her findings that whites with a criminal record were more likely to get jobs than blacks without one.[1] Blacks in the audience responded positively: heads were nodding, and there were a few "mm-hmms" heard. The white Republicans in the audience were less comfortable, laughing nervously. Nelson, who would speak next, looked on, stone-faced. Jones closed by focusing on five structural issues that face blacks: education, entrepreneurship, home ownership, prison reform, and the continuing color line. He warned the crowd that he was unsure which political party would own these issues, but he had no doubt that the party that could best address them would deserve black voters' support.

•   •   •

A central theme of this research is the way that African American Republicans are challenged with resolving the perceived inconsistency between their racial identity and their partisan choice. Chapter 3 focused on the color-blind strategy, highlighting how some African American Republicans draw on a pathological construction of blackness to connect their black racial identity and Republican partisanship. The color-blind approach argues that too narrow a focus on race has been detrimental to black people. From this perspective, black interests are consistent with a race-neutral brand of conservative social policy. This chapter turns to African American Republicans who also feel a sense of connection to other black people but, unlike their color-blind counterparts, also emphasize that racial connectivity in understanding how the world works.

The centrality of race in their worldview has consequences for their image of black people and the way that they frame Republican policy positions. They construct black Americans in a way that highlights the impact of racial discrimination and disparate treatment on their life chances, creating a respectable picture in need of economic policy changes and framing *conservative* values as the ones best suited to create those solutions. These Republicans are *race-conscious* rather than color-blind.[2]

PATHWAY INTO THE PARTY

Given the prioritization of race and racial inequality in the Republican Party's politics and their perceived animosity toward "identity politics," the migration of race-conscious African Americans away from the Democratic Party might seem surprising. Many reported growing up in Democratic homes and identifying as Democrat for most of their adult lives.[3] While color-blind activists motivate their migration to the Republican Party by appealing to their values, this was less common among race-conscious African American Republicans. It did occur. And, similar to the stories of the color-blind activists, these conversion narratives often involve engagement with a white conservative:

> My political views are consistent with my basic values of life. And I, I guess, a couple of decades ago, I was sitting and having lunch and we were talking, much like we are, with a colleague of mine.

And we were solving the problems of the world! We were talking about, "And this has got to happen. And this. And why don't people realize this?" And as we got into the conversation, he leaned over and patted me on the arm and said, "It's okay to be a Republican." And it wasn't until that time that it clicked in my mind that my views, in terms of our two-party system which it basically is, were more consistent with the Republican Party than the Democratic Party. So it wasn't that I came up and everybody in my family is Republican, yadda, yadda, yadda, because that's not the case. But when I looked at what my values are and then had to make a choice.... As I begin to apply those core values and begin to see how others applied their values that was when my thinking began to change.

Conversion accounts like this were rare among race-conscious African American Republicans, though. Rather, race-conscious black Republicans fled the Democratic Party, believing that the policy solutions it has offered black communities have failed. They understand economic empowerment as key to black power and view the social programs they associate with the Democratic Party as inhibiting that development.

Race-conscious African American Republicans often spoke about their exasperation with social welfare programs. For them, these programs were facile attempts to paper over the challenges facing the black community without addressing the fundamental drivers of black inequality. They were sensitive to racial inequality and didn't believe that black people were the primary cause of unequal outcomes. Yet their frustration with the ineffectiveness of existing liberal social policy drove race-conscious African American Republicans to look for political alternatives. Primarily, the state-centered Democratic policy solutions they most often took issue with were welfare programs and public housing. Joseph asked rhetorically: "How long can we keep doing the same thing over and over and not seeing results? We've [blacks] been voting for Democrats for as long as I can remember and what have we got from it? We still have the same problems in the ghetto. I don't think the answers to black folks' problems are going to come from the government." His is a common sentiment among race-conscious African American Republicans—a combination of so-called "black problems" with distrust for government solutions (broadly coded as "white" solutions, removed from the realities of black life). Considering the aggressively "pro-black" nature of their political orientation, they embrace the small-government calls of the GOP while remaining ambivalent about the party as a whole.

Still, distrusting government as the solution to the challenges within black communities and demonstrating their commitment to black economic empowerment, these race-conscious black voters see few alternatives to Republican partisanship. Of course, this perception is grounded in the reality of the two-party structure of the U.S. political system. The Republican Party seems in favor of small government and the interests of business *compared with* the Democratic Party.

Devon, who works with both Republican and black political organizations in his city, weighed the relative merits of the two parties and ultimately decided that Republicans' economic policies better fit his ideas about what black people needed. He told me that he saw how the more generous social programs supported by Democrats provided a safety net for those at the bottom of the social ladder, but he feared that such well-meaning social programs would do little to build lasting black wealth: "The Republicans do a better job about issues relating to the economy, and that's where I think we need to focus our energies. We need to be focused on ways to get some real money in people's pockets to support black-owned businesses in black communities. A welfare check is not going to do that." In the context of just two realistic alternatives, Republicans are the most appealing to race-conscious African American Republicans who combine a pro-black political orientation with a pro-business policy preference.

This is not to say that Republican partisanship is a forced decision. Without exception, my respondents in this group also agreed with the GOP's social conservatism. Where the Democratic Party seemed an untenable home for commitments to small government and the long-term economic empowerment of black communities, the Republican Party seemed a more natural political fit. Without foregrounding social issues in their motivations for identifying as Republican, though, across a range of issues like abortion and gay rights, the race-conscious Republicans also found the conservative positions of the party aligned with their personal beliefs.

Pragmatically, many saw Republican politics as working toward increasing the power of the black electorate. If the black vote is so solidly and reliably Democratic, they argued, it loses power. Devon wondered, "If the Democrats know that they are going to get ninety percent of the black vote in every election, what incentive do they have to do anything for us?" This is a lay version of political scientist Paul Frymer's "captured voter argument," which suggests that because Republicans are not actively trying to solicit black support, Democrats have little incentive to make concessions toward black interests. Another respondent put it this way: "When we have all our eggs in one basket, we have less power." Republican partisanship, then, can be positioned as a part of a broader strategy to strengthen the power of the black vote.

In "explaining" their Republican partisanship, both color-blind and race-conscious African American Republicans shared the notion that Republican policies will benefit blacks and the idea of re-empowering black voters, of putting the black electorate "back in play." The key difference is that, for color-blind African American Republicans, these factors are secondary explanations for their partisanship that emerge only after probing. Among race-conscious African American Republicans, these are the primary motivations for a party switch. They did not have some political awakening; the Republican Party represents a new means to a dearly held end.

THE PERSONAL MEANINGS OF
RACIAL IDENTITY

For race-conscious African American Republicans, race is salient (or top-of-mind) across all domains of life. Being black and identification with that blackness are central to their experiences. In their personal narratives, they call attention to how being black and realizing others' perceptions of what it means to be black have been consequential in the paths their lives have taken. All of the respondents I spoke with had relatively good life outcomes: they were educated, professional, and middle class. Race had not stymied their success. But, consistently, race-conscious African American Republicans stressed how they had to overcome racial discrimination or use race as a resource in helping them achieve.

Andrea articulated this sentiment in a casual conversation. An attorney for a government agency, she had recently been promoted to a supervisory position. I offered up congratulations and asked how she was dealing with the new responsibilities of management. She talked about how she was really excited about the opportunity and was ultimately looking forward to further advancement within the agency. However, one aspect of the new job had given her pause. She felt that she was having problems managing some members of her team, getting much more push-back than her predecessor. When I asked Andrea why she thought she was having these issues, she gave me a knowing look and arched an eyebrow. It was the incredulous question "Really?" physically embodied. I stared blankly, hoping she would verbalize a response. Pausing a beat, Andrea said the white attorneys who worked under her were not used to taking orders from a black woman. She patted me on my shoulder: "You know how it is."

Color-blind African American Republicans shared similar stories, but they didn't see these occurrences of discrimination as defining their life experiences. It was the opposite for race-conscious respondents. Their black identity shaped their experiences of home, work, and politics. This is not to say that they were "militant" or obsessed with race and racial discrimination. Recall that I had to tease out Andrea's racialized perception of differential treatment at work; ironically, race-conscious activists' black identity was most acutely noticed through an absence. Where color-blind African American Republicans assumed that the default assumption was that race was important and often made a point of asserting that racial identity played a marginal role in *their* identities and worldviews, race-conscious African American Republicans rarely spoke explicitly about the role of race in their own lives, leaving intact the assumed primacy of race.

I observed this orientation most keenly when my race-conscious interviewees tried to relate to me as a fellow black person. Throughout our talks, it was assumed that I was "in" on the racial realities of the workplace and the world. Race-conscious respondents felt that our shared racial status was accompanied by a shared understanding of what it meant to be black in majority-white spaces—Andrea's "You know how it is." Often these comments referenced the idea that blacks had to work harder than their white counterparts to achieve the same levels of success or that blacks were under special scrutiny their white counterparts didn't face. In an intense interview, Joshua used me to illustrate a bigger point about how the deck is unfairly stacked for black men: "You know what I'm talking about. I bet you have to deal with the same thing being an educated black man. The world isn't used to us. The world is afraid of us. You, young man, are the worst nightmare for all those peckerwoods out there: an educated black man."

At fifty-seven, Joshua was one of my older respondents, and he spoke of a lifetime of white scrutiny. Despite decades of social and political change, he didn't think that the way black people experienced society had changed much. He wasn't alone. When asked about whether he felt comfortable at Republican events, one respondent hesitated: "You know what it's like being around white folks all the time. You have to constantly be watching your back." Another, talking about the challenges of navigating the very white context of the Republican Party, drew a parallel to another very white space, graduate school. He rubbed his hand, calling attention to his black skin, as he said, "I'm sure you know what it's like since you're over there at Northwestern. I'm guessing there's not many over there like you getting PhD's." The belief that, as a black man, I had a tacit understanding was commonplace in my interactions with African American Republicans. Central to that understanding, they believed I would "know" that being black means facing a greater set of burdens in life, particularly when it comes to working and living in majority-white contexts.

"BLACK PEOPLE" AS RESPECTABLE:
CONSTRUCTING THE BLACK SUBJECT

> You know that saying about how black folks got to
> work twice as hard for half as much? Well, it's still true.
> Look at Obama. That's a black man that's had every
> advantage, mainly 'cause he grew up around white
> folks. But just take the average brother on the corner.
> He's got the same hope and dreams. He probably wants
> to be President too. But he can't because he doesn't
> have opportunities to be all he can be.

Jeffrey, a blue-state voter, was among the race-conscious Republicans I interviewed. The way he and others constructed "black
people" was a stark contradiction of the image of a morally flawed
subject presented by color-blind African American Republicans;
this construction saw blacks as sharing "mainstream" values of
hard work, traditional families, and patriotism. For the race-conscious Republicans, black people are far from pathological (and
those individuals who might be are the exceptions).

While color-blind activists obsess over black pathology, this
perspective treats blacks as a group facing social and political
barriers to success—blocked opportunities that constrain their
life chances. Furthermore, blacks are positioned as having been
ill served by a series of social policies that have weakened the
black family and increased their dependence on the government. On balance, this portrait is of a respectable community
constrained by racism.

While the color-blind vision of blacks focuses attention on
the urban poor, the race-conscious African American Republican's vision of black people privileges the working and middle
classes' efforts. Rather than tell the "story" of black people
through a narrative of urban decay, this more uplifting vision
draws on success stories: blacks' efforts to maintain dignity and

achieve material success in the face of crime and poverty in their communities. Blacks are presented as having special and unique cultural traditions, but as sharing fundamentally mainstream attitudes toward work and family. The difference, according to race-conscious African American Republicans, is that black people are forced to engage in their hard work and express their traditional values in the face of societal racism.

Often this vision of black people is juxtaposed with media images. When race-conscious African American Republicans offer up their perspective on black people, it is often an attempt to counterbalance what they perceive as inaccurate portrayals. Jeffrey reflected on his experiences in an integrated suburb of a large midwestern city with a reputation for urban crime. When he would go downtown, he said, "They [white residents] see me and my friends in baggy jeans and Tims [Timberland boots] and old ladies start grabbing their purses!" We both laughed knowingly and Jeffrey added, "But we're just minding our own business. Hanging out. Just like that group of white kids outside the Urban Outfitters. That's what is so frustrating sometimes. I wanted to scream out: 'Don't be afraid of the skin. It's just skin. I'm just a regular teenager.'"

I asked Jeffrey if he thought that white people responded to him and his friends differently than to other racial groups. His considered answer was a surprise:

> Now that you ask, I don't really think there is much of a difference. I mean, you just get programmed to think if a group of black kids are hanging on a corner, they must be up to something. I'm not gonna lie. If I saw a group of boys hanging outside my house I might get suspicious too. I'd be peeking out the blinds. [Imitates timid resident peeking out the window.] How can you not? We've been programmed to be scared of black men.

We both laughed again, though the sober words mixed uneasily with the humorous tone, reflecting the tension between Jeffrey's belief about what black people are "really like" versus their perception in the public imagination.

For those subscribing to this vision of black people, the challenges that blacks face are social and political, not cultural or moral. These African American Republicans link blacks to contemporary racial discrimination, not a historicized discrimination that was overcome in the civil rights era. However, this is not to say that they don't evoke black history—indeed, race-conscious African American Republicans make explicit ties to a tradition of hardworking and determined blacks facing (and overcoming) adversity. As one respondent put it: "Look, I know black people, and the problem isn't that black folks don't want to succeed. We want the same things everybody else does whether you are black, white, yellow, green, whatever! So the problem is[n't] not wanting to do better.... It makes me so sick when you get some of our own even saying that." These respondents see the civil rights movement as unfinished and believe that racism still shapes the daily experience of being black in America. Devon said: "We've come a long way, for sure. And that came on the backs of years and years of protest. But it doesn't diminish that success to recognize that there is still a lot of discrimination that black people face. Probably more so than any other minority group." Devon sees, and appreciates, the historical strides that blacks have made, but his experiences (and those of his friends and family) still point to the daily relevance of race.

Even our meeting became an occasion for gauging the role of race in America. I met him in a glass-walled room at a local library. Devon wondered aloud what the white patrons thought when they saw us:

I mean, people see us in this room and you know they are thinking "What are those niggers up to?" White folks see two black men together and they get scared thinking that we are plotting. And I'm not saying that excuses any behavior from our young black men, 'cause a lot of what we're doing has nothing to do with white folks. But you can't just pretend like racism is not out there.

Devon and others expressed a deep skepticism about ending racism by changing individual beliefs, going so far as to say that no matter how hard any given individual works, anti-black attitudes constrain the lives of black people. Still, they believe that black people have to be accountable for improving their situation. In this sense, they see blacks as ultimately responsible for their own improvement. Put another way, when race-conscious African Americans center the reality of racism in their worldviews, they still hold blacks collectively responsible for having not met racism's challenges. Devon, for instance, was adamant that black people must do a better job of dealing with deviant behaviors within black communities. And Roland, introduced at the beginning of the book, had a generally positive, almost idealistic, view of the black community, but he too challenged fellow African Americans to meet their own needs when he spoke of "bad apples" spoiling the bunch: "We want the schoolteachers to raise our kids. We want the [public housing authority] to give us a place to live. We got a few of us making us all look bad. We have to get our own house in order before we can start hollering about all that's been done to us."

Like their color-blind counterparts, these African American Republicans construct black people as facing problems of their own making; unlike the color-blind, though, they see these "problems" as outliers that are not representative of the black experience and must be solved by black communities. To them,

African Americans cannot trust whites—and by extension, the government—to improve their lives. In this sense, a similar concern for responsibility and respectability animates the thinking of both types of African American Republicans. It is simply that the race-conscious group looks less to a notion of lax personal responsibility and instead to an extra responsibility to take care of each other.

Race-conscious African American Republicans see black people as morally worthy but politically constrained and, consequently, do not invoke any real difference between themselves and other black people. They see themselves as representative of black people, carrying the concerns of the collective and speaking on behalf of those who cannot speak for themselves. And more optimistically, these Republicans see the collective identification of blacks as a resource enabling individual black people to survive and thrive, overcoming the explicit racism and discrimination of the past and the challenges of today. To the extent that blacks are a people in trouble, it is because they are walking away from the collectivist orientation that once served them so well.

This image is socially conservative, hardworking, and in tune with the value system of broader, whiter American society. For the race-conscious right, black people need freedom from the constraints of an interventionist state and access to the means of success. With these things in place, black success is almost a foregone conclusion.

In many instances, this more uplifting vision competes with the vision of moral failure offered by color-blind African American Republicans. In chapter 5, I address how that tension makes organizing difficult for African American Republicans. But for now, I turn to how race-conscious black Republicans engage with Republican policy positions. Given their construction of the black political subject, the very racialized political outlook that accompanies their version of Republican politics is not surprising.

WHAT DOES IT MEAN TO BE REPUBLICAN?

In contrast to the color-blind framing on display in chapter 3, the race-conscious framing of Republican beliefs explicitly presents conservative social policies in light of how they affect black people. That means racializing some seemingly race-neutral social policies by asserting their appeal in terms of how they will put black people on the path to middle-class success. Policies are perceived as "good" when they work toward improving the lot of blacks and lifting up the race. In this sense, race-conscious African American Republicans are very much engaged in a form of identity politics that privileges race over other potential interest groups. This often leaves them at odds with the national Republican Party, since they are more than willing to stray from the "party line" when it diverges from what they perceive as the best interests of blacks. However, this framing still works to align black racial identity with Republican partisanship by positioning conservative policies as best for black people.

Real Communications is a website started by self-described "Radical Republicans." Its goal is "to educate African American voters on the wisdom of being open to voting for Republican candidates, and to persuade the Republican Party to make achieving racial equality and social justice political priorities." This commitment to winning blacks back to the Republican Party informs the site's framing of key political issues. In some instances, the site reads as a manifesto. For instance, on business:

Real [Communications] supports Black entrepreneurship. Government assistance should be used only when necessary. However, it's necessary more than many people realize. Real recognizes that in their quest to become entrepreneurs, Blacks face racial discrimination that Whites do not have to contend with. One of government's duties is to aggressively remove barriers erected by racial discrimination. One such barrier is redlining by banks. Redlining denies its victims equal access to capital, and in a capitalistic society, such a denial puts the victims at an unfair disadvantage in the marketplace.

Its perspective on crime strikes a similar tone:

Real [Communications] believes in law and order. One of government's duties is to protect its citizens from criminals who prey on innocent people. Unfortunately, criminals sometimes carry a badge and a gun. This is an unfortunate truth that the Black community knows all too well. So, Real supports enforcing the law on both civilians and law enforcement. The police should not be permitted to discriminate in their enforcement of the law, neither should government adopt unnecessary policies that have discriminatory effects against racial minorities.

And black parents' concerns are prioritized in their perspective on education:

Real [Communications] supports school vouchers to give parents more educational choices for their children. Several studies reveal that most Black parents support vouchers, though most Black leaders oppose them. Teachers unions also oppose vouchers. Ironically, one of the strongest arguments in favor of vouchers comes from the choices of public school teachers themselves. In several of America's big cities, up to 40% of public school teachers send their own children to private schools. So, if public schools aren't good enough for the children of public school teachers, then why should low-income parents be forced to send their children there?

Even an issue like same-sex marriage gets the race-conscious spin:

> Real [Communications] opposes gay marriage. We believe that marriage is supposed to be between a man and a woman. Real believes that a fair and balanced review of the available evidence does not support the argument that homosexuality is genetically determined. We believe that homosexuality is learned behavior. And what can be learned can also be unlearned. Homosexuality is particularly damaging to the Black community.... The effects of rampant racism [have] depleted the pool of available Black men, meaning that most Black women will never get married.... Assuming that homosexuality is learned behavior, we must do what is necessary to help Black male homosexuals unlearn it. We must give them back their social testacies *[sic]*. That can be done by removing, or at least significantly decreasing the racism that makes it difficult for Black men to fulfill the traditional male roles of provider and protector.

Real Communications is in no way the "public face" of African American Republicans, but it certainly captures the sentiment of the race-conscious African American Republicans featured in my research.

Alongside the founders of Real Communications, the other African American Republicans I spoke with also positioned Republican partisanship and its corresponding policy positions as beneficial for blacks *as* blacks. Jeffrey's take on tax policy is emblematic. Growing up in a big city brought Jeffrey close to the effects of economic deprivation and, although he never lived in what he called the "ghetto neighborhood," he recalls taking the bus with the kids who did. Now he believes that black neighborhoods suffer from a lack of investment and commercial activity: "Look around. You don't see no businesses. No kind of economic development. Everybody always talks about the b-boy on the corner being the problem in black communities. But the real problem is that he taking his drug money out to the suburban mall 'cause ain't no stores in the hood." So when Jeffrey echoes the broader Republican call for lower taxes, he frames his support in terms that stress the relevance of low taxes for black people specifically: "When taxes are lower there is more money to invest back into the community. How can you support black businesses if you're losing half of your paycheck to taxes?"

Steven, an African American Republican active in a decidedly blue state, draws on very similar rhetoric when discussing the benefits of conservative fiscal policies: "When taxes are low, that encourages business development and entrepreneurship in black communities. When taxes are lower, there is more money to encourage business. And that's what we need in our communities. All these empty storefronts could be filled with black-owned companies. Black folks think high taxes are good for social programs, but we're really shooting ourselves in the foot because it doesn't encourage black businesses." Steven goes so far as to compare low taxes against social welfare programs, calculating to his satisfaction that lower taxes will ultimately provide more resources for black communities in the form of more money to spend. Consistent with Republicans' general preference for tax cuts, the point is refined by these race-conscious African Americans in terms of how it is beneficial for black communities.

Education was also ripe for the race-conscious framing. As in the education statement from Real Communications, one activist saw school vouchers as a way of empowering black parents: "You know why I love school vouchers?" he opened, reminding me that *all* African American Republicans seem to love rhetorical questions, "You know why I love school vouchers? Because they give black parents control over their kids' schools. It puts black parents in charge of black kids. Not some white person from the school board who doesn't have any idea of what black children in black communities need."

Sandra, a red-state southerner, agreed: "Vouchers let us take back our schools. They put us in control." Where her color-blind counterparts saw school vouchers as just a free-market approach to education, Sandra went further, stating that the vouchers are about providing *black* parents with choices. In fact, she never called on the generic free-market framing; her preference is linked to her estimation of the policy's capacity to lift black people out of poverty and empower black parents. Sandra's support is pragmatic rather than ideological: support for school vouchers is just a means to a racially defined end.

Race-blind African American Republicans expressed skepticism about faith-based initiatives, telling me they build on a troubled infrastructure within black communities. Recall from chapter 3 that their position on this issue was that the black church, itself riddled with problems, could not be trusted to shepherd black people onto the right path. For those employing the race-conscious framing, though, faith-based initiatives are a boon for black churches and the broader black community, since black institutions are considered best suited to address the problems of black people. Jeffrey even thought faith-based initiatives would improve the image of the Republican Party among black people:

> I thought the faith-based initiatives would go over well [with blacks]. What's not to like? The government is saying instead of some bureaucrat in Washington coming and telling you how to fix your community, we'll take that same money and invest it in resources already there. If you been growing up in the church since you was a baby, your pastor has a better idea of how to help you than some social worker. That's not to knock on social workers, per se.

He went on, saying that in some instances, professionally trained individuals might be needed to intervene (particularly in cases of child endangerment or domestic abuse), but it was a good idea to "build up the resources already in the community" as a sort of first-responder network. For Jeffrey and race-conscious African American Republicans like him, GOP policy positions lessen the intrusion of outsiders—the "government"—into the lives of black people. The limited-government, pro-business rhetoric of the GOP is molded into a platform that simultaneously acknowledges local expertise and invests in black institutions.

Putting the lie to the perception of African American Republicans as sellouts, race-conscious African American Republicans are engaged in a fairly mundane form of identity politics: their racial identity structures their political behavior. They are connected to blackness and to a collective identity of it, privileging racial identity in political calculations. The interests of blacks, constructed to play up the positives, further calibrate their policy preferences and help justify their "unique" choice to align with the GOP.

For the race-conscious, being black is not just one among many social identities that define them. Race is more meaningful than other potential axes of categorization like gender, class, or sexuality, and racial identity is believed to fundamentally shape their experience of the world. In this sense, they share with their color-blind counterparts an experience of race as a constraint. However, for race-conscious African American Republicans, the sources of that constraint are externally imposed through racism and discrimination, rather than internally cultivated by individual bad apples. Going further, the most effective response they see to the reality of racism and discrimination is not to abandon race as an axis of identity, but to turn the personal and institutional bonds of shared racial identity into a path to the salvation of black communities. Often the master status of race is left unspoken, its reality a taken-for-granted component of being black in America. But even tacitly, race animates their politics, extending personal experience into political preference on behalf of black people as a group. If color-blind African American Republicans stress their difference from other blacks, these Republicans act as if they are black ambassadors to "mainstream" politics. They paint blacks as conservative, hardworking, and upstanding, acknowledging individual exceptions but insisting that if black people are to be faulted collectively, it is only that they have allowed themselves to become too reliant on state intervention, when, really, *limited* government would allow blacks to flourish.

Race-conscious African American Republicans resolve the perceived inconsistency between blackness and Republican partisanship by constructing a narrative within which being Republican is in the interest of black people. They articulate a very pro-black form of political conservatism that draws on Black Nationalist thought and has deep roots within the black community, even if that conservatism rarely translates into contemporary Republican partisanship.[4] So, despite the aggressively pro-black nature of their political reasoning, race-conscious African Americans remain subject to the sellout critique while also finding themselves at odds with color-blind black and white Republicans.

Despite perceptions of them as a monolith, African American Republicans proffer competing approaches to linking black identity to Republican partisanship.[5] The differences between race-blind and race-conscious activists in this study highlight the need for political analysts to examine how variations in the meanings and importance of racial identity might inform African American political behavior. As Sellers and colleagues note, "The process by which individuals' beliefs regarding the meaning and significance of race can influence the way in which they appraise and behave in specific events has not been delineated in the current literature on racial identity."[6] Such variation in meaning or importance could have very serious implications for how individuals shape their political decisions, how political behavior is organized collectively, and how identities are leveraged for political use.[7] For some African Americans, racial identification is not only important for self-understanding, but also central to their understanding of the political world. For these African Americans, race provides a frame that shapes understandings about social problems. Other African Americans, less racially oriented, might foreground their class status or sexuality in understanding the social world. For them, race would be less important in structuring political decisions. As the preceding chapters demonstrate, this is precisely the dichotomy that divides African American Republicans.

When examining the link between race and political behavior, race is almost exclusively understood as a marker of identity. As such, many analyses of the relationship between race and politics among black actors are constrained by (at least) two prospects. First, these approaches treat race mostly as a characteristic of individuals. It is measured by individual-level identification. "Race" is something people do (or do not) have, while the meanings and importance of race are often assumed, but left unexamined. Second, assumptions about the nature of "black interests" are treated as relatively self-evident and naturally fall out of group identification.[8] In reality, the interests of any given black person (or subset of blacks) are mediated by the intersecting social identities that exist among all blacks, as well as the shape of the political landscape at any given time. So while a great number of African Americans might agree that what happens to blacks as a group affects their own lives, this insight sheds very little light on what individuals are identifying with. Indeed, as we see, the ideas about black people are also central to how African American Republicans construct black interests.

In this regard, when analyzing the relationship between race and politics among African American Republican activists, it is useful to think of race as both an identity and a cultural object. What does it mean to say that race is a cultural object? Wendy Griswold argues that cultural objects give form to shared significance.[9] A cultural object "is a socially meaningful expression that is audible, visual, or tangible or that can be articulated. A cultural object, moreover, tells a story, and that story may be sung, told, set in stone, enacted, or painted on the body."[10] Accordingly, one way to think of race as a cultural object in the political arena is to examine the narratives that political actors invoke about black people. These narratives provide a way to understand the social meaning of blackness, as well as perceptions of black people themselves.[11] When African American Republicans talk about "black people," they reveal the meanings that attach to black identity. Their talk reflects the often unspoken ideas about the political subject who benefits (or loses) from social policy.

Treating race as a cultural object draws attention to the shared meanings associated with race and how those meanings fit within a broader political system—how those meanings get enshrined in policy, in relations between political actors, and in the attitudes and belief systems of actors. Doing this foregrounds the "story" of race, specifically the story of who black people are and what they need politically. Such an analytic move is inherently cultural, and is vulnerable to the critique that it emphasizes meaning and meaning-making over structural conditions.[12] However, without attending to the cultural meanings attached to black racial identity, it is difficult to determine how political actors engage in the boundary-making process.[13] Central to that boundary-making are the stories that black people tell about themselves.

Race-blind and race-conscious African American Republicans operate with competing visions of the black political subject. Both groups operate with a set of ideas that provide a "prototype" of who black people are and what they need politically. Instances when people talk about blacks as a collective (like "black folks," "our people," "us," or "we") or when they speak of a generic "black community" are occasions where respondents are constructing the black political subject. They draw from a multiplicity of cultural narratives about black people, some more positive than others, when constructing the black political subject. Sometimes the black political subject is conceived as an "other" and other times black Republicans talk about this political subject as if it were them. These ideas about black people provide a heuristic that guides thinking and helps actors navigate the political waters around issues of race. In this way it is similar to other aspects of culture in providing an orienting schema for acting in the world.[14] Because these ideas are central to the construction of black political interests, a full analysis of black political behavior requires understanding how African American actors deploy these ideas within the political context.

My engagement with African American Republicans highlights the importance of attending to both the presence and the *content* of black identity. Race also operates as a collective set of meanings for the subjects of my research. While these two formulations of race are interrelated, each influences political behavior in different ways. As a system of meanings and beliefs about who black people are, race structures multiple aspects of the political action of African American Republicans. Among African American Republicans, this process begins with battles over who *represents* black people. Here, I'm not referring to who speaks for black people or who their elected representatives are, though there is disagreement about that. Rather, African American Republicans are often disagreeing on the symbolic representation of black people. Answers to the question "Who are black people?" shape how black interests are defined among African American Republicans. As we have seen, different answers to that question have implications for politics from ideological positioning, but the meanings attached to racial identity also structure political behaviors related to organizing and alliance building. The next chapters explore how divisions among African American Republicans are manifested within these political activities.

CHAPTER FIVE

Like Crabs in a Barrel

At 7:50 in the morning the lobby bustled with activity, signs in red, white, and blue announcing the politically conservative group hosting its annual conference. A sea of overwhelmingly white men in khakis, navy-blue blazers, and loafers—accented, of course, with patriotic neckties—milled about. The scene was almost a little *too* on the nose for what a conservative conference would look like.

Not far from this busy scene, a ballroom was set up for a panel session and a crowd of 150 to 175 people. It was almost empty. A raised platform with a table and chairs was positioned at the front of the room, while two hotel staffers put out coffee and muffins in the back of the room. This was an early-morning session, and there were three people hurriedly unloading boxes, finalizing the setup. One unpacked a suitcase of merchandise—pendants, bracelets, and buttons with Republican imagery, as well as pamphlets and promotional materials—for display. Some of the fliers promoted the Democrats' historical role in supporting legalized slavery and vigilante violence against blacks. One noted Democratic senators' resistance to civil rights legislation in the 1960s; another called the Ku Klux Klan "the terrorism arm of the Democratic Party."

Slowly, a small group entered the room and made its way to the platform. The panelists were all black. The contrast became more noticeable as white faces from the lobby made their way into the ballroom. The room never reached capacity—far from it, in fact. But for every black attendee, there were at least 3 white ones. As a panelist delivered a prayer, I noticed that there were as many black people on the panel as in the audience. After a collective "Amen," the annual meeting of the National Black Republican Association (NBRA) got underway.

In a fortunate coincidence, Republicans for Black Empowerment (RBE) was holding its annual meeting in the same city, on the same weekend, in a different downtown hotel. This lobby lacked the energy and the pomp of the first. There were no red, white, and blue banners, no bright-faced college students handing out pamphlets. It was just a nondescript hotel plated with what patrons were supposed to think was a lot of gold and brass. The meeting I was observing was on the second floor, where no one hurried to unpack promotional materials and there was nary a muffin to be found. From the hallway, I saw two guys from the hotel staff breaking down the previous event, removing a projector, and stacking the last of the chairs on a cart. Another team was setting up tables, heat lamps, and a bar for catering, with the event scheduled to start at 6:00 P.M. Five minutes after six, nothing was yet under way.

Inside the room, a young black man—probably in his early thirties—was talking with a white woman and a black man, both about twenty years his senior. They were all dressed in business suits, and the overhead lighting reflected off the young man's

American-flag lapel pin. He explained to the couple that the event's start time had been misprinted—it would start at 7:00, and he said he hoped the snafu would not reduce the expected high turnout.

A smattering of people had started to arrive by the time I went back into the hall. When a woman made eye contact and gave me a broad smile, I smiled back, putting out my hand to introduce myself. Leah was short and slightly heavyset, with long hair, a black business suit, and perfectly manicured fingernails. Her handshake was crisp and professional. She asked how long I had been involved with RBE, and I told her frankly that it was my first meeting—I was there researching African American Republicans. "Really?" she asked incredulously. "That is so interesting. I don't think I've ever really read anything that was like a study, study about us. Just newspaper articles. And you know how that goes." I didn't know how that went. As I was about to ask, Leah smiled at a pair of identical twins coming up the stairs. Both twins were dressed in suits that looked to be about half a size too big, and scuffed dress shoes. They looked very young and unpolished compared to the other people I had encountered so far. Leah waved them over to introduce me: "He's doing a research project on black Republicans. He's a sociologist."

By seven, the twins were still lecturing me on the perils of government dependency for black communities. Leah had begged off a while ago. The expected big crowd had turned out, with several dozen people mingling and a line forming at the buffet. There was no wait for the cash bar, and the buzz of conversation filled the room. With the exception of three white people standing awkwardly at one table, the crowd was entirely black. The atmosphere was relaxed and jovial, more family reunion than business meeting. Someone stepped to the lectern to introduce the first speaker. After an impromptu rendition of the Negro national anthem, "Lift Every Voice and Sing," the RBE began their annual meeting.

The differences between the meetings of the NBRA and the RBE were stark. The audiences were overwhelmingly white at the NBRA event, while black people populated the RBE function. With each panelist, the NBRA created an environment hostile to "race talk," while members of the RBE reveled in their same-race community. The NBRA event occurred at the center of the conservative movement's network of power, while the RBE was putting on its own event at the margins of the conservative scene. The NBRA could afford to host lavish events at nice hotel ballrooms. The RBE had cash bars at a hotel well past its prime. Despite these differences, though, the members of both groups were all black and all Republicans. At one point there was no difference between the two groups—they were, in fact, the same organization.

·   ·   ·

Chapters 3 and 4 explored the strategies that African American Republican activists use to manage the links between black racial identity and Republican partisanship. I found two broad approaches: a color-blind approach that depoliticizes race and relies on an ideological commitment to conservative principles, and a race-conscious approach that foregrounds blackness and links it to conservative policies by trumpeting the benefits of Republican policy for black communities. These two strategies are very different and rely on distinct meanings surrounding blackness and black interests, but the activists share the challenge put to them by other blacks and by white Republicans: to reconcile race and politics. This common ground is not one they build on to unite.

When thinking about political behavior, the focus is often on individual-level acts. Did you vote? Did you go to a protest? Did you write a letter? This is important because actions matter. As I've shown, individual-level policy framings have serious consequences for how African American Republicans express their partisanship. However, exclusive focus on individual-level behaviors obscures a great deal of other political behavior. Among the activists I spoke with, the convergence on policy positions—even though they get there through very different channels—directs attention to the other aspects of political behavior affected by the divergent visions of black people. In particular, political organizing is one arena where different ideas about black people and their problems lead to conflicting political behaviors.

Organizing is central to black political behavior. Collective action has been central to the political and economic achievements African Americans have fought for throughout the history of the United States. Additionally, organizing is a context in which identities are not only expressed, but also constructed. Through the processes of organization, groups come to define who they are and set a political agenda.[1] And, of particular importance for African American Republicans, organizing gives legitimacy. These organizations make African American Republicans seem real—not untethered unicorns, but a substantial and important group. Only "for real" things have conferences. Organizing is also a way of concentrating power and letting us see black Republicans interacting with one another and with other audiences. In this chapter, I consider intra-group interactions and how variation in the ways that African American Republicans understand black people's problems and political interests can stymie organization; in the next, I turn to these activists' experiences interacting with white audiences.

A consistent theme among my respondents was their feeling of isolation and misunderstanding. The stories from chapter 2 are a testament to these feelings, and other research on African American Republicans has found similar sentiments.[2] To hear the activists tell it, no one understands what it's like to be a black Republican. Their political location requires constant affirmation of the link between racial identity and political identity in a way that simply doesn't happen for white Republicans and African American Democrats, whose "existence" is taken for granted. They experience alienation from their white Republican counterparts and fellow African Americans. Sometimes there is even a sense of psychological alienation from their black racial identity.

In this context, African American Republican organizations could offer shelter from the storm—a safe place to commune with like-minded fellow travelers—and it's easy to imagine that black Republicans would have little trouble organizing. They share a general agreement on most policy issues—no one here is *cool* with abortion, gays, or taxes. And there certainly are not enormous numbers of people to organize—I imagined their biggest problem would be finding one another.

Given the strong sense of isolation and appetite for community expressed by *individual* African American Republicans, I was surprised to find constant contention and friction among the activists when they tried to act collectively. Put less delicately, African American Republican organizing was a mess. Groups that tried to organize across the race-blind/race-conscious divide had short life spans and were riddled with constant infighting. Groups that managed to not implode eventually adopted either race blindness or race consciousness as a guiding philosophy and sought to present their version of black Republicanism as the *only* legitimate form of black conservatism. This frequently produced competition among black Republicans for the same limited resources.

Race-blind activists who just want to "be Republican" and race-conscious activists dedicated to "staying black" struggle to work together to build organizations that will promote the social policies they all agree on. Further, my respondents often spoke of fractious personal relationships. They regularly disliked their fellow African American Republicans and felt they actually had little in common beyond that shared label. After watching them interact with one another and hearing them talk about their organizations, I learned that the only thing worse than the loneliness of being a black GOP member was the frequent disappointment that came with engaging with another one.

UNSUCCESSFUL ATTEMPTS

Many right-wing black organizations can be described as "inorganic" in the sense that they have little grounding in black communities or black leadership. Organic organizations arise from sentiments within black communities, whereas inorganic groups are thought to be driven by external, primarily white interests, generally unconcerned with the needs and interests of black communities.[3] In reality, the boundary is messy: across organizational types, groups are open to taking resources from white Republicans and frequently contest what exactly is "best" for black communities. Recent African American Republican organizations have a reputation as "fronts" for white activists, and their proliferation risks undermining the success of any individual group's efforts. Given that the black political community has shown little interest in supporting their efforts, and black voters show low levels of support for the GOP, more groups mean more competition for limited attention and resources. This is partly why I expected some "banding together." Instead, I found rivalry.[4]

African American Republicans have yet to produce a long-standing national organization. Often ideology is used to account for this difficulty. African Americans who join the Republican Party, it is argued, are less interested in a racialized identity politics. Therefore, they are unlikely to organize on the basis of race. As I began my data collection, Orville, one of my first interviewees, warned that I might have difficulty in my search for African American Republicans. I patiently said that I understood there was a relatively small number of black Republicans and that I would have to really dig and draw on black organizations. Orville stopped me—that was *why* it would be difficult, he explained: African American Republicans were not into "race politics."

Tacitly adopting a race-blind approach, Orville presented his engagement in Republican politics as conditioned on abandoning identity politics. He and others position organizing around racial identity as incongruent with the appeal of being in the Republican Party. According to their logic, blacks come to the GOP when they've moved past identity politics. So why would they organize groups based on blackness? There is some merit to such claims. Similar ideas support the race-blind strategy among African American Republican activists who frequently de-emphasize the role of race in their worldview and their understanding of life outcomes. In some ways, race is less "important" to African American Republicans. However, claims that they do not pay attention to race are inaccurate. African

American Republicans are very much aware of their racial status and display a feeling of linked fate with other African Americans. Even in their harshest critiques of other blacks, African American Republicans often discuss the motivation for their political ideas and behaviors as racially defined. Moreover, their relative rarity in the Republican Party forces a racial consciousness onto African American Republicans whether they like it or not. To say that African American Republicans are not "into identity politics" is a little misleading.

The idea that African American Republicans are not interested in organizing as African Americans is also undermined by the fact that, time and time again, African American Republicans have attempted to form groups with explicit racial agendas. This suggests that at least some African American Republicans see value in organizing *as* African American Republicans. For sure, there is recognition among black Republicans that they are in a unique political position, and there are benefits to be gained from pooling their numbers and resources. David, an investment banker from New York and a one-time leader of an African American Republican political organization, spoke openly about the importance of organizing to expand the visibility and viability of the Republican Party in black communities: "One thing we need to do better is get organized. We need to work together to show black people that other black people are positively involved in the party and that the ideas of the party are relevant to the black community. Being a part of this group is one way to do that."

The problem is that these groups have had relatively little long-term success. The various organizations that have aimed to bring black voters into the GOP have had different focuses and targeted different audiences; they have been sometimes aligned with party leadership while others challenged platforms; and they have had different plans for the future, with some groups aiming for a lasting effect and others coming together for one-off conferences or around single issues in specific elections. Across the board, though, they have had minimal impact within the Republican Party and among the black electorate.[5]

Given the sustained attack that black conservatives have launched on the inadequacy of organizations associated with what they call the "civil rights establishment," it is not surprising that they have made repeated attempts to organize over the past twenty-five years. Yet efforts at producing a conservative organization to counter the influence of more liberal black political institutions have failed. Even the groups that have avoided explicit partisan links in an effort to broaden conservative appeal among black audiences have gained little traction. Obviously, many reasons contribute to organizational failure, including factors external to the groups, but certainly infighting among black Republicans has been a major hurdle to gaining an organizational foothold.

THE CHALLENGES OF ORGANIZING: THE NATIONAL BLACK REPUBLICAN ASSOCIATION

Founded in 2005, the NBRA is a fairly recent attempt at organizing at the national level. Its trajectory is emblematic of how tensions over race and politics become manifest in organizing. Started with funds from the Palm Beach County Republican Party in Florida, the NBRA's mission is "to be a resource for the black community on Republican ideals and promote the traditional values of the black community which are the core values of the Republican Party: strong families, faith in God, personal responsibility, quality education, and equal opportunities for all." To this end, the group works to conduct grassroots education campaigns in black communities. The group launched with a great deal of fanfare and, on the backs of high-profile appointments of African Americans in the George W. Bush administration, expectations for it were high. Bush had been reelected, and though the Republican Party and the broader conservative movement faced stiff opposition, conservatives were setting the national policy agenda. Even with low black voter support, Bush was perceived as a "friend" of black conservatives. One former board member of the NBRA told me, "When the group started, we were all really excited about the possibility. There was a sense that 'now is the time.'" Then Republican National Committee Chair Ken Mehlman said of the upstart group: "In reaching out to African Americans to give them a choice, what [the association] is doing is more important than what I am doing."

However, unity within the organization was short lived. Within months, over half of the NBRA's board of directors had resigned. Media coverage suggested that these departures stemmed from disputes about how race informed the understanding and analysis of Hurricane Katrina. For instance, after the hurricane, the organization issued a press release supporting President Bush's handling of the emergency, while also invoking controversial language to describe the storm's victims: "President Bush is to be commended for deploying all of the resources of the federal government to help the refugees," Frances Rice, chairman of the NBRA, wrote at the time. "The President turned an unacceptable situation in New Orleans into a massive relief effort," Rice continued, "including deploying all of the assets necessary to provide immediate help for the people and long-term planning to rebuild communities." This infamous press release went on to suggest that those who would use the event as a pretext for a discussion of race were the "real" racists. In the words of another NBRA officer, "As African Americans, we are deeply concerned about efforts of President Bush's critics to politicize, for their own partisan political agenda, a disaster that affects so many of our fellow African American citizens." The NBRA still defends the Bush Administration's attempt to shift blame for the catastrophic response and protracted rebuilding in New Orleans to local Democratic officials:

> While criticizing President George W. Bush, Democrats turn a blind eye to the failures of the Democrats running the city of New Orleans and the state of Louisiana. The black Democrat officials in New Orleans did not execute the emergency evacuation plan and allowed over 1,000 school buses and city transit buses to stay in parking lots and become ruined by the flood.... The Democrat governor of Louisiana, a white woman, refused to cooperate with President Bush when the president asked for her consent to begin a mandatory evacuation four days before the storm. The Democrats in the Louisiana homeland security office also refused to let the Red Cross bring truckloads of food, water and supplies to the Superdome. Since 1980, Louisiana emergency personnel knew that the levees in New Orleans would not withstand a category 3 or 4 hurricane. Yet, the Democrats in Congress filibustered President Bush's energy bill which was introduced in 2001 and contained $540 million for repairing the levees in New Orleans.

The NBRA narrative tried to have it both ways: praise for the Bush administration for turning around an "unacceptable situation" alongside blame for local Democratic officials and the governor ("a white woman") for failed emergency efforts. There was not a problem in New Orleans, they seemed to say—but if there was, it was the Democrats' fault.

In Katrina's aftermath, the high expectations for the still-new NBRA came crashing down. Former NBRA board members were gracious, telling media outlets that the split was amicable, and the former communications director for the organization downplayed it. "The organization and its current leadership is heading down a much different direction than was envisioned by myself and the other board members," he wrote in an email to media outlets. "I personally wish nothing but success for the organization." The former board members were, however, less polite in my private interviews.

In response to the NBRA's efforts to diminish the role of race in Hurricane Katrina, one departing board member asked, "How can we say that as black people? It [the mass resignations] was about that, but it was also about who is in charge of this group and who gets to decide what we do." It had been that way since the very beginning: questions of identity and interests were problems among the membership. Questions about the role of race in structuring political action are linked to issues of organizing, and conflict over race and identity played out in organizational failures. Media coverage of the board members' departure pointed to conflict over the group's unwavering support for President Bush, while departing board members linked that support to the more mundane organizational management issues already plaguing their fledgling group.

The resignations, presented in the conservative press as a surprise, were, according to one informant, a long time coming. The discontent had fomented around organizational finances, authority within the group, and the NBRA's ties to the broader Republican Party's agenda and operators.

Yet these practical concerns grew from more fundamental questions about the goals and directions of the NBRA. Rice, the then and current head of the organization, reported that the split was due to board members refusing to sign a form pledging loyalty to the group. This aligns with what my informant reported. However, the *reason* they refused to sign, I was told, was that they felt the organization was headed in a different direction than they could support. Rather than being an organization attuned to the concerns of African Americans and how the Republican Party could meet those concerns, the former board members I spoke to felt that the group was much more attuned to the *publicity* needs of the Republican Party, that the NBRA was quickly called upon only when Republican policies needed the "blessing" of black faces. One interviewee questioned the racial authenticity of its leadership: "Look at who is in charge of that organization, and look at what kind of person they are married to." The implication was that Rice's marriage somehow embodied the less-than-pure racial commitment of the group.

The NBRA in Action

The early resignations of half the NBRA's board members did not destroy the organization, which exists to this day (though it does not appear that there is a huge active membership).[6] The organization regularly holds an annual conference—though as noted at the start of this chapter, most of the attendees are white—and occasionally publishes a magazine, *Black Republican*. Its leaders are quoted in conservative media outlets. Although the stated mission is to be a resource to the black community, the efforts of the organization have been focused on advertising campaigns during elections. That is, rather than working as a grassroots group, the NBRA is an explicitly political organization. Its central work revolves around speaking out on behalf of the GOP in general and black Republicans specifically. Seemingly operating under the assumption that "no press is bad press," the NBRA has courted controversy and is probably better known for its announcements and advertisements than for championing any specific policy program or political candidate.

In 2008 the NBRA sponsored a series of radio ads and billboards aimed at drawing blacks into the Republican Party. Martin Luther King, Jr., they pointed out, was a Republican.[7] The advertisements, which ran in multiple media outlets, were positioned as educating voters, and used history to reframe the GOP as a long-standing, reasonable, even natural home for African Americans. The NBRA often brings up the Democratic Party's history of supporting lynching and the contrast of Republican support for, and Democratic recalcitrance to, civil rights legislation in the 1960s.

This tactic elicits a range of responses, from shoulder shrugging to mouth frothing, but none of them are positive. The use of King was cynical and distorted the facts by stripping them of context—including the all-important reality that both parties have shifted dramatically since the 1960s and that racial-equality issues have found a home in the Democratic Party. However, most responses were less concerned with the historiography than with the appropriation of King in what was perceived as a cynical means of supporting a racist party.

The tight relationship between the conservative establishment and the NBRA is cemented in the group's public meetings. The NBRA holds its annual meetings in conjunction with the Conservative Political Action Conference (CPAC) sponsored by the American Conservative Union. The meeting I attended reflected the attendance of the conference, with its white crowd and black panel. A series of black speakers issued sharply worded critiques aimed at getting black people to better understand the history of the political parties—but they were speaking to white

people. The fact that the audience for their message was white
people was highlighted in a talk given by a former official from
the George W. Bush administration. The high-ranking official
spoke about the dangers of "political correctness," arguing that
the reasonable fear that white people had of urban black men
was being unfairly coded as racism. He absolved the audience
members of any guilt that they might feel by animatedly describing his own fear when he sees a group of young men dressed in
"urban" clothes walking down the street. As a black man myself,
it was certainly unnerving to see a high-ranking federal official
telling an audience full of white people that people should be
afraid when they encounter young black men. But beyond my
own discomfort, the instance illustrated how the NBRA's message was tailored to appeal to white conservatives.

It is, of course, difficult to measure the success of the NBRA's
efforts to reframe history and construct African Americans as
mostly responsible for the problems in their community. Not
only do they seem to reach far more white Republicans than
black voters whose affiliation might be in play, but they seem
uniquely focused on media stunts meant only to produce attention. To some extent, that works. The group has gotten noticed,
though the attention beyond the conservative media was and
remains far from positive. When some white Republicans found
it difficult to support the group, it was hardly a shock that many
black Republicans could not.

Even among African American Republicans I spoke to *at* the
organization's annual meeting, the NBRA's rhetorical strategy of
invoking the histories of the Democratic and Republican Parties
was not particularly well received. I shared a table with Ted,
Hakeem, and Mike, three African American men attending
the CPAC conference. All identified as Republican and all were

interested in the NBRA. Before the event started, they talked to me about what it was like to be black and Republican. They spoke passionately about alienation among other blacks, and Hakeem insisted that this black resistance to the Republican Party was grounded in an ignorance of history. He said that people just needed to know the history of the Democratic Party and its relationship to the Ku Klux Klan, that the Democrats have a terrible history on civil rights, and that it was Republicans who teamed with President Johnson to get the Civil Rights Act passed. He complained that people attacked Strom Thurmond as racist, but Robert Byrd was a former member of the Klan. The conversation was intense, and everyone seemed startled when Hakeem lightly banged the table. Mike nodded sympathetically but countered that most people don't care what happened a hundred years ago. Ted trumped him: people "don't care about what happened forty years ago!" We all laughed and the tension dissipated. The fact remained, while Hakeem was a faithful believer in the power of history (however decontextualized), Mike and Ted were less convinced.

In a way, the conversation was a micro-demonstration of the NBRA's macro problems: the group's purpose is to change the way we "see" the past and understand the present, to change black people and their perception of their own history. The goal is not to change what white Republicans do or change understandings of what it means to be a Republican. My experiences at the NBRA meeting highlighted a new possibility: the efforts of the NBRA, nominally designed to speak to other blacks, were actually intended for white audiences. In this sense, the NBRA has definitely failed to live up to the initial hype surrounding the group. Even though the group never positioned itself as a champion of black communities, it did set up a goal of taking the Republican message to black communities. There were always concerns that it was just an AstroTurf organization, and its activities seem to confirm that description.[8] The organization now has a more complicated relationship to the party leadership. While it is still relatively active with the more conservative elements of the party, relations with party leaders are strained. So, white audiences still populate their conferences, but their outrageous rhetoric draws fire from some Republican leaders.

The Community of Republicans for Black Empowerment

After the NBRA's internal post-Katrina discord, some of the departing board members started their own organization. They chose a name that signaled the priority this group would place on racial uplift: Republicans for Black Empowerment (RBE). In their explanation of the name, RBE explicitly takes on black conservative organizations like the NBRA:

> RBE has "black" in its name precisely because at the time of its founding in 2007, there were no organizations adequately filling the need of offering a non-hierarchical, online, grassroots social platform for black conservatives to (i) easily discover one another nationwide, (ii) discuss issues of the day and share information of interest, (iii) inspire one another to get more involved in their local party apparatus and (iv) connect the dots for critically thinking blacks considering switching parties and desiring a support group or intellectual ammunition.

The friction between the RBE and organizations that appear to cater to the interests of the white Republican establishment—groups like the NBRA—is obvious, not just because the RBE was founded as a breakaway group from the NBRA. For the RBE, the goal is not to rewrite history, but to link conservative principles with black interests, because "when conservatives take our message directly to the black community in a manner that is authentic, deliberate, strategic and speaks directly to its concerns, we will take steps toward eliminating misconceptions and capturing a new generation of black conservative voters."

Both organizations are dedicated to raising the profile of the Republican Party in black communities. One of the goals of the RBE, in fact, is to chip away at the stranglehold the Democratic Party has on the black electorate. They hope to "raise awareness, provoke greater critical thinking and increase Republican elected officials." This looks similar to the NBRA. But the RBE takes a very specific position on the cause of black people's problems, describing itself as "on a mission to raise the value of black America's political capital by increasing awareness of the upside offered by conservative solutions to the black community's concerns."

Like the NBRA, they invoke the language of improving the lot of the Republican Party, but RBE places race and racial uplift at its heart. Far from a symbolic nod, the group works to build networks and train younger activists to create "a robust and connected community of black Republicans" who can then become embedded within the GOP's power networks. The organization is not a tool for the Republican Party but, instead, aims to bolster the community of black conservatives as a mechanism for improving black communities.

True to its mission, RBE's annual meetings, described at the opening of this chapter, are mostly black. The atmosphere is a bit difficult to describe: one part political rally, one part networking event, one part family reunion. It was unlike any other event I experienced during my fieldwork. From its late start to the opening prayer to the singing of the Negro National Anthem, the meeting's rhythm produced a comfort and familiarity that reminded me of black events I have been attending all my life.

All the people I met through RBE were eager to build personal connections, even if those connections were strained. Casual introductions morphed into elaborate narratives that often included details of the person's plans for empowering the black community. Meeting Keith is a good example: when he found out I lived in Chicago, he excitedly told me that he was originally from Gary, Indiana. That led him to telling me about a trip he was planning to Gary to attend a friend's birthday party—a big reunion of high school friends, where Keith's presence would be a big deal, since he rarely goes back to Gary. Others had accepted the invitation, he said, after they heard he would be there. Going with the flow, I said it sounded like fun and mentioned that my stepfather had family in Gary.

Keith got excited: "You have people in Gary?" I added that while I had been to Gary, the quasi-relatives I knew there were not very close to me and I didn't know them well. Soon I was hearing of Keith's plans to start a scholarship and mentoring fund for students at his old high school, using himself as an example of someone who "got out of Gary and made it." Then he lamented that the town no longer offered any opportunity for anyone with a high school education and worried whether enough of Gary's kids were attending college.

Interactions like this were encouraged by the informal, networking vibe of RBE meetings. The evening event was explicitly framed as a networking opportunity. When one of the RBE leaders welcomed everyone, he told the crowd we were there to honor the keynote speaker and to create a forum for blacks to learn more about the Republican Party. He added a third purpose: to give black Republicans a chance to network with one another.

Even the ostensibly political speech from the keynote speaker placed strong emphasis on the power of good networks. After apologizing for being late, the speaker's talk explored his past involvement with civil rights litigation and his work in the White House. He presented himself as a political pragmatist who consciously built connections with members of both political parties (and joked that these connections were responsible for an important presidential honor he once received), but he said he was serious about networking among blacks—blacks had to take care of one another, and networking was central to that. The keynote speaker closed with an invitation for people to drop by his office to talk: "You never know when I might have a connection that could be useful." Audience members lined up to meet him.

Some of the RBE's tactics were similar to those the NBRA is known for. At the same evening event that encouraged members to network, another RBE speaker delivered a mini-sermon in full "black church" style. She mentioned that she had come north from Georgia as part of a civil rights march, and she liked it so much, she never left. As "we all know," she joked, Dr. King was a Republican, and his dream was that people were not to be judged on the basis of their skin color. She then talked about a song she sang in church about how "Jesus loved the little children. All the little children of the world. Red ... AND yellow ... black AND white." And she lamented the fact that blacks were now doing "the same thing that whites had once done to them"— discrimination was bad, no matter who was doing it. This received a rousing applause from a crowd that knew all too well that she was alluding to the suspicion their political leanings evoked from their own families and friends. Unlike the NBRA,

however, the RBE has a much lower media profile; her proclamations did not end up in newspapers.

THE BLACK REPUBLICAN
ALLIANCE: A PATTERN OF FAILURE
AT THE LOCAL LEVEL

The challenges that hastened the splintering of the NBRA are
not unique to national organizing. One could argue that, at the
national level, there are more challenges to organizing a group for
African American Republicans. The stakes are higher in many
ways: there is media attention, a lot of resources have been dedicated to the cause, multiple sets of local interests have to be rec-
onciled, and so on. Yet similar experiences occurred at the local
level when African American Republicans tried to organize. For
these local groups, organizing can be even more critical. There
are fewer resources, and banding together would help more. In a
blue state in particular, Republican resources are strapped, so
there is not a lot to go around. Working together would make a lot
of sense. Yet, even in this context, African American Republican
organizations have trouble maintaining momentum.

The Black Republican Alliance—an effort in a blue state to
organize African American Republicans—met with initial success but dissolved quickly into internal bickering. Derrick and
Devon, introduced in chapters 3 and 4, respectively, were found-
ing members of the organization. At the start, all of its members
thought they were united in both their partisan and racial identities. Derrick recounted, "We had a good turnout. Spirits were
high. Here we were in the belly of the Democratic beast, and we
had a room full of Negros hand-raising as Republicans. That
alone felt like an accomplishment."[9] Devon said separately,

"Everything was on point in the beginning. Folks were serious about the group. Nobody had time to be playing games. We were trying to make something good happen." Despite their shared optimism about the group, in interviewing Derrick and Devon, I was taken aback that they had ever gotten along under a single organization. They articulated extremely different visions of how Republican politicians should relate to the black community. The divisions I saw between Derrick and Devon were, in fact, the divisions that tore the Black Republican Alliance apart.

Derrick, who initially praised the broad range of members, recalled that he was dismayed almost immediately with the ideological differences within the group. Some members were far less committed to what he termed "core conservative principles"—a commitment to individual equality, personal responsibility, and small government—than seemed right to him:

> Early on, it was kind of clear that we didn't see eye-to-eye on a lot of stuff. To put it honestly, a lot of those guys were Republican in name only. They sounded more liberal with a lot of "down with the man" talk. That's not really my thing. I mean, I'm not trying to say racism doesn't exist, but that's not really where I want to put the focus. I think we need to get black people back to core conservative principles. That's what the community needs.

Derrick also felt that some members of the group were cowed by their minority status as Republicans in the black community. He suggested that the stigma of the Republican label tempered some members' open commitment to the organization. "They were Republicans when it was convenient.... You can't call yourself Republican and then publicly support Democratic candidates," he said. This timidity was seen as evidence of their ideological cowardice.

Derrick also felt that the group should take its message directly to the African American community by educating them on the benefits of conservative social policies. He believes the GOP is not interested in working with blacks because there is no political "upside." To change that, it is necessary to get more blacks interested in the GOP: "Look at it from their perspective. If you have a group of voters where if you're lucky you get ten percent of the vote, why would you invest any effort in trying to reach out to those voters? It's not about racism. It's about votes. We have to show blacks how the principles of the party are the same conservative principles of the black community."

For Devon and others, the split was not driven by social policy debates but, rather, by broader questions of loyalty and accountability. To whom was the group beholden? That was the central question on which the group's leaders could not agree. Devon, and the members who aligned with him, saw the Black Republican Alliance's role as challenging GOP officials in the state. Rather than fit themselves into the party leadership's agenda, Devon wanted to upend that agenda. Like Derrick, he thought the group should direct their resources toward an education campaign, but Devon wanted that campaign to be directed at white Republicans. He felt they needed to be educated about how the GOP was founded "literally on the backs of black folks" and how state party leaders could work to reintegrate African American voters into the party. The leaders of the party needed to acknowledge its racist past and atone to black voters, as well as prioritize the uplift of black communities.

Devon felt that Derrick was content to allow the organization to be nothing more than a mouthpiece for the state's Republican Party. But he believed their goal should be to persuade party officials to extend (and improve) their outreach efforts in black communities. Devon contended that his camp was motivated by a concern for black people as a group. They felt they couldn't stand by silently while the Republican Party traded on racially motivated rhetoric or while the group ignored chances to support policies and candidates working to uplift the black community, regardless of party affiliation. Consequently, Derrick, a staunch supporter of GOP candidates, was openly ridiculed, his racial authenticity called into question, and was labeled by more than one of my interviewees as an Uncle Tom.

It would be fair to say that in the most abstract sense, both factions within the Black Republican Alliance understood the organizational challenge similarly: to close the gap between the state's black electorate and the Republican Party. They just had incompatible ideas about how to close that gap. Derrick wanted to change black people by making them more conservative. Devon wanted to change the party leadership by making them more sensitive to the material and symbolic concerns of black voters. Members balkanized around these perspectives, and this made working together collectively nearly impossible.

Derrick and Devon's difficulty in working together was grounded in a number of things. Each came with his own ideas about black people, black history, and blacks' relationship to the Republican Party. While acknowledging the reality of contemporary racism, Derrick was a color-blind Republican who underplayed the role of race in structuring the lives of black people. He called on his people to embrace conservative principles to allay the problems of black communities. Devon, on the other hand, was a race-conscious Republican who Derrick believed could not see the world through any lens other than race. Devon countered that Derrick knew little about black history—automatic evidence that Derrick was racially inauthentic. But at a basic level, they just didn't get along.

Recall that, in *any* local political context, the universe of African American Republican activists is tiny; this situation was no different. Thus, an active fight between just two people can cripple an organization. A personality clash like the one between Derrick and Devon can easily inflame an ideological disagreement, and a big ideological division can drive personal animosity. It was impossible to tell whether activists didn't like each other because they disagreed over how race should be integrated into life and politics or if their distaste for one another was manifested in disagreements about how central race should be to life and politics. Either way, the personal animosity was often articulated in race-based attacks over who was legitimately black or legitimately working for the good of black people.

However, the grievances between race-blind and race-conscious African American Republicans, and the ways those disagreements manifest themselves, are not all lofty debates about race and politics. On the contrary, the fights within the Black Republican Alliance were often about the down-and-dirty aspects of running a group. At the same time that the group wrestled with questions of accountability, members struggled over who actually was in charge. They fought over mundane responsibilities, like who was tapped to monitor group finances and who should be in charge of finding space to meet. These fine-grained issues about responsibility and control were also critical to the group's undoing. George was one of the members jockeying for a leadership position, but even he could identify the danger of having "too many generals." He told me, "In spirit it could have been a great organization. In reality, [it was] these same conflicts. In anything you've got the clashes of the egos.

We truly don't want to be subservient to anyone. I don't know where people get off thinking they don't have to be a servant to someone at any point…. Therefore, we're wasting time trying to give people titles and positions within our group. We're missing the prime time of going out and doing what we need to do."

George drew on the vaguely spiritual language of "subservience" to lay the blame on the lack of a giving mindset. This was a generous way of saying that people were power hungry. Everyone wanted to be in charge and lead the group. Tim himself recognized this: "We take so much time trying to set up and fighting about who going to run what. Again, that's one of the main things I saw with [the Black Republican Alliance] … a bunch of people who were fighting about who was going to do what." According to George, this fighting touched leadership duties as well as more mundane tasks: "There's plenty of work to go around—you know, logistics. That was my thing in a previous job. It was my job to make sure things got somewhere in a timely manner. I can look at a map and tell you exactly what we need to do and how it's going to go. Quick, fast, and in a hurry. But we had already had a logistical person, so who was I to come in and say, 'Oh, I want that position.'"

Having interviewed most of the players in the Black Republican Alliance drama, I was not surprised they weren't friends. What was surprising, though, was their inability to move past these divisions in the name of their shared interests and goals. For an outsider, the depth of the animosity between African American Republican activists was a shock, and their inability to overcome that animosity would spell the end of the group. It was not only ideological and identity issues that undermined the Black Republican Alliance. Indeed, to focus exclusively on those divisions probably misrepresents the lived experiences of

African American Republicans. Focusing on the ideological would cast the intra-group experiences of African American Republicans as a bit too high-minded. Yes, they disagree on broad ideological principles, but they also fight over incredibly mundane and petty things as well. One key to the importance of color-blind and race-conscious worldviews is the way they infuse both the interpersonal and the more mundane organizing interactions among these activists. At an interpersonal level, these "small issues" can be as simple as not liking or respecting one another. The organizational tasks can range from things like who gets to decide how much is spent on copying fliers, to the wording of what should go on the flier itself.

One way to think about the failure of black Republican organizations like the NBRA and the Black Republican Alliance is that there are "big" reasons why these activists have trouble organizing and there are "small" reasons. The big reasons are related to ideology and the meanings connected to race. These are important because they are the places where people stand on principles and espouse grand platitudes. The activists I spoke with did not talk in terms of a divide between color-blind and race-conscious Republicans, but they acknowledged that differing approaches to thinking about race and politics made—and continue to make—organizing difficult. It was a challenge to bring together activists with such diverging ideas about what the organization is even supposed to address. For some, a good black Republican organization is oriented toward promoting black interests, and that often requires clashes with the state's party leadership. Of course, as we have seen, determining what counts as a "black issue" is itself contentious. And for others the organizational goal is the promotion of conservative politics—and positive, uncontentious relations with the white Republican leaders in the state were central to meeting that goal. While the Derricks and Devons of the party are far from the monolithic oddity so many conjure when they think "black Republican," those very differences can stymie mobilization efforts.

Anyone who has dealt with political organizing understands the potential for frustration and burnout, but African American Republicans talk about their organizing experiences like soldiers remembering a tour of duty. Insults, mutual recriminations, personal slights, and racial animus animate their stories, and their very body language reveals the heavy tolls they've taken: weary sighs, slumped shoulders, fists shaking in anger as they recalled efforts to build a community among black conservatives. My informants may have varied in how they went about linking blackness to Republican partisanship, but they were consistent in their grousing about other African American Republicans and their inability to work together. When I asked one activist how he responded to calls to organize black Republicans, he unabashedly rejected the prospect: "When I answer the phone and somebody is talking about doing a Black Republican group, the first thing I do is hang up. Been there. Done that. Not going anywhere," he said.

Why do African American Republicans have such difficulty getting along and organizing? The short answer is that they often don't like one another. Personal animus makes it difficult to work together, and just because people share some similar characteristics does not mean they should be expected to get along. This is often how African American Republicans themselves will account for their discord. But their accounts of organizational strife reveal more than differences of personality. It is true that African American Republicans in any one location often dislike one another. It is also the case that organizing among African American Republicans stalls over the role of race within their organizations. More specifically, it seems to stall over how race manifests itself—no one seems to want a "raceless" African American Republican group, but no one has found a way to effectively bridge the race-blind and race-conscious approaches. Previous chapters detailed how African American Republicans are called on to reconcile their commitment to blackness with a dedication to Republican partisanship. There is variation in how this reconciliation is practiced among the activists in this study. The manner in which African American Republicans link blackness to Republican partisanship structures a range of political behaviors. It is crucial to how they frame and present Republican social policies, but it also informs how they organize.

Multiple respondents—well beyond the participants in the Black Republican Alliance breakdown—described the situation among African American Republican activists as like "crabs in a barrel," cramped together and all competing to rise to the top. Black Republicans do inhabit a narrow space in the public imagination, squeezed between the black community and the GOP. And, from my observations, there was certainly competition for attention and resources; internal squabbling and backbiting were par for the course. Over the course of these fights, one might expect African American Republicans to come to some clarity about organizational goals. Sociologist Amin Ghaziani has shown how infighting can provide clarity and consensus around organizational identity and goals within the LGBT movement.[10] Why does infighting have the opposite effect in African American Republicans' groups?

To answer that question, it is necessary to examine African American Republicans' relations with their white Republican counterparts. White Republicans control resources that allow some African American Republicans to opt out of internal organizing struggles. In this context, relations with white Republicans are incredibly important. And when white Republicans and institutions are the primary sources of material support, African American Republicans have little incentive to resolve conflicts within and among groups. The next chapter explores how the presence of white Republicans often works to amplify divisions among black Republicans. Lacking coherent, organized power as a group, they are especially dependent on their white counterparts even when that dependence keeps African Americans on the fringes—good for the "optics" but rarely given real voice and real power.

CHAPTER SIX

Whither the Republican Party

"It's demagoguery," Mia Love, a Utah Republican of Haitian descent, told the *Deseret News* in 2012. A candidate for the U.S. House of Representatives, she was describing the Congressional Black Caucus (CBC), continuing, "They sit there and ignite emotions and ignite racism when there isn't." Love was on a tear: "They use their positions to instill fear. Hope and change is turned into fear and blame. Fear that everybody is going to lose everything and blaming Congress for everything instead of taking responsibility."[1]

Love lost in a close race but would go on to win a House seat in 2014. Her position on the CBC had, by then, softened. When she was asked by the Capitol Hill news website Roll Call whether she would join the group, she said, "I think I will. I will consider joining because I think that in order to effect change, you can't do it from the outside in. You have to do it from the inside out. I'm going to see if I can make a difference there."[2] Her decision to join the CBC did not grow out of any change to her general attitude on issues of race. As both a candidate and a congresswoman,

Love has consistently spoken out against identity politics, while still standing by the language of personal responsibility and downplaying structural accounts of racism and discrimination. On election night, Love assured a cheering crowd that "I was not elected because of the color of my skin."[3]

On that night in 2014, the Republican National Committee (RNC) was celebrating the victories of three black candidates, calling the wins "historic."[4] In a surprise victory, William Hurd became the first African American Republican congressman elected in Texas, and Tim Scott of South Carolina won a Senate seat, making him one of two African Americans serving in that body. Like Love, Hurd and Scott have distanced themselves from any notion that their racial identity is politically relevant. Scott positions his victory as a rejection of Democrats' attempts to "play the race card": "The lowest common denominator of fear and race-baiting is something that the other party has tried to do, and the voters said 'No.'"[5] Like Love, he said his election was based on his values, not his racial identity: "South Carolina voters vote their values and their issues—and not my complexion."[6] Hurd has been less deliberate in downplaying his race,[7] even joking about the likelihood of a "black dude" winning his congressional seat. Still, Hurd has framed his success as appealing to issues that cross racial boundaries: "We [won the election] by engaging people on the issues that they care about. Whether you're Hispanic, black, white, you know, you care about putting food on your table, having a roof over your head, and that the people around you that you love are healthy and happy."[8]

Love, Scott, and Hurd present a world where race does not matter, where an overt focus on racial inequality ultimately undermines the possibility of black success like theirs. Further, they have become the contemporary face of African American

Republicans, held up as examples of how the party is reaching out to minority voters and increasing its diversity. In that all three use color-blind narratives for linking black identity and Republican partisanship, even taken together, these leaders provide a limited, and GOP-sanctioned, image of the black Republican. Compared to the race-conscious respondents in my sample, African American Republicans who take a color-blind approach (like Love, Scott, and Hurd) are more consistently channeled into leadership roles.

The previous chapter explored how these competing notions of black interests become embedded in organizational practice and hamper the organizing capacity of African American Republicans. This chapter examines how these differences structure relationships among Republicans, particularly between black and white Republicans. African American Republicans' ability to form alliances with other political actors often rests on the extent to which both individuals agree on the appropriate role of race in the lives and politics of black people.

It is important to attend to how African American Republicans interact with their white counterparts because these relationships are so politically important. For instance, there have only been six black Republican House members since 1971. None was elected from districts that were majority black; with the exception of Hurd, all of these representatives have been elected from majority-white districts. Beholden to their voters, they must talk about race in ways that are consistent with what those people want to hear. Further, alliances with white Republicans are important for securing resources. Groups like the National Black Republican Association are dependent on money that white Republicans control, and even race-conscious black Republican organizations understand the importance of winning over leaders within the GOP.

African American Republicans' relationships with other black political actors, of course, are also informed by how they conceptualize black people and their interests. However, very few in my sample had *sustained* interactions with non-Republican black political activists. Occasionally, informants reported participation in neighborhood and community groups primarily concerned with challenges in the black community, and they indicated that, in those spaces, they downplayed their Republican partisanship. They made little effort to build bridges between African American Republicans and politically liberal black organizations. Put bluntly, black people are not providing a forum for African American Republicans. Instead, it is the political opportunity structure within the GOP that creates an avenue for African American Republicans' success at the individual and organization level.

In many ways, white Republicans set the terms for the relationships they have with their black counterparts. White leaders in the GOP structure outreach efforts and control resources within the party. When there is a shared understanding of how race should be folded into the political discourse and framing of Republican policy, African American Republicans and their white counterparts enjoy a mutually beneficial relationship, and African American Republicans and their organizations gain access to resources (material, network-based, and symbolic). However, when African American Republicans endorse an explicitly "pro-black" version of Republicanism, as is often the case with race-conscious activists, relations with white Republicans are contentious and adversarial. Finally, the more functional relationship that race-blind African American Republicans enjoy with their white counterparts exacerbates tensions with their race-conscious black compatriots.

WHAT'S THE GOP UP TO?

Black voters' rejection of the GOP stems, in no small part, from the perceived racism of Republican politicians and representatives. Cataloging all the instances of racially inflected rhetoric from the GOP would create a book of its own, and multiple websites are devoted to tracking Republicans' racial flubs.[9] The sites are part tongue-in-cheek satire, part inventory, and they give a sense of the sheer volume of racially insensitive remarks, posters, images, and jokes emanating from Republicans. Today the RNC offers candidates training to avoid gaffes—racial or not.

One driver of the deployment of racialized language is the presidency of Barack Obama. Indeed, just weeks into the Obama presidency, the Tea Party emerged as a vocal and ardent source of criticism of the president and his policies. However, the most striking impact of the movement has been the internal policing of Republicans. In many ways, the Tea Party movement has become the standard-bearer for the Republican Party in the Obama era. Within the movement, Tea Party protesters and activists have used race as a symbolic weapon against his political aims.[10]

For instance, politicians, activists, and protesters on the right were staunchly opposed to Bill Clinton's efforts to reform the health-care system. So to call opposition to Obama's health-care reform racist would be misleading. However, the *form* that opposition took could manifest itself in racist ways. For instance, the Obama "witch doctor" poster only makes sense as a way to voice opposition to the Affordable Care Act (once derisively called "Obamacare," today the ACA is certainly best known to supporters and opponents alike as Obamacare) because it links Obama's blackness to stereotypes about African tribal traditions. An image of Bill Clinton in the same poster could not have "landed." The distinction between racist intent and racist approach is certainly a fine one, and it doesn't matter when you're on the receiving end of that language. But it is an important *analytic* distinction because it exemplifies race as a symbolic resource that politicians can mobilize (and an association that can stick with the GOP and shape its image among voters).

Racially charged rhetoric makes black Republicans' efforts to link black racial uplift to conservative social policy and Republican partisanship even more difficult. Many report that they try to show how their Republican partisanship is grounded in a "pro-black" politics, but for every argument won over the dinner table, another is lost when white Republicans do something construed as racist. As Richie, a self-employed entrepreneur, told me over lunch, "It [was] hard enough trying to convince blacks to support Republicans when Bush [had] Colin Powell and [Condoleezza] Rice in there. Imagine what I look like on the block when Trent Lott is talking about how the country would be better off if a segregationist had been president."[11]

Richie was not alone in feeling that the tentative advancement made by his personal example was far outweighed by racially insensitive rhetoric from GOP leaders. Dinner-table outreach is of little consequence when it is countered by constant public affirmation of the notion that Republican and black "don't go together." Why would anyone be in a party that could produce—possibly encourage—politicians who would make such glaring racial missteps? Indeed, as noted earlier, the perceived hostility of the Republican Party to black people and their interests is a critical aspect of what makes the politics of black Republicans so unexpected—and makes white Republican outreach efforts to black communities seem disingenuous at best, and ridiculously insulting at worst.

Despite being met by general skepticism, GOP leadership has made no secret of its desire to increase its appeal to black voters and reverse its anti-black reputation. In a 2005 speech to the National Association for the Advancement of Colored People (NAACP), then RNC Chair Kenneth Mehlman issued an apology from the Republican Party for the "Southern Strategy" that many feel leveraged racist ideas and intentions to woo southern whites to the GOP and win elections for Goldwater, Nixon, and Reagan. Mehlman conceded that "Some Republicans gave up on winning the African American vote, looking the other way or trying to benefit politically from racial polarization. I am here today as the Republican chairman to tell you we were wrong."[12] Not everyone was happy with the apology. Rush Limbaugh, a conservative radio personality, likened Mehlman's words to sexual assault and was infuriated that the party chair would "go down there and basically apologize for what has come to be known as the 'Southern strategy,' popularized in the Nixon administration. He's going to go down there and apologize for it. In the midst of all of this, in the midst of all that's going on, once again, Republicans are going to go bend over and grab the ankles."[13] Many on the left, too, felt that it was a meaningless, cynical gesture.

In 2010 the first black RNC chair, Michael Steele, broached the Republican Party's history of deploying racism to win white votes by arguing that "For the last forty-plus years we had a 'Southern Strategy' that alienated many minority voters by focusing on the white male vote in the South. Well, guess what happened in 1992, folks, 'Bubba' went back home to the Democratic Party and voted for Bill Clinton."

Steele's comments were not any better received than Mehlman's. Protectors of the party's history pushed back against the insinuation that the Republican leaders had knowingly played on racial animosity to secure votes.[14] And Steele himself was not beyond racial gaffes. In one instance, while fielding questions from a group of local bloggers during a Young Republican Federation convention in Indianapolis, Steele was asked about plans for inclusivity and replied that he would say, "Y'all come." Perhaps it was the informal vernacular, so casually southern, that prompted the questioner to reply sarcastically, "I'll bring the collard greens." Or maybe it was a zany one-liner. Either way, Steele, in what even critics must admit was quick timing, said he'd bring "the fried chicken and the potato salad." Steele was lambasted when the video inevitably made its way across the Internet. But lost in the collective cringing was the fact that a black party chair was out in the public expressing commitment to increasing the racial diversity within the Republican Party.

More recently, Reince Priebus has used his RNC chairmanship as a platform to call for increasing the numbers of racial and ethnic minorities within the party. "I think it's the right thing to do for our party ... fighting for every vote in America is the right thing to do in our party," Priebus said. "I want to see us increase the numbers of Republican votes in the black community so that increase actually has a clear impact on the outcome of the election."[15] Of course, these comments came amid the lowest levels of support the GOP had seen since the Goldwater campaign. Priebus allowed for the fact that previous outreach efforts had been less than sincere, and he assured voters that post-2012 efforts would be different. It wasn't about just throwing money at the problem, but about truly reaching out to black citizens: "I think we can do much better with black voters for our Republican candidate if we do the things that I've been talking about for the last three years, and that increase can be an impact increase that people can point to, and say: See, this is what happens when you fight for every vote." Later Priebus added that "Money isn't the answer, it has to be long-term engagement."[16]

The RNC hired a field director for African American initiatives, a communications director for black media, and a senior advisor for black media. Along with beefing up its communication staff, the GOP launched "#CommittedToCommunity: Engage, Empower, Uplift" as part of an effort to educate and recruit black voters. A press release described the social media campaign as a partnership with black media outlet Radio One, aimed at "recruiting, activating, and mobilizing black voters ahead of the 2016 presidential election through a series of engagement activities, issue forums and other events in communities of color."[17] On their website, the RNC wrote of the initiative: "First, it's the right thing to do. We never want to take any voter for granted. Secondly, our goal is to incorporate metrics-based engagement to recruit, mobilize and activate black voters ahead of the 2016 presidential election so that we position the Republican nominee for President with the best opportunity to win new voters and ultimately the White House."

More generally, Priebus commissioned a report from the Growth and Opportunity Project to grow the party and improve Republican campaigns. Its initial report in 2014 noted the GOP's failure to appeal to a wide range of voters, including women, Latinos, Asian Americans, and African Americans, and acknowledged that Republicans would have to improve messaging to these voters to achieve long-term success in national elections. In relation to African Americans specifically, the report stated that "the RNC must embark on a year-round effort to engage with African American voters. The engagement must include not only persuasion based upon our Party's principles but also a presence within community organizations."

The committee offered ten recommendations for connecting with black voters. specifically:

1. The RNC should hire African American communications directors and political directors for key states and communities across the country.

2. The RNC should work with the Republican State Leadership Committee to develop best practices of Republicans who were successfully elected in districts with a high population of African American voters.

3. The RNC should establish a presence in African American communities and at black organizations such as the NAACP. We are never going to win over voters who are not asked for their support. Too many African American voters have gotten in the habit of supporting Democrats without hearing anyone in their community making a case to the contrary.

4. The RNC should create a program that is focused on recruiting and supporting African American Republican candidates for office.

5. The RNC should engage historically black colleges and universities (HBCUs) with the goal of educating the community on Republican ideals and the party's history.

6. The RNC should conduct a pilot project in several targeted urban markets to identify potential target groups of voters and to enlist support from demographic partners and allies in voter contact efforts. Big-city mayoral races provide our best 2013 opportunities for these projects. The findings of these pilot projects can inform a more robust effort in the 2014 governors' races to build coalitions and greater support in urban areas.

7. The RNC should develop a nationwide database of African American leaders.

8. The RNC must improve on promoting African American staff and candidates within the party. The GOP should utilize African American elected officials as surrogates both in their

communities and with the national media. At the staff level, the personnel should be visible and involved in senior political and budget decisions and not be limited to demographic outreach.

9. The RNC must develop a national African American surrogate list to promote a high-level presence in African American media.

10. The RNC and state parties should make every effort to feature and use diverse committee members.

By calling for the hiring of communication directors, building relations with black organizations like the NAACP, developing a nationwide database of black leaders, and supporting more African American Republican candidates for office, the Growth and Opportunity Project is attuned to messaging but does little to address any substantive policy issues. In the years since the report's release, Priebus has gone on to affirm the GOP's commitment to community-based outreach efforts: "My point is this to our party, and what I think we've changed over the last two years: we can keep whining about this all day long. But, until we get into the community talking about the things we believe in, nothing is going to change.... I think it is impossible [to reach these communities] if you don't show up."[18]

Community outreach is effective only insofar as what you say when you "show up" connects with its intended audience. It seems that Republican efforts to speak to African American voters have not hit their mark. I had occasion to interact with white Republicans engaged in such efforts, and they often displayed very little insight into the communities they were trying to reach. Larry, a representative of the Republican Executive Committee of an urban city, cornered me at an event to discuss outreach efforts to black voters. He had heard that I was conducting a study of black Republicans and their experiences within the GOP, and he was eager to know what I'd learned. He told me that "it looks good when we can be more diverse." A few years before the higher-profile efforts of Priebus and the RNC, Larry's questions put me on edge. I was guarded in my response, explaining that I had only recently begun qualitative exploration of the topic. Switching tactics, Larry asked if I had looked at any quantitative data. Continuing to be evasive, I told him that I had only examined publicly available data—as a part of party leadership, he would certainly have access to better data than mine. Larry assured me that was not the case, even when I expressed surprise that he would have less knowledge about black Republicans than a graduate student. He shared his frustrations about what he saw as his committee's inability to "move the needle" on the number of black Republicans and was clearly pessimistic that they could attract more blacks to the party. Larry knew that black voters were important but stated flatly that Republicans just didn't know what to do to get more blacks involved.

Not all white Republicans were as pessimistic as Larry, but even those who were able to articulate a plan for reaching black voters mostly relied on nonspecific, amorphous appeals. Rather than link Republican policies to the concrete concerns of black voters, outreach efforts have generally been grounded in vague, race-blind language. Betsy, another white Republican tasked with black outreach, chatted with me at a political event after Michael Steele, then making waves as a prominent African American Republican, spoke. Betsy praised Steele for being "articulate and well spoken" (words often recognized as a racially back-handed compliment) and was enthusiastic about him, though she was quick to note that she would like him whether he "was black, white, red, or orange." She went on to say that the biggest barrier to getting

more blacks involved in the Republican Party was education—
stressing that, to her mind, when other groups like Jewish, Italian,
and Polish immigrants had been underprivileged, education
offered a "way out." Even when these people were uneducated,
Betsy said, they made sure that their *children* were educated.

I asked how education would increase black people's Republicanism. She explained that once black people were educated,
they would realize the affinity between their beliefs and the
Republican Party. There was a palpable shift in the tone of our
conversation, and Betsy became very serious, shaking her head
and hitting the table to emphasize her points. She said that education would lead to more success and less "dependence on the
government." She paused. "Don't you agree?" I tentatively
responded that it was hard to argue against education. With her
triumphant look, the tension in the conversation dissipated.
Smiling, Betsy assured me that she was not going to give up on
black voters just because it was hard to win them over.

RELATIONS WITH WHITE REPUBLICANS

The activists I spoke with were divided in their responses to
GOP outreach efforts. Some had benefited from the party leadership's openness to black involvement, but others had nothing
positive to say about their experiences with white Republicans.
Across the board, however, there was a shared belief that while
party leaders might want more black *faces,* they were less interested in tailoring policies in a way that might be informed by
the racial identity of black voters.

For many, the GOP's black outreach efforts are too color-
blind. Gwen had campaigned for Congress in a majority-black
district in a politically conservative state, and she felt good

about her chances in the race. She had run previously, without the backing of the party, and had, by her account, garnered about 30 percent of the vote. Given the solid Democratic Party foothold in this particular district, she felt this was a good showing. By the 2008 elections, the incumbent was facing a series of ethical scandals and challengers in the Democratic primary, and Gwen had managed to secure promises of support from the state's Republican Party apparatus.

Undertaking the campaign, Gwen felt that it was crucial that she link the party platform to the interests of the black people in her district. Indeed, she had good reason for concern on this issue: in an earlier run, she had secured the majority of her donations from contributors outside of her district. Gwen was concerned that national support from Republicans outside of her state could be used by opponents to frame her as unfamiliar with the concerns (around education, abortion, and business, in particular) of what she claimed was her community. In 2008, though, she felt that state party officials were unwilling to recognize the unique situation of her candidacy and would be miserly in their support if she refused to "stay on script" as a "one hundred percent Republican Party, go President Bush kind of Republican." She sensed she had to separate the GOP message from the GOP messenger, and that the party would not understand why she had to call upon her racial identity and distance herself from the Republican Party even while running under its banner. The lack of understanding when it came to black voters was a big problem.

For activists like Gwen, relations with white Republicans are strained and often contentious. Gwen wants to place race—her own *and* her take on the concerns of black people—at the center of her efforts. She fits well with the race-conscious respondents considered in chapter 4. However, it would be inaccurate to think of Gwen's race consciousness as reflecting a built-in resentment of white leaders in the party. Gwen's issue was that the candidate training did not seemed designed with the specific needs of black candidates in mind. She was more than happy to take resources from white conservatives, even when they came from potentially questionable sources.

When Gwen spoke about working with white Republicans, the most positive experience she relayed was about a group in her state dedicated to preserving the memory of the Confederacy. "The Sons of Confederate Soldiers were so supportive of me. I could not believe it. When they invited me to one of their meetings I went with a, I have to say a modicum of trepidation, you know…. But because we had basic beliefs that were the same, they were so welcoming of me. They campaigned for me. I couldn't believe it. But it was based on we had the basic beliefs that were the same really. That was a shock to me." While it is questionable whether or not someone running in a majority-black district would want the Sons of the Confederate Soldiers campaigning for her, Gwen's experience with the group suggests she was open to working with white Republicans—it would be naive and unrealistic to be a black Republican and not be willing to work with white Republicans—but, in general, she feels that the leaders of the party are not willing to work with her.

Gwen's issues with the party were not limited to state-level officials. As a congressional candidate, she participated in a Republican-organized "candidate camp" to identify, train, and cultivate relationships with possible African American Republican candidates for congressional office. For Gwen, the event was a bust. She went to the camp expecting to hear about strategies relevant to minorities running as Republicans:

I guess there was something less than a hundred of us that were picked from across the country to come to a candidates school that the RNC held. And I'm not sure how I got picked. I still don't know anything about that. And here I was with about eighty other blacks and some Latinos from around the country running for various offices. Of course, Ken Mehlman was head of the RNC. He comes in and gives the rah-rah speech and other people come in and [say,] "These are things you can look forward to. These are the things you need to know about being a candidate." It was a candidate school, and as far as I was concerned, it wasn't particularly any better or worse than any other candidate school. All the information was about the same.... It was certainly a pleasure to smile and get a photo-op with Ken Mehlman. But some of the other nitty-gritty stuff, like how do you deal with white Republicans who look at you askance, saying "Why are you in this party?" That was missing.

The information Gwen wanted was not readily available from the candidate school. She wanted to hear from Republicans with experience running as racial minorities, or at least hear from those who had been involved in the campaigns of minority candidates. To find that information, Gwen had to search on her own:

Black Republicans didn't come to talk to us. They didn't invite and pay for any black Republicans running for any of the higher-level offices, be it senator or governor. But they still didn't have any black folks come and talk to us. And there were no sessions—only afterwards when I got entrée to other people by other inroads of people that I knew, I would sit down and have them say to me, "You know in principle we're right Gwen. In principle this is the party we need to be behind. This is how we need to advance black people. But you know, the party is not going to do anything for you." So it was in other venues that people sat down and said, "Don't be discouraged. You already know. Do the right thing always. So just keep doing the right thing no matter what everyone else is doing." But it would have been nice to have some of them have their way paid to D.C. to have them come talk to us there.

The experience was disheartening and left Gwen feeling as if the national leadership of the party was as oblivious to the importance of race as the Republican leaders in her home state. Despite calls from Republican leaders for increased diversity within the party, Gwen was not optimistic that the GOP would put in the time and effort required to make real inroads with black voters.

There is no long-term strategy. And because of that I think that's why there's no investment although that's supposed to be a Republican principle. You know? [laughs] You know, you start here. You put stuff into it. You grow it. You put some more stuff into it. You strive for excellence so that other people will want your product and you continue to grow it and that's how we thrive in this capitalistic society or whatever. But they don't do that with regards to black people. And so then they get to the situation where we're at when ninety percent of black people vote Democrat.... I said during the campaign, "The Democrats pimp us. The Republicans ignore us." And that's the way it is. The Democratic Party, they don't have to do anything to keep the black vote.

Gwen was very vocal with her feelings about the state of black partisanship and her desire that the party be more sensitive to her specific needs, but she was not alone in finding little support for efforts that centered on a candidate's race or the race of minority constituents.[19] Concern about assistance to minority candidates was a constant theme among these activists, even those who had some success in gaining traction within the network of power. One activist who would go on to become a high-profile candidate with substantial support from conservative backers sounded a lot like Gwen when he talked about the support black Republican candidates got in 2006 campaigns:

They talk about outreach to blacks running as Republicans and in the last election you had Lynn Swann in Pennsylvania, Blackwell in Ohio, and Steele in Maryland. Okay. High-profile, qualified, intelligent blacks. And the Republican Party wouldn't break an old rule of getting behind them and really trying to get behind them and help them to the finish line. So don't talk to me about how you're going to do black outreach when you've got opportunities like this and they just sit back like, "Well, let's just see if he can swim." It's like throw him in the pool and let's just see if he can swim on his own and if he does, "Look what we did as the Republican Party." Then claim credit. That ain't outreach.

There was also concern about the party's openness to the framing of outreach efforts. Marcus, another African American Republican candidate, told me that, if he could get people to focus on the issues rather than partisanship, he would do fine in his municipal-level election. He explained that he was taking a tough-on-crime stance, particularly around juvenile auto theft, and would campaign on his support for an alternative "boot camp" program for juvenile offenders over jail time or probation. This all seemed reasonable enough to me, but it didn't address the fundamental issue of having to run as a Republican.

Marcus was hoping that his different approach would be effective in gaining black votes, suggesting that most approaches tried to change the way blacks thought about the Republican Party, whereas his approach was to link the party to existing attitudes in the black community. You have to meet black people "where they are," he said, and make the Republican message appeal to them. He called this "an insight-driven marketing perspective" that focused on the best way to sell Republican beliefs given blacks' current attitudes.

Outreach was an area that was emblematic of the challenges in deploying a race-conscious perspective within an official party context, but it was difficult in general for race-conscious African American Republicans to deal with their white counterparts. Devon, whose organizing efforts were discussed in the last chapter, spoke passionately on a number of occasions about this difficulty. He found himself consistently arguing with how his state's Republican Party structured their outreach efforts. In Devon's opinion, GOP outreach needed to relate conservative social policies to the lived experience of black people, but he felt that the party too often relied on an abstract appeal to the inherent "rightness" of Republican policy preferences. He would regularly confront state party leaders with data—once he showed me a binder filled with newspaper articles, academic texts, and a meticulously detailed historical timeline of black involvement in the GOP. The file highlighted the rocky and distasteful relationship and comprised the facts with which he armed himself to "make sure that they take me seriously. They expect me to come in all angry and loud. That's what they think of us. But I go in cool and have my facts in order. They can't argue with that." Devon engaged in an internal brand of respectability politics, but constantly finding himself at odds with party leadership, he noticed that he was increasingly not being invited to speak at panels that explored issues of race in the context of the Republican Party.

Despite the *volume* of outreach, race-conscious African American Republicans find very little to recommend about official efforts to reach black voters. In the absence of explicit efforts to link conservative social policy to black interests, the GOP would seem to have very little that appeals to black voters. African Americans have been disproportionately affected by the poor economy, yet Republican candidates have been vocal in their desire to cut taxes, slash government spending, and repeal the Affordable Care Act. Across the board, these changes would have a negative impact on the material conditions of African Americans. Support for aggressive voter identification and silence on issues related to police brutality and the criminal justice system are further strikes against the party in most black-majority communities. So, although organizations like the National Black Republican Association like to frame black voters as misunderstanding the GOP's history, there are plenty of rational reasons for black voters' skepticism. In failing to directly address these policy concerns, the party consistently troubles the race-conscious African Americans in its ranks.

In contrast, African American Republicans who are willing to downplay the significance of race in the politics of black people find the mainstream conservative movement quite supportive. As noted in chapter 2, a common attack on African American Republicans is to describe their relationships with white conservatives in terms of patronage. However, among African American Republicans, there is a belief that patronage is mainly bestowed on a certain *kind* of African American Republican. Recall that, in chapter 5, I discussed Derrick's problematic relationship with other African American Republicans. His experiences with white Republicans were very different, and he counted a number of white Republican leaders among his supporters. To him it made perfect sense that his white counterparts preferred his de-racialized approach. Over multiple discussions, Derrick stressed that his approach was less antagonistic and that he did not understand why anyone would expect that white Republicans would endorse a pro-black version of Republican politics: "No one will say it 'cause it's not politically correct, but if only ten precent of a group votes for you, why would you bend over backwards to try to reach out to them? If you go into talking about 'black this and black that' people are going to question your commitment to the party. It seems like you are putting race before values." A red-state black Republican said in another interview: "Nobody in the party is going to listen to you if you sound like a radical. We're conservative, not radical. So if you are coming at them with a lot of talk about Black Power, they'll just look the other way. This is not a 'black' thing. It's about conservative values. When you show you believe in that, people will respond to you."

African American Republicans like Derrick, who question the role of racial discrimination in limiting the lives of blacks, experience much more positive relationships at the individual and organizational levels of the party. On multiple occasions throughout this research, I attended events sponsored by state or local Republican Party organizations or independent conservative groups. Often they were advertised with titles like "Race and the Republican Party" or "Race and the Conservative Movement." Their stated goal was always about increasing understanding between black voters and the conservative movement. Rarely, however, were actual black voters present.

Generally, these events consisted of African American Republican activists or political candidates soliciting financial support from white Republicans or speaking as representatives of the "black position" on a panel. At one of these events, early in my fieldwork, Marilyn, an older white woman who regularly attended the meetings, explained how things work. Every month, the group meets to discuss a different topic. Speakers come—often presenting a pro and a con position on the topic. After the speeches, the session is opened up for a question-and-answer, or as Marilyn put it, "They let us have at 'em!" She was enthusiastic about the group and very welcoming to me.

At one meeting I attended, the topic was the black vote in 2008, and an African American Republican congressional candidate was one of the speakers. Ostensibly, he was there to talk about the best way to reach black voters, but he was also there to promote his own candidacy in a heavily Democratic district against a fairly strong incumbent. His chances of winning were slim. He began his talk by stating that government isn't the savior—no, his savior "is THE Savior, the Lord and Savior, Jesus Christ." The line got vigorous applause from a few in the audience, but when he railed against the complacency of black voters, the entire audience responded positively. In particular, he was lauded for his argument that black voters had been brainwashed by "Democrats and the civil rights establishment." He closed with a plea for support of his campaign. As the crowd clapped, an older white woman caught my eye, looked at me expectantly, and asked, "What did you think? It's nice to finally have someone willing to stand up and tell the truth."

Similar events always featured African American Republican representatives engaged in discussion of the pathological vision of black people, followed by a race-blind framing of conservative policies. I heard more than one African American Republican explain how it was reasonable to be afraid of young black men dressed "in sagging jeans." I saw activists mimicking the urban speech patterns stereotypically associated with black youth to illustrate the challenges facing black communities. Tellingly, these sorts of themes emerged only when the majority of the audience at an African American Republican organization's event was white or when black Republican activists were speaking at a white event. By the end of my fieldwork, I could almost perfectly predict the tone of speeches by the racial makeup of the audience. If white people were present in significant numbers, I could expect to hear a lot about black pathologies, failures of black leadership, and the ills of race-conscious social policies. But there would be very little about how conservative social policies were good for black people *as* blacks.

Though race-blind African American Republicans also see outreach efforts as devoid of a race-based message, this is not particularly troublesome to them. In fact, it works to their advantage, producing a mutually beneficial relationship whereby race-blind African American Republicans gain access to resources and the GOP gets to have the appearance of diversity. This is a consequence of ideological consistency: a black subject constrained only by personal choices is consistent with the broader GOP platform that stresses personal responsibility and questions the validity of using racial status to distribute state resources.

Despite the generally positive relations between white Republicans and their race-blind African American counterparts, white Republicans do not *always* marginalize race-conscious African American Republicans. The Black Family Values Summit presented its mission as supporting the advancement of public policy that promotes responsible government, liberty, economic empowerment, and family values within urban communities. The "summit" was convened two years in a row—no small accomplishment, given the track record of African American Republican organizations discussed in chapter 5. At the conference I attended, concern about black communities was front and center, manifest in the panels and activities. There were panels related to "Our History," as well as sessions exploring how to economically empower black communities, the role of race in Constitutional interpretation, and giving grassroots organizers tools to promote Republican leadership in their communities.

I attended the first summit, where the conference hall evoked a pro-black feeling. The program was filled with black speakers addressing issues directly related to black communities and few discussions about the Republican Party specifically. Even informal interactions with attendees brought to mind the "family reunion vibe" at the Republicans for Black Empowerment meeting. More often than not, I was greeted with familiarity that evoked an in-group racial connection: "What's happening, brother?" was combined with a half-handshake, half-hug introduction. Several actual families with children mixed among about a hundred attendees, and I overheard a group of women praising the showing of "strong black families."

Given this environment, I was surprised at the level of *white* attendance. Most of these events had audiences that were either pretty much all white or all black (depending on the organization hosting it). This crowd, though predominantly black, was mixed—you might even say interracial. More tellingly, it did not feel like the event was "for" the white people there. This was surprising, given the strong emphasis on race and, more specifically, the racial-uplift tone of the promotional materials for the event.

With "family values" in its title, it was not surprising that the summit was focused on social issues, but I was taken aback by how often the speakers used their platforms to chastise the black community. Over two days, speaker after speaker lamented the decay of the black family and aligned it with a range of social issues. Blacks were called to task for getting abortions and blamed for supporting candidates who supported marriage equality (which the speakers felt undermined black families). Even blacks' religiosity was impugned, with churchgoing presented as hypocritical if black people were also supporting the

Democratic Party. To their credit, the speakers skillfully managed to indict the entire black community *except* the attendees at
the summit. The failure of *most* blacks to hold the line against
contemporary social decay was set against a backdrop of a mythical past in which black families mimicked the Cleavers. American blacks were even called to task by a white woman working
for a Christian relief agency for not supporting abstinence-only
education efforts that might slow the spread of HIV and AIDS
in Africa. The pro-black nature of the summit operated in conjunction with an incredibly pathological construction of the
black political subject.

At the Family Values Summit my research was challenged:
here I saw a direct focus on social issues by black Republican
activists *and* white attendees engaging with a race-conscious
form of black Republicanism. Despite its antagonistic language
with regard to "black people," the summit framed its *goals* in the
language of racial uplift. Conservative social policy and Republican partisanship were presented as good for black people *as*
black people.

The leadership of the Republican Party has made it very clear
that they want more people who identify as black among their
ranks—as voters, activists, and candidates—and it has dedicated time and money to outreach efforts. At the same time,
Republicans stubbornly stick to a very particular set of ideas
about black people. Representatives of the party have consistently been linked to events that reflect an anti-black sentiment,
to racist statements, and to ideas about black pathology. While
this tension certainly is present in the public discourse, from my
observations, white Republicans are actually quite encouraging
of the efforts of their black counterparts. They talked about the

presence of African American Republicans as a key component of the party's outreach efforts and an important symbolic marker of the "big tent" image the GOP wants to create. However, almost all of my interaction with white Republicans occurred in contexts where the African American Republicans were either committed to a race-blind politics or wanted to use conservative politics to reform the black community. African American Republicans who embraced a more race-conscious application of conservative ideology reported much more contentious relations with white Republican leaders. Hearing African American Republicans discuss the range of their relationships with white Republicans lent credence to the idea that race-blind African American Republicans generally have more positive relations with the party leadership.

To disgruntled race-conscious African American Republicans, the GOP seems to want more people who identify as black to become Republicans, but *without* Republicans changing their preconceived notions about black people and black communities. So, while the Republican Party is incredibly welcoming of the black activists I spoke with, there is one critically important caveat: those who articulate a "race doesn't matter" brand of Republicanism are embraced, whereas those who support a "Black Power through conservative principles" perspective are difficult to integrate into GOP networks. However, I found one pathway to center race and still gain acceptance from white Republicans: linking blackness and Republican partisanship via the "spoiling" of a nostalgic, imagined community of black people and Republicans' ability to help reclaim it.

African American Republicans' relations with their white counterparts call attention to the importance of distinguishing between thinking about race as an identity and considering the meanings that are attached to race. Republican leaders want people who identify as black, sure. But they also have a particular set of ideas about black people that the party is committed to. Making sense of this contradiction is difficult for black Republican activists, and their experiences often reflect the GOP's conflicting responses to African Americans. For African American Republicans, participation in the party closes off certain ways of understanding their own racial identity. Only one way of thinking about black people and their political motivations is validated by GOP leadership. So the GOP's color-blind ideology might preclude success for African Americans who espouse race-conscious policy preferences, unless those preferences are attached to a pathological image of black people. It is certainly the case that color-blind African American Republicans and race-conscious Republicans motivated by pathological ideas about black people are drawn to—and into—the Republican Party. The rewards structure of the party, though, encourages lower racial consciousness among African Americans. That is to say, organizational constraints endemic to the Republican Party structure how African American partisans express both their blackness and their Republicanness.

If they are so troubled by their experience within the GOP, why do these African American Republicans stay around? This is a potent question that few of my respondents had a clear answer to. For most, it was built into the broader political system within the United States. In a two-party system, if you are frustrated with one party you are limited in your alternatives. With internal party politics weighted so heavily against a form of Republican partisanship that centers black identity, African American Republicans began to question this logic, and even true believers are skeptical about the GOP's ability to welcome

African Americans. As one respondent glumly assessed: "Now, if I were long-thinking in terms of four hundred years from now, I might say let's start another party. I'm not quite willing to wait four hundred years. I'm hoping that there are changes that can be made to help, especially black people, sooner than that. So, I think that the Republican Party is the vehicle but it may be four hundred years anyway going through the Republican Party if there is not some support given beyond lip service by the Republican hierarchy."

Conclusion

By the end of the 2016 Republican primaries, the African American Republican angle to the race had shifted away from making fun of Ben Carson. Instead, the country collectively scratched its head at the idea of black supporters of Donald Trump. Whether puzzling over the antics of Diamond and Silk, the African American sisters from North Carolina who gained notoriety and laughs in their efforts to "Stump for Trump," or chuckling at a panel of black Trump supporters explaining themselves on *The Nightly Show*, black Republicans may have reached peak ridiculousness in 2016.[1] Given the way African American Republicans rise to prominence within the party, it should not come as a surprise that the carnivalesque atmosphere of the primaries was reflected in the black Republicans who captured our attention during them. Still, in a campaign built upon racially exclusionary rhetoric, it does beggar belief that someone with commitment to black racial identity could support a Trump presidency. But who's to say that black people should center their racial identity in their political decision-making? Furthermore, why is it so laughable that someone could find a way to direct pro-black commitment toward support for a candidate like Trump?

The jumping-off point for our discussions about blacks in the GOP is often a comical take highlighting the incongruence of black people supporting the Republican Party in its current form. When we are not laughing at African American Republicans, we are expressing outrage or dismay at the political positions of high-profile politicians like Ben Carson, conservative academics like Shelby Steele, or idiosyncratic celebrities like actress Stacy Dash. Occasionally, we are amused and offended by African American Republicans at the same time. While humor and outrage are certainly legitimate responses to the African American Republicans we encounter in the popular media, that group presents a limited picture. As we saw in chapter 6, African American Republicans are *selected* into success when they have a particular way of talking about black people and their problems—specifically, one that fits with what white Republican power brokers want to see in office and on stage.

To some, these African American Republicans are saviors who refuse to stay beholden to shallow identity politics. To others, they are sellouts willing to betray other blacks for their own self-interest. Both arguments treat race as an identity that drives political behavior. So, in the same way that being wealthy might make an individual seem like an "automatic" Republican, being black makes one seem more likely to vote Democrat. Under this sort of thinking, the unexpected politics of African American Republicans presents a curious case: political behavior does not match the expectations associated with a social identity. Accordingly, African American Republicans have a reputation for *lacking* racial identity or, at the very least, being willing to ignore their racial identity in service to their partisan beliefs.

I find some support for this reputation among the activists I spoke with, but the story is more complicated. I find meaningful, or meaning-filled, divisions among the group. By focusing, primarily, on nonelite African American Republican activists across multiple political contexts, I have been able to explore the differences in their beliefs, rhetoric, and political strategies. I have shown how African American Republicans often engage in a heated debate about what is "best for black people" and the appropriate way to conceptualize Republican partisanship as a solution to the challenges black people face in the post–civil rights era.

After spending time with black Republican activists, I am convinced of the need to shift the focus to exploring the meaning that African Americans attach to their racial identity and how political context facilitates and inhibits the meaning-making process. My conversations and observations reveal that, contrary to perception, nearly all African American Republicans express high levels of racial identification. They see themselves as linked to a broader black community and, to some extent, see their fates as linked to other African Americans. Some experience this connection as empowering; others assert individualism and work to distance themselves from the broader black community. All understand that they are connected to the black community and black identity regardless.

In response to claims that social factors play an increasingly smaller role in postindustrial political life, Manza and Brooks defend the usefulness of the "sociological" approach to political behavior.[2] Their approach looks to social divisions in American society to account for variations in partisanship and policy support. Social categories like race, class, and gender act as cleavages that divide the electorate, calling attention to how social status structures individual political behavior. That is, the groups with which we identify shape not only the lenses through which we see the world, but also the programs of viable and acceptable political behavior available to us. Political scientist Katherine Cramer Walsh writes: "Social identities occupy a central role in the perspectives people use to think about public affairs. They are not simply another consideration that people take into account when making sense of the world around them. Instead, identities color the lens through which other considerations and factors in opinion—things such as interests, attachments to political parties, and political values—are understood."[3] One danger, of course, is that social categories become taken for granted, their meanings assumed as self-evident by virtue of membership in the category. As Brubaker and Cooper note, a social identity is expected to "manifest itself in solidarity, in shared dispositions or consciousness, or in collective action."[4] As such, sociological approaches shed light on differences between different social groups but, to date, have less to say about differences *within* social groups.[5]

This model serves as the backdrop to a great deal of the discussion about U.S. politics. For instance, discourse around identity politics illustrates how the identity model has come to dominate our understanding of political behavior. Most basically, identity politics represents political arguments, attitudes, and preferences as shaped by a person's social identity. Some see identity politics as a natural outgrowth of recognizing the reality of how social identities like race, class, or gender shape life chances. If your racial status strongly determines the likelihood that you will be pulled over by police, it makes sense to organize your political claims and protests around an idea like Black Lives Matter. Opponents of identity politics often object to the prioritizing of social identities and claim that identity politics balkanizes political interests and motivations and impedes political collaboration. Identity politics, for these critics, is shortsighted and focused on minor slights. It is a politics of accommodation. Interestingly, critiques of identity politics emerge across the political spectrum, looking surprisingly similar.[6]

Rather than support or critique identity politics, we need a deeper exploration of the phenomenon. As African American Republicans show, black racial identity can be used to support a wide range of political behaviors, ideologies, and social policies. Under the right circumstances, this can include conservative politics and Republican affiliation.[7] As Melanye Price argues: "Attachment does not equal or even necessitate action. Nor is there any logical behavioral end that results simply from feeling attached to other blacks. Does linked fate necessitate mass Democratic support? Does it increase voter apathy? Does it create a set of criteria for weighing candidates against each other?"[8] Just as African American Republicans have to work to link black identity to conservative politics, we would expect it to take work to link blackness to liberal policies. Any social identity, in fact, can be channeled into a broad range of political actions and strategies, in part based on how that identity is perceived in relation to other collective identities or individual characteristics. As such, to fully understand the relationship between black identity and political behavior, we must understand how particular *political* behaviors are linked to *racial* identity. Political analysts should direct attention to the mechanisms through which racial or other group identity is brought to bear on political decisions.[9]

We must also assess the importance and meaning that individuals place on their identities. We cannot assume that within any identity category, importance and meanings are constant. The diversity of the African American experience—across workplace, family, and political arenas—has been well documented.[10] Indeed, as the lived experience of blackness becomes more complex and inconsistent, within-group variations become truly important.[11]

Yet the complexity of racial identity and racial group membership is rarely manifested in our measurement of race, and rarely are differences in attitudes about black people accounted for in analyses of black political behavior.[12] Race is often treated as a static, phenotypical characteristic. When analysts explore the social-psychological components of racial attachment, a feeling of group membership comes to represent the totality of racial identity. But as scholars of politics and political behavior turn to "identity" as a way of understanding the political world, it behooves analysts to move beyond race as a static characteristic with consistent meanings and importance; race is neither consistent nor constant.[13]

Capturing the varying importance and the variety of meanings that people attach to racial identity is central to this move. My analysis shows that the importance attached to racial identity varies among African American Republicans and that this variation is associated with important political choices. To truly capture the effect of racial identity on political behavior, the presence of racial identification has to be contextualized by *salience,* or the importance an individual places on that identification. Generally, I found that African American Republicans express relatively high levels of racial identification. They see themselves as connected to a broader community of black people, and—whether they like it or not—they see their fates as linked to this broader black community. Where I did find a difference was in the centrality of racial identity. Just because a person feels a subjective sense of group membership does not mean that this membership is central to how they understand themselves or the political word. I found significant variance in how much African American Republicans used race as a personal identity and a lens for understanding how the world works. Some activists treated their black identity as a primary identity and the lens through which they made sense of the political world. Others treated their racial identity as culturally, but not politically, important. For these activists, just because they wanted to go to a black church did not mean that they thought about tax policy through the lens of race. Acknowledging that identification and consciousness are aspects of racial attachment that do not always go together allows for analysis of the effect of identifying as black, but also accounts for variation in how respondents prioritize their racial identity. Importantly, this approach does not assume that everyone who identifies with a group places the same importance on that identification.

This insight is applicable across racial groups and social identities, though the research presented here has focused on black racial identity. For instance, it is quite possible that non-blacks have a consciousness about the role their racial identity (and black racial identity in general) should play in their political behavior. Nor is it difficult to imagine that other social-group memberships could play orienting roles in political behavior. However, the strength of that effect might vary among members of any group.

While the importance, or salience, of an identity matters, the experience of African American Republicans illustrates the need to attend to the content of identities as well. The importance placed on an identity is influenced by the meanings attached to that identity. In turn, the content of an identity is critical to linking it to political behavior. Among African American Republicans, the relationship between identity and politics is fundamentally shaped by competing ideas about black people. The activists in this study, like all black political actors, exercise a great deal of agency in constructing meanings around black identity.[14] What does it mean to be black? Who are black people? The answers to these types of questions vary among African Americans, and that variance has consequences for political behavior.

Like other researchers, I found multiple expressions of conservatism among African American Republicans. The *color-blind* Republican activists, while acknowledging racial discrimination, think that black people are mostly held back by their own individual life decisions. The *race-conscious* activists see racial inequality as fundamentally structuring the lives of African Americans; for them, conservative social policy is the best response to the social conditions that blacks face. Table 1 summarizes the differences between color-blind and race-conscious African American Republicans.

Both groups offer up ideas that seriously constrain who black people can be—blacks are either demonized or valorized, with seemingly little room for a nuanced gray area attuned to the specific contexts in which people live or the individual decisions they make. Within both constructions of blackness, there is a very selective picking and choosing of who will come to represent black people. Consequently, black interests are very much contested among African American Republicans.[15] Additionally, though never explicitly invoked in interviews or observations, the idea of whiteness hung over all discussions about black people. For both color-blind and race-conscious interviewees,

TABLE I

Comparison of African American Republicans (AAR)

	Race-conscious AAR	Color-blind AAR
Pathway into GOP	Frustration with Democratic politics	Recognition of alignment between attitudes and Republican policy/values
Vision of black people	Respectable	Pathological
Republican policies	Good for black people	Race-neutral/ideologically motivated
Relations with GOP leadership	Tense conflict	Positive and affirming

"white" served as an implicit comparison to black people. Both sets of activists envisioned whites as an unquestioned normative marker. For color-blind Republicans, whiteness is a model most blacks fail to live up to (though they could, with the right political alignment).[16] For race-conscious Republicans, whites and blacks share a commitment to American values that must be enshrined in policy and correct past wrongs. Neither group interrogates the idea of whiteness.

As a consequence, both visions also rely on some form of what Evelyn Higginbotham has termed a "politics of respectability."[17] In its conservative form, the politics of respectability avoids identifying root causes of racism and discrimination and instead attributes blacks' problems to their own "negative" behaviors. A politics modeled on respectability presents blacks as good and decent to try to gain approval from mainstream society. These efforts include promoting family values and shunning outcasts and deviants.

For the race-conscious Republicans, the link to respectability is more obvious. They draw on a respectable vision of blacks in presenting their case for the black political subject. Blacks are "just as good," "the same" as everybody else, rather than demonized deviants. This approach is consistent with the presentation of "the best and brightest" that accompanies the politics of respectability. Yet the color-blind African American Republicans are engaged in an inverse politics of respectability. Rather than presenting the black subject as respectable, color-blind Republicans chastise the black subject for failing to live up to the standards of respectability. The same expectations that accompany the politics of respectability lie beneath the expectations of color-blind Republicans. It's just that they don't envision the black subject as capable of meeting those expectations. But for both types of Republicans, the politics of respectability guide their constructions of the black subject.[18]

Spending time with African American Republicans, it becomes clear that within some political dynamics, *ideas about black people* are more important than actual black people. In *Desire for Race,* Daynes and Lee stress that *ideas* about race are a key component of what they call the "racial ensemble." In the midst of reintroducing the body into the theorizing of race, these authors engage in a fruitful analysis of the meaning of race and how it is related to racial practices in any society. For them, ideas about black people intervene in our understanding of phenotypical markers of race: "Indeed, ideas intervene in the way we perceive 'things in nature,' in the sense that they come to stand between what we see and how we see it. Here 'ideas' could be replaced by 'meaning': *we do not perceive outside of meaning.* Hence what we see is a product of our ideas: and what we see can be different from the actual object we are looking at."[19]

Daynes and Lee then tie racial ideas to practice. Other research has shown how ideas about blackness animate within-race conflicts and tensions, as well as individual-level social psychological processes.[20] Politics is no exception. Extending this to politics, I submit that differences among African American Republicans are, primarily, driven by different ideas of how much and by what mechanisms race exerts power over the lives of black people. Cathy Cohen convincingly illustrates how African American political and religious leaders' commitment to an idea of respectable blacks slowed their response to the HIV/AIDS crisis. Black leaders' efforts to "redefine and indigenously construct a new public image or understanding of what blackness would mean" led them to resist designating HIV/AIDS as a black issue.[21] In a similar vein, McDermott and Hughey each details how the meanings attached to whiteness influence the political beliefs and behaviors of whites across a range of economic classes and ideologically diverse groups.[22] Chavez compellingly illustrates how ideas about Latinos are leveraged for political gain.[23] In short, my findings are consistent with a range of research that suggests we should attend to the varying ways that racial meanings structure political behavior.[24]

There is certainly a precedent for exploring how ideas about black people affect political behavior. Research in the *symbolic racism* tradition suggests that whites' attitudes about blacks lead them to oppose racially redistributive social policy. While not explicitly framing itself as research into "ideas about blackness," the symbolic racism scale draws heavily on respondents' perceptions, assumptions, and beliefs about blacks. Tarman and Sears argue that symbolic racism is a belief system with four tenets. Two of the central tenets are specifically keyed in to ideas about black people: "(1) racial discrimination is no longer a serious obstacle for blacks' prospects for a good life, so that (2) blacks' continuing disadvantages are largely due to their unwillingness to work hard enough."[25] These are ideas about what it's like to be black in America, and scholars in the symbolic racism tradition have produced a large body of evidence suggesting that they inform white people's policy preferences.[26]

For all its contributions, however, symbolic racism research focuses, almost exclusively, on how whites' attitudes about blacks affect policy preferences. In a notable exception, Bobo and Johnson show that scores on the symbolic racism scale predict blacks' attitudes toward the death penalty.[27] Their findings suggest that attending to the variation in how "blacks" are constructed can be a fruitful addition to research on black political behavior. There is no reason to think that all black people feel the same way about being black. Political analysts must build this variation into their understanding of black political behavior.

It is time for political analysts to recognize the wide range of ways of "performing" blackness.[28] This is certainly not anything new to black people. Within black communities, there has always been a range of people with diverse interests, attitudes, beliefs, and preferences. However, there is an increasing acknowledgment of the internal diversity of black people outside of black communities. Generally this is seen as a good thing. The association of group membership with particular behaviors is rightly often called out as stereotyping. Stereotyping leads to unfair treatment and drives the racial inequalities that still plague the United States. Indeed, people often push against the expectations that constrain them. For instance, not many women want to be told they cannot be good at science. Central to the struggle for civil rights has been an insistence that group membership alone does not define African American individuals. This recognition has not fully penetrated conversation around political behavior.

Competing perspectives on how race influences the lives of black people also lead to divergent expressions of Republican partisanship and very different experiences within the context of the GOP. The work of linking black identity to conservative political behavior occurs within a broader political context. While their feelings about racial identity condition their political behavior, African American Republicans' political location shapes their feelings about racial identity. Their "unexpected" partisanship *forces* the efforts to link racial identity and politics that this book has examined. But more proximately, African American Republicans' understanding, attachment, and expression of racial identity are constrained by the demands and desires of politicians and leaders within the Republican Party. In other words, black Republicans have to engage in their identity work within the context of a markedly white Republican Party, committed in rhetoric to racial diversity but in practice to (perhaps unrecognized) alienation of racial minorities. A similar tension marks many organizations on issues of diversity and incorporating difference.[29] The organizational demands of the Republican Party structure the expression of both racial identity and conservatism among African American Republicans. This reality illustrates the importance of institutions in shaping the expression of political action.[30]

White Republicans, for their part, appreciate what blacks bring to the GOP, so long as it echoes the party line about race and politics. While both the color-blind and race-conscious strategies rely on certain attitudes about black people, the strategies are not equally embraced, nor are they equally effective in allaying white Republicans' concerns. Not all of my respondents invoked the color-blind strategy, but those who did were more embedded in political networks that included white Republicans, and they reported less conflict in their relationships with white Republicans. African American Republicans who invoke the color-blind strategy are better able to capitalize on the political and discursive opportunities surrounding blackness within the GOP.[31]

My assessment of the experiences of African American Republicans suggests that the GOP needs to reconsider how it incorporates blacks into the party. It is not enough to incorporate blackness only on terms that are comfortable to white leaders. This creates an echo chamber that leaves little incentive to shift the rhetoric and actions around race-related issues. As a group, African American Republicans suffer from the process that elevates color-blind activists while leaving the race-conscious ones at the margins. As a group, they are left vulnerable to negative impressions because the GOP endorses such a limited picture of the universe of black Republicans. More distressingly, my research suggests that, in its current form, the Republican Party's approach to incorporating black people alienates the black people who are already involved in the party.

Furthermore, in its current form, the incorporation of blacks—along with additional "othered" groups in the GOP like Latino, Asian, women, and LGBT voters—is hard to see as genuine. When incorporation efforts resist framing Republican positions in ways that might be relevant to the very people whom the outreach efforts supposedly target, it raises questions about the actual target audience of these diversity efforts. Is the goal to increase minority participation in the party? Or is the purpose to have minorities around to provide cover to the more unsavory racial conservatism that has taken root within the GOP? For the black Republicans who benefit from that patronage, the resources are perceived as being fairly distributed to party loyalists. Those on the other side of the patronage reward system view it as undermining efforts to make Republican partisanship relevant to the lives of black people. At a minimum, the party must do a better job of listening to the diverse perspectives among African American Republicans. Certainly, many African American political actors are constrained in how they can talk about blackness, as white sensitivities often constrain black political agency.[32] So although this is not unique to black Republicans, the experience is particularly heightened because control of resources is thoroughly dominated by whites in the Republican Party.

Beyond the Republican Party, this book speaks to the ways that political environments shape how people understand their identities. Sociologist Nicholas Danigelis convincingly argues that the political climate will mitigate the effects of race on political participation.[33] In some political contexts, racial status might inhibit political participation; in other historical moments, African American political participation may be buoyed. The central premise of the theory—that historical context informs the effects of race on political behavior—provides an important corrective. For African American Republicans, being a good Republican often means limiting how and when you talk about the ways that racial identity informs your life. This absolutely *inverts* the way we think about the relationship between identity and politics. Rather than identity driving politics, politics—here, political location within the Republican Party—drives the way African American Republicans think and talk about their black identity. This is consistent with research that shows how political participation can produce personal, as well as collective, identities.[34] So instead of thinking of identity driving politics, political circumstances can produce identities where none may have existed before, or strengthen the salience of weak identities.

Recognizing this allows for a range of relationships between race and politics that move beyond causation. Race might not "cause" politics and politics might not "cause" race. We can think of race as a tool that political actors use to justify political behavior. We can think of race as something used to mobilize hesitant actors behind certain policy positions. We can think of race as a set of narratives deployed for political purposes. Such formulations might be necessary for a full understanding of the relationship between race and political behavior. More research is needed to explore these possibilities, but the broader call—for theories and research open to a multiplicity of relationships between race and politics—is one that should be incorporated into our political analyses.

Although the case of African American Republicans highlights issues surrounding our understanding of the link between identity and political behavior, it would be a mistake to think that the issues raised in this research are only relevant with regard to people engaged in unexpected politics. Political analysts must be sensitive to the possibility that some identities might be (or can be made to be) more relevant to political behavior than others. Also, the political relevance of any identity might vary across members of the social category or across different contexts. By examining the ways that race structures partisan affiliation among African Americans, this research suggests that it is not enough to claim that race matters in politics. Rather, it is necessary to explore questions of when and why race matters in political behavior and the processes through which social identities like race are linked to a particular political program.

METHODOLOGICAL
APPENDIX

This project draws on a range of research methods to collect and analyze data. I collected extensive data from the field, immersing myself in the world of African American Republicans for about four years. This included ethnographic observation, interviews, and monitoring the online world of African American Republicans. Drawing from multiple data sources allowed for a triangulation of insights.

INTERVIEWS

Interviews were used to gather data about African American Republicans' political attitudes, their perceptions of other Republicans and other African Americans, and their own sense of racial identity. The interviews also illuminate the ways in which African American Republicans manage the uniqueness of their partisan choices, as well as their perceptions of the responses that other political actors have to them. Initial respondents were recruited through a convenience sampling. My contacts with interviewees were made through connections I made while conducting ethnographic observations of African American Republican political events (panels, conferences, organization meetings). In addition, I recruited participants through political organizations and postings soliciting respondents through online forums dedicated to African American Republicans, political conservatives in black communities, and forums dedicated to discussing black politics more generally. Respondents were also recruited through a snowball sampling method whereby existing interview subjects were used to locate and recruit future subjects. Such an approach, while not providing a random sample, has many merits. There is the obvious convenience factor: given the small absolute number of African American Republican activists, trying to find a random sample is beyond the material and time constraints of this research. Furthermore, this approach to sampling allows for flexibility in recruiting subjects. I took an iterative approach to recruiting respondents that relied on theoretical sampling methods. As the study progressed, respondents were selected on the basis of the theoretical needs of the study and in an attempt to gather as broad a range as possible of interview subjects. Respondents were recruited on the basis of a theoretical sampling procedure that samples for the purposes of theory building rather than for making statistical generalizations to an overall population of African American Republicans.[1]

The interviews focused on respondents' experiences with the role their racial identity plays in their political beliefs and behaviors. Key areas included how they came to hold their political beliefs; the centrality of their political beliefs to their everyday lives; their experience with friends and family reacting to their political beliefs; and their experience of being a minority within the Republican Party and their identity group. To be included in the interview sample, respondents had to express partisan identification as Republican. Respondents were also required to have some involvement with politics either at the local or the national level. This included respondents who were active in African American Republican–themed organizations, respondents who were involved with "mainstream" Republican groups, respondents who had been (or were, at the time, currently) running for political office, and respondents who identified as Republican but were active in African American–oriented political groups. Many respondents were active in more than one type of group or organization. While this limits the sample to "semi-elites" (respondents do not necessarily have to be high-level, political elites), it provides the benefit of controlling for an "engagement in politics." Good answers to the questions motivating this study require having people talk about the nature of their politics, and given the difficulty most people have in expressing their political beliefs, it seems reasonable for this study to limit analysis to people more likely to be able to engage in articulate discussion of their politics.

Whenever possible, interviews were conducted face-to-face. However, due to geographical distance and timing constraints, some interviews were conducted over the telephone. Interviews typically lasted more than two hours, and some interviews had to be conducted over the course of two or more sessions. I transcribed all interviews verbatim. The transcripts were coded by hand into the various themes that animate the research. Respondents were promised anonymity, and this promise was crucial in securing participation. Given the small and intensely overlapping nature of the world of African American Republicans, many respondents knew one another (even when they did not direct me to one another). The closed networks of African American Republicans (and often the small network of GOP activism more generally) made many respondents concerned about the content of our interviews being connected to them personally. The small-world aspect of African American Republican circles is illustrated by the fact that, on more than one occasion, when I "cold called" a potential respondent or sent an unsolicited email requesting an interview, I was told that they had heard about "the guy researching Black Republicans." As I demonstrate throughout the findings, the social world of African American Republicans is often contentious. Respondents expressed very little interest in having their words used against them in interpersonal and organizational disputes.

In each of the primary locations, I had key informants who connected me with other African American Republicans in their area. These informants also stayed in contact long after our initial interviews and offered, often unsolicited, their thoughts and opinions on current events, national political figures and politicians from both parties, and the "inside scoop" on their local networks of African American Republicans. All were made aware that these conversations would also be considered "data" for my research, and, accordingly, these conversations—over phone, in person, and by email—are considered in the present analysis.

In total, I conducted forty-five formal and informal interviews with African American Republican activists. To protect their anonymity, I've attempted to disguise all revealing characteristics. In some instances, this necessitated altering descriptions of their professional activities. For instance, rather than describe a respondent as a "computer programmer," I might use the more generic IT professional. Or rather than describe someone as a "doctor," I might use terminology like "medical professional." All such changes were designed to both protect anonymity and give a general sense of the respondent's professional occupation.

Although they were not the focus of this study, I also conducted informal interviews with white Republican Party elites. I want to briefly discuss the exposure to white Republicans throughout my fieldwork. These observations help frame the broader discussion of the relationship between white and black Republicans. Finding African American Republicans to interview and observe was quite difficult, but finding white Republicans willing to talk about black Republicans was even more challenging. In each of the primary field sites, I made interview requests with state and local GOP officials. In each instance those requests went unanswered. A similar fate befell my requests to the Republican National Committee. Although I never spoke with any GOP leaders in an "official" capacity, I did have multiple encounters with white Republicans throughout the course of this research. None would agree to a sit-down interview, but they did share their thoughts on the party's relationship to black voters.

Overall, my exposure to white Republicans occurred in two settings: events targeted at a general Republican or conservative audience and events sponsored by ostensibly African American Republican organizations. Despite their different stated audiences and purposes, both types of functions often had majority-white audiences. This afforded me a chance to speak to white Republicans about issues of race and outreach to black voters, but it did not afford an opportunity for in-depth interviewing. However, this type of exposure to white Republican audiences did afford an opportunity to compare how the different kind of African American Republican activists acted in front of white audiences.

ETHNOGRAPHY

The fieldwork for this project was conducted from June 2006 to August 2013. Fieldwork involved attending a range of political rallies, organizational meetings, conferences, and panel discussions. I also spent time with several key informants in nonpolitical settings. I made every attempt to observe group meetings, social activities, and any other organizational functions. Additionally, I treated the context of each individual interview as an occasion for ethnographic reflection and attempted to take notes during each of these ethnographic events. As most of these occasions were political events involving speakers of some sort, I did not stand out by taking notes. When note-taking on site was not feasible, I attempted to record my thoughts immediately after the events. From these notes (and, when relevant, transcripts from recordings), I wrote detailed field notes for each observation. Various "artifacts" from each event were also included in the analysis. This often included flyers, mailings, conference notes, and articles that recount events from the perspective of various participants.

In addition to ethnographic observation where I was physically present, I immersed myself in the virtual world of African American conservatives. This work mainly consisted of monitoring discussion boards, receiving emails from various listservs, and monitoring the content of a range of African American Republican and conservative websites. In general, efforts were made to "be present" in the world of African American Republicans throughout the duration of data collection. With such small absolute numbers, being present often meant observing interaction and discourse in virtual settings. I also made a point to consume and catalog media accounts of African American Republicans. This included examining newspaper articles (from 1952–2012) drawn from both mainstream and black newspapers, radio and television reports, speeches by influential political elites, autobiographies, scholarly work, and political texts written by African American Republicans.

SURVEY DATA

To examine the demographic and attitudinal characteristics of African American Republicans, this study uses data from multiple sources. The primary analyses shown draw from the 2008 and 2012 American National Election Study (ANES), but supplemental analysis was conducted using the 1996 National Black Election Study (NBES) and the 2004 National Politics Study (NPS). Drawing from different data sets allows for measuring the demographic characteristics of African American Republicans in multiple contexts across different times.

The ANES provides the most recent data, but the sample has the smallest proportion of black Republicans. However, it is helpful for examining the demographic characteristics of African American Republicans in relation to their non-Republican counterparts. The ANES is a national survey of political attitudes conducted with preelection and postelection cross sections. The time series conducted in 2008 is unique in that African Americans and Latinos were oversampled and some questions were self-administered through ACASI (Audio Computer-Assisted Self Interviewing) to reduce social desirability bias.

The NBES provides information on the attitudes, preferences, and behaviors of the black electorate during the 1996 presidential election. Unlike most political surveys, the NBES offers a sizable sample of African American respondents ($n = 964$) and asks questions about both respondents' attitudes about race and their political behaviors. The 2004 NPS gathered data on political attitudes, beliefs, and behaviors on a nationally representative sample between September 2004 and February 2005. This analysis draws on the sample of 756 African Americans (from a total sample of 3,339 respondents). Although they are each over a decade old, the NBES and NPS are well suited for this analysis. Large-scale data sets with African American samples are rare. Both studies provide survey data with a comprehensive battery of questions about both black political ideology and subjective feelings of racial identity. Furthermore, because of the richness of these two surveys, many previous empirical studies of black political behavior have drawn on these studies long after their initial fielding.

In all data sets, respondents who described themselves as Republican and independents who described themselves as "leaning Republican" are coded as Republican and all others are coded as non-Republican (Democrat, independent "leaning Democrat"). Consistent with actual voting results, very few blacks identify as Republican; 7 percent of NBES and 9 percent of NPS respondents are in the Republican category. Only 5 percent of black respondents in the ANES could be categorized as Republican. Given the small number of African American Republicans in the sample of all the surveys, the analyses presented here must be used with caution and for illustrative purposes only.

Table A.1 draws from the NBES and NPS studies to compare the demographic characteristics of African American Republicans to those of blacks who are Democrats or left-leaning Independents. As noted in the main text, the data suggest that African American Republicans share many demographic characteristics

Demographic Means and Proportions by Partisan Leaning ("Other" vs. Republican)

	NBES 1996		NPS 2004		ANES 2008/12	
	Other	Repub	Other	Repub	Other	Repub
Male	.37	.42	.35	.53**	.44	.70**
Age	39.6	34.0**	46.3	42.8	43.7	40.6
Income						
Less than $15,000	.24	.23	.10	.19*	.27	.26
$15,000–$24,999	.21	.17	.21	.10	.15	.14
$25,000–$39,999	.26	.28	.16	.17	.19	.14
$40,000–$74,999	.21	.23	.32	.27	.23	.31
$75,000–$104,999	.06	.04	.11	.07	.07	.04
$105,000 and over	.02	.04	.10	.20*	.09	.11
Education						
Less than high school	.11	.16	.12	.19	.15	.16
High school	.59	.57	.25	.20	.58	.44
Associates degree	.09	.04	.36	.34	.11	.20
College degree	.16	.14	.15	.12	.13	.12
Graduate school	.06	.09	.12	.15	.05	.08
Church attendance						
Never	.06	.04	.05	.07	.24	.45
A few times a year	.20	.19	.21	.36*	.16	.07
Once or twice a month	.25	.28	.20	.09*	.19	.19
Almost every week	.19	.14	.48	.46	.15	.08
Every week	.30	.30	.06	.03	.11	.09
Twice a week or more	.02	.04	.05	.07	.15	.11
N	895	69	596	59	1,242	64

SOURCES: National Black Election Study (NBES) 1996, National Politics Study (NPS) 2004, American National Election Study (ANES) 2008.

NOTE: **$p < .01$ *$p < .05$, difference in proportions tests and difference in means t-tests between those who lean Republican and those who lean Democrat.

with their Democratic and Independent counterparts. Consistent with the analysis presented in the main text, there are not a lot of significant differences between the two groups.

While it is rare to observe significant differences between African Americans who are Republicans and those who are not, it is important to be aware of the limitations of existing survey data in addressing this question. Assessing the characteristics of African American Republicans is surprisingly difficult. The central challenge is their rarity. Because so few African Americans identify as Republican, they are difficult to capture in large-scale surveys. In general, African American representation in survey research can be a problem. Often, nationally representative samples still do not have enough black respondents to slice and dice the population to explore within-group differences. Even when a survey delivers a nationally representative sample of black respondents, the absolute number who identify as Republican is quite small. This makes it difficult to examine the demographic characteristics of African American Republicans. So it is possible that there are significant demographic differences, but the sample size is too small to see them. Still, even keeping these limitations in mind, the available data suggest that the difference between African American Republicans and other blacks is not demographic.

SOME GENERAL NOTES ABOUT THE RESEARCH

The interviews, observations, media content, and survey data combine to provide a rich, all-inclusive picture of the populations under study. This multi-method approach allows for a triangulation of data sources. Information gathered from one source can be confirmed or rejected by other collection methods. This provides a fuller picture of African American Republicans. It allows the research to take seriously the statements and beliefs of interview respondents, while at the same time confirming or rejecting those statements through participant observation and media/textual analysis. Outside of any particular method of data collection or analysis, there are a few things worth noting about the process of completing this research. Over the course of the research, I encountered some particular issues in attempting to access the social and political worlds of African American Republicans.

Throughout the fieldwork for this project, I was quite sensitive to how my own "situatedness" informed not only how I thought about and analyzed the data, but also what I got to "see." However, the effect of my various social statuses rarely worked consistently, making it difficult to situate any knowledge claims in relation to my own social status. In some contexts, the fact that I'm black opened doors and created a spirit of trust between black respondents and me. In other contexts, black respondents were quite skeptical of me because of their previous experiences talking politics with nonconservative blacks. Undoubtedly, my own racial identity helped secure access to individuals and organizations, as well as shaped my understanding of what I learned from them. Often, my connection to an elite university was far more salient. Furthermore, the assumed class similarities that respondents projected onto our relationship often left respondents feeling a sense of shared experiences.

Throughout the fieldwork, I was confronted with challenges of gaining access to African American Republican spaces, as well as politically conservative spaces more generally. Assumptions about my own politics were a constant source of tension in my efforts to gain access to the world of African American Republicans. These assumptions did not seem to be patterned in any interesting way. Some respondents assumed that I shared their conservative political leanings, while others figured me for a political liberal. On occasion, these assumptions made building rapport with individual interview subjects and participants at African American Republican events difficult.

Because of the perceived inconsistency between black racial identity and Republican partisanship, African American Republicans are often subject to withering criticisms that call into question their racial allegiances, as well as their political savvy. As such, when attempting to contact various African American Republican groups, I encountered a great deal of skepticism about my project. People feared that I was motivated by liberal politics and was only interested in presenting them in an overly critical light. In an equally problematic vein, some respondents assumed that I shared their conservative politics, that I myself was an African American Republican, and that the project was essentially an effort, under the guise of academic research, to promote African American Republicanism in a tacitly partisan way. To the extent that these assumptions impeded access, I would correct them. Otherwise, I was quite conscious of "erasing" my politics from any discussions with respondents. Yet, despite my best efforts over the course of long and involved conversations (often over multiple sessions or across multiple events), it was sometimes inevitable that I would be asked about my personal politics. I always answered honestly, while attempting to reaffirm that my politics were not relevant to research project. For every respondent, I would stress that the project was not partisan in any way. It was not designed to be a puff piece or a takedown. On the whole, I think subjects were convinced of my commitment to objectivity in conducting this research.

Another difficulty with the fieldwork was driven by the rarity of African American Republicans. As a consequence, the number of African American Republican organizations is small in any given location. This also made it difficult to find field sites in which to observe African American Republicans, and ensured that the absolute number of people I encountered would be small. This was unavoidable, and although it limits the ways I can generalize from the data I collected, the reality of the small world of African American Republicans does present some advantages to a field researcher. Because the network of African American Republicans is so small in any given location, I was able to get much greater coverage of the "universe" of African American Republican goings-on in each field site. Additionally, I often heard multiple versions of the same story from the perspective of everyone involved. With such tight networks, everyone often knows who all the African American Republican players are. This effect was further highlighted in contexts where Republicans were not the dominant party or where party dominance was highly contested. This often produced a Rashomon-like effect: I would hear about the same event from the perspective of everyone who was involved. Not surprisingly, different tellers have different perspectives. The small number of African American Republicans, while limiting the number of respondents, increased the possibility of delving deeply into their world.

Although respondents were difficult to find and I encountered quite a bit of resistance from some participants in this research (in particular white Republicans and the African American Republicans most strongly aligned with them), on the whole, African American Republicans displayed an openness to the research and showed a willingness to discuss their politics and have their stories told. The project would have been impossible to complete without that openness. Individual respondents and organizations alike were very much positively disposed to having their lives and institutions treated as an object of scholarly study. Their willingness to open up and share their stories certainly added to the sense of responsibility I felt to accurately portray their experiences.

NOTES

INTRODUCTION

1. See www.theguardian.com/us-news/gallery/2015/nov/07/ben-carson-house-homage-to-himself-in-pictures.

2. The Carson organization was incredibly successful in at least one regard, raising $57.9 million over the course of his campaign. That was more than any of his Republican rivals, and over three-quarters of his donations came from small donors. The Carson candidacy spoke to big funders and small givers alike. Equally surprising, Carson managed to spend more than any of the other candidates in the primary race. Much of the spending went to fundraising and marketing firms owned by his top consultants. See www.slate.com/blogs/the_slatest/2016/03/04/ben _carson_s_fundraising_machine.html; http://bigstory.ap.org/article /2297ea3b600648e3a35581572c67447f/ carson-spent-heavy-consultants-light-2016-campaigning.

3. Throughout the text, the terms *African American* and *black* are used interchangeably. However, it is important to note that interview data were collected from native-born blacks exclusively. See the Methodological Appendix for further description of data-collection practices.

4. Steinhauer (2010).

5. See www.nationalreview.com/article/422237/ben-carsons-gentle
-virtuous-rhetoric-elevated-gop-debate-david-french.

6. Jimmy McMillan, formerly chairman and leader of the Rent Is
Too Damned High Party, entered the race in August 2015. He was a
perennial candidate, and no political observers took his candidacy
seriously. He was, however, the only other African American candidate. He ended his campaign on December 9, 2015. McMillan would go
on to endorse Donald Trump in the 2016 Republican primary.

7. Sheridan (1996); Reed (1997).

8. All respondents' names and identifying characteristics have
been altered to protect their anonymity. Additionally, when respondents discussed participation during one-on-one interviews, the names
of those organizations were changed. When organizations had public
meetings that I attended, the actual names of those organizations were
used. See the Methodological Appendix for further discussion of
research protocols and respondent concerns about revealing their participation in this research.

9. Polling before the 2012 election suggested an even worse outcome
for Romney among black voters. In an NBC/Wall Street Journal poll,
the percentage of black respondents supporting Romney was so low as
to register at zero percent. While this was largely a statistical quirk, it is
indicative of the low levels of support the GOP garnered from black voters over the past few presidential elections. See http://firstread.nbcnews
.com/_news/2012/08/21/13399788-nbcwsj-poll-heading-into-conventions-
obama-has-four-point-lead?lite.

10. In a 2012 nationally representative survey, the Pew Research
Center found that 87 percent of Republican respondents identified as
white, but only 2 percent of Republicans identified as black. Gallup
polling from the same year provided similar results. Two percent of
Republicans in the Gallup survey were classified as Non-Hispanic
Blacks.Seewww.people-press.org/2012/08/23/a-closer-look-at-the-parties
-in-2012/; www.gallup.com/poll/160373/democrats-racially-diverse-
republicans-mostly-white.aspx.

11. Kabaservice (2012).

12. A number of theories suggest that particular behaviors can be
associated with members of a particular social group. "Expectation

states theory" suggests that social statuses come to be associated with particular behaviors (Berger et al. 1972; Ridgeway 2011). Although the theory was developed to explain hierarchies within task-oriented groups, the broader principle is applicable in any range of social contexts, and the theory has been used to account for the formation and functioning of status hierarchies (Correll and Ridgeway 2003). Status beliefs—the beliefs associated with a social category (or status)—center expectation states theory. The surprising nature of Republican partisanship among African Americans reflects, in part, the expectations associated with black attitudes and behaviors.

13. Similar analyses of the 1996 National Black Election Survey and the 2004 National Politics Study, both of which have large samples of black respondents, yielded very similar results. See Methodological Appendix for a more detailed analysis.

14. Given the centrality of social conservatism to the contemporary Republican Party, this might be surprising. It also runs counter to Republican outreach efforts to African Americans that have focused on churchgoers as most open to conservative overtures (Kirkpatrick 2004). However, given the combination of the African American church's traditional role in progressive politics (Morris 1986) and African Americans' consistently high support for Democrats, one might expect that church attendance would be strongly correlated with Democratic affiliation.

15. Gay and Tate (1998); Dawson (1994); Weakliem (1997).

16. Countering claims that social factors play an increasingly smaller role in political life, Manza and Brooks assert the continued relevance of social cleavages in political behavior. In a series of works (Manza and Brooks 1999; Brooks and Manza 1997), they show a continued relevance of social cleavages in shaping party coalitions, voting, and nonvoting behavior. In particular, they show that race represents the largest cleavage during the period since 1964. Interestingly, African Americans are the only members of the New Deal coalition whose support for the Democratic Party has actually increased. Their analysis shows that racial identity is a key factor in shaping American political behavior, but it sidesteps any systematic evaluation of race as an ideological cleavage.

17. Research suggests that this is not just the case for black voters. In general, racial divisions remain strong in U.S. politics (King and Smith 2011). Racial identity, white or black, is a powerful predictor of political behavior and attitudes. In fact, much research suggests that the phenomenon is only getting stronger. In other words, race is strongly correlated with political attitudes, policy preferences, and voting behaviors.

18. Characteristic of structural approaches to race and political behavior, Orum (1966) argues that African Americans' level of political participation is suppressed through social isolation. Segregation, both through legal and informal mechanisms, keeps African Americans isolated from the larger political structure. This isolation inhibits full integration into politics and depresses political participation and voting among African Americans. As a result of their isolation, African Americans do not develop routines that contribute to political participation and lack the political resources to effectively benefit from politics. In a similar vein, community resource theories argue that social isolation of African Americans is central to their higher levels of political participation. Olsen (1970) argues that social pressures exerted within ethnic communities encourage political participation. Members of an isolated racial community are more likely to be aware of their common bonds and share similar material and political interests. Social isolation builds race specific motivations and reinforces group commitments. Furthermore, social isolation results in race-specific institutions that can be leveraged for political ends. Along these lines, Morris (1986) locates much of the formative work of the civil rights movement within African American churches. Again, structural location is central to the effects of race on political behavior, but here African Americans' position outside the political structure produces opportunities for consensus building within the group and mobilizing community resources more effectively. Empirical tests of each theory produce mixed results, with support for each approach found in the actual behavior of African American voters (Danigelis 1977).

19. In *Behind the Mule* (1994), Dawson presents a comprehensive theory of black political behavior. His approach draws on the work of social psychologists (see Turner 1987; Tajfel 1981) in using the concept

of identification. *Identification* refers to an individual's sense of belonging or attachment to a social group. The concept can refer to how one locates or identifies oneself, as well as how one is located or identified by others. In general, studies of political behavior focus on the self-identifications individuals use to place themselves into groups. Identification captures an individual's subjective sense of sameness or similarity to members of a group. This sense of sameness produces "a feeling of closeness to others who identify with the group label and involves the acceptance of the belief that individual life chances are inextricably tied to the group as a whole" (Simien 2005). Under various guises—racial solidarity (Verba and Nie 1972; Olsen 1970), interdependence (Conover 1984), or linked fate (Dawson 1994)—studies of African American politics have examined the extent to which an individual's identification with the racial group informs their political decisions.

20. Dawson (1994, p. 199).

21. Tate (2003).

22. Tate (2003, p. 50) cites Dawson (1994) and Gurin, Hatchett, and Jackson (1989).

23. See www.politico.com/story/2016/02/ben-carson-obama-was-raised-white-219657.

24. Seewww.bloombergview.com/articles/2011—06—13/herman-cain-on-why-the-black-guy-is-winning-jeffrey-goldberg.

25. Sellers et al. (1998).

26. See Smith (2014), Waters (1999), Roth (2012), and Rogers (2006) for a more detailed examination of pan-ethnic diversity among blacks, and how the politics of Caribbean and African immigrants (and their descendants) differs from that of native-born blacks.

27. Reed (1999); Price (2009).

28. Hogg et al. (1995, p. 257).

29. Sellers et al. (1998).

30. There have been a number of studies illustrating differences among African Americans (Anderson 1990; Pattillo-McCoy 1999; Lacy 2007; Young 2004; Smith and Moore 2000). The suggestion that there is a monolithic "black culture" would certainly draw scorn from anyone who lives in or studies black communities. While there has been a

great deal of descriptive illustration of intra-group differences, less attention has been given to how these differences inform political behavior.

CHAPTER ONE. FROM MANY TO FEW

1. For a more detailed historical analysis of black Republicans, see Walton (1975), Fauntroy (2007), Thurber (2013), and Rigueur (2015).

2. Walton (1975, p. 297).

3. According to Walton, "Free Blacks had the legal right to vote in all of the New England states except Connecticut; more than 1200 qualified as voters in New York City and environs, and those with a greater admixture of white blood had the right to vote in Ohio. In several places within some other states, such as Wisconsin and Michigan, Blacks were permitted to vote illegally due to a laxity of law enforcement. And from 1838 to 1860, Free Blacks voted illegally in Rapides Parish, Louisiana, even though the state legislature had curtailed the right in 1812" (Walton 1975, p. 3).

4. Dawson (2001).

5. Walton (1975).

6. Quoted in Walton (1975, p. 4).

7. Quoted in Walton (1975, p. 5).

8. Walton (1975, p. 17).

9. Frymer (1999).

10. Walton (1975).

11. Key (1949).

12. Walton (1975).

13. Walton (1975, p. 164).

14. Walton (1975, p. 166).

15. Key (1949).

16. Weiss (1983); Fauntroy (2007).

17. Lemann (1992).

18. Fauntroy (2007, p. 45).

19. Weiss (1983, pp. 45–48).

20. Weiss (1983); Walton (1975).

21. Weiss (1983, p. 51).

22. When blacks saw tangible benefits from New Deal programs, it was often through the efforts of individual administrators. In particular, Harold L. Ickes and his management of the Public Works Administration (PWA) worked to ensure that African Americans received their fair share of the New Deal. Although the PWA had a very limited effect on national economic recovery, it was the agency where blacks were most likely to find New Deal relief (Weiss 1983). Ickes also ended segregation in the cafeterias at the Interior Department and in restrooms (Stikoff 1981).

23. Fauntroy (2007, p. 48).

24. This is mainly representative of voting outside of the South. In the South, the Democratic Party dominated, taking advantage of Jim Crow racial divisions in the region. Republicans in the South offered little in terms of an alternative because the region was dominated by a racially divisive politics that drew on anti-black sentiment. Neither party offered much in terms of policy or patronage to black voters and politicians. Furthermore, the majority of blacks in the South were disenfranchised.

25. Morris (1986); Berlin et al. (1992).

26. Morris (1986).

27. See McAdam (1988, 1999) for an explanation of whites' shifting public opinion and participation in the movement.

28. Frymer (1999).

29. Given the resistance of southern Democrats, the support of moderate and liberal Republicans was crucial to the bipartisan passage of civil rights legislation. Bipartisan support for the legislation was important to Johnson (Loevy 1997).

30. Kabaservice (2012).

31. Fauntroy notes that "the Southern Strategy refers to Republicans' efforts to win conservative white support by distancing themselves from progressive and moderate positions on racial issues of importance to African Americans" (2007, p. 129). Unsurprisingly, some Republicans have contested this interpretation of the Southern Strategy, arguing that it misrepresents the party's commitment to smaller federal government as anti-black sentiment. This defense has gained little traction among political historians who study the era.

32. Rigueur (2015, p. 53).

33. Brooke was vocal in making civil rights and the fight against racial inequality central to his political platform. He might be the last highly placed African American Republican politician to engage in such an unabashed "pro-black" politics. He is vocal in his skepticism about the prospects of the contemporary Republican Party welcoming black voters (Brooke 2007).

34. Rigueur (2015).

35. Fauntroy (2007); Frymer (1999).

36. Bracey (2008, p. 126).

37. Sowell (1980).

38. As I will demonstrate later in this book, tensions still exist between proponents of a race-blind brand of Republican politics and those African American Republicans who endorse a race-conscious style of engagement with Republican ideology and policy.

39. Dillard (2001, p. 28).

40. Fauntroy (2007, p. 49).

41. Philpot (2007).

42. Philpot (2007); O'Reilly (1995); Mendelberg (2001).

43. Philpot (2007).

44. Bolce et al. (1993).

45. Mendelberg (2001); O'Reilly (1995).

46. The Bush campaigns in 2000 and 2004 garnered around 10 percent of the black vote nationally. However, in several key swing states, Bush managed to chip away a few percentage points from the black voting block. While this only amounted to a few thousand votes in absolute numbers, in tightly contested swing states every vote made a difference.

47. Thurber (2013).

48. Frymer (1999).

49. Frymer (1999); Weiss (1983); Walton (1975).

CHAPTER TWO. BEYOND UNCLE TOM

1. Philpot (2007).

2. Fields (2014).

3. Sheridan (1996, p. 167).

4. I first encountered this joke in J. C. Watts's autobiography (Watts and Winston 2003), but by the end of completing fieldwork for this research I had heard it multiple times, often from African American Republicans. As we'll see, humor is a frequently deployed coping strategy among black Republicans.

5. LGBT Republicans often encounter similar accusations of group betrayal and questioning of political loyalties. However, there the axis of betrayal is sexuality, not race (Goldstein 2003; Robinson 2005). The negative reaction to Caitlyn Jenner's comments in support of Ted Cruz is just a recent illustration of this phenomenon. See www .advocate.com/media/2016/3/03/caitlyn-jenners-ted-cruz-comments-blow-internet.

6. Accessed on June 14, 2010: www.theroot.com/views/whatever-happened-black-republican-wave#comments.

7. Accessed on June 14, 2010: www.theroot.com/views/black-republicans-more-ripple-wave.

8. Dawson (2001); Harris-Lacewell (2004).

9. Kennedy (2008, pp. 4–5).

10. In his study of the consequences of German unification on identity, Glaeser (2000) endorses an approach to identity that focuses on the process of identification. *Identity construction* revolves around creating meaning ("My identity to me is what I mean to myself; my identity to you is what I mean to you"; Glaeser 2000, p. 9). *Identification* is the process of connecting the self with particular meaning structures: "The meaning of self (i.e., identity) is produced by identifying (i.e., connecting) self with itself at other points in time; with other persons; with beliefs, ideas, and values; with the world in the widest sense…. If identifications are repeated and reconfirmed by others and thus stabilized, they congeal into parts of identities" (pp. 9–10). This approach shifts the focus of study from the "whole to its parts" and from the "product to the process" (p. 10). Making this move allows observers to see how various aspects of space, time, work, and morality are drawn from in constructing identity. This inside-out approach certainly adheres to the basic constructionist principles, but it imbues individuals and institutions (broadly defined) with

agency that must be recognized by the observer of the identity-construction process. Rather than assuming a category—say, black—an identification approach looks to the things individuals use to identify as black. Connecting with historical moments is a key part of the identification process. By placing themselves in a long line of black politics, African American Republicans lay claim to black identity.

11. Bonacich (1973); Pattillo (2007); Kanter (1993).

12. Kennedy (2008).

13. In his exploration of racial betrayal, Randall Kennedy argues that black political conservatives have been much less successful at deploying the "sellout" rhetoric. However, he suggests that their attempts to use such rhetoric across the political spectrum work to "spread and deepen its overall influence" (Kennedy 2008, p. 67).

14. Dillard (2001) shows that this is common talk among black conservatives. Direct connections between the rhetoric of influential and well-known African American political conservatives and African American Republicans working on the local level was surprisingly rare. In fact, many respondents expressed frustration with the incendiary language often used by black conservatives in the media. With titles like "Bamboozled," "They Think You're Stupid," "It's Okay to Leave the Plantation," "Pimps, Whores, and Welfare Brats," and "What's Race Got to Do with It?" the writings of black conservatives are designed to court controversy (Elder 2008; Parker 1997; Weaver 1998; Cain 2005; McGlowan 2007).

15. Accessed on May 25, 2016: www.politico.com/blogs/jonathanmartin/1008/Limbaugh_Where_are_the_inexperienced_white_liberals_Powell_has_endorsed.html.

16. The reliance on rejecting affirmative action to prove party loyalty obscures the Republican Party's complex relationship to the issue. Although its exact role is debated, actions of the Nixon administration were critical to the development of affirmative action policy in the United States.

17. See Schreiber (2008) for a discussion of how the issue of abortion is a similar instance where a policy runs the risk of putting one

constituency (women) at odds with the GOP platform (opposition to abortion).

18. Faryna et al. (1997).

19. Dawson (1994).

20. See the Methodological Appendix for an analysis of other data sets that present similar findings.

21. Although racial identification is important in understanding African Americans' political behavior, theory and research suggest that identification is only one way in which attachment to an identity group manifests itself. As researchers of identity have demonstrated, any "identity" is made up of a number of components (Brubaker and Cooper 2000; Stryker and Burke 2000; Hogg et al. 1995). Identification is one, but there are others. *Salience* is also a measure of attachment to an identity (Stryker 1980). A salient identity "is conceptualized (and operationalized) as the likelihood that the identity will be invoked in diverse situations" (Hogg et al. 1995, p. 257). The level of attachment to any identity can vary across identification and salience measures. Together, these two components may reflect attachment to an identity. Race is no exception. For African Americans, the centrality of race is distinct from the presence or absence of identification with a racial group (Sellers et al. 1998). With this in mind, extensive focus on racial identification obscures how the salience of race might affect political behavior.

22. Reed (1999); Price (2009); Chong and Rogers (2005); Rogers (2006).

23. African American Republicans are not rising out of black communities; as a consequence, they are dependent on white Republican patronage. Their inability to convince other African Americans of the racial sincerity of their politics, ironically, makes them more dependent on white Republicans, who often demand that racial sincerity goes on the backburner in exchange for patronage. Chapter 6 explores this reality in more depth.

24. Granted, it's possible that these concerns exist only in the heads of the African American Republicans I spoke with. That seems highly unlikely, though. Their concerns are consistent with other

accounts of African American Republicans. Their concerns also ring true given the public responses that others have toward black Republicans.

CHAPTER THREE. RACE DOESN'T MATTER

1. Bonilla-Silva (2010, p. 29).

2. Consistently throughout my conversations with African American Republicans, they would use the phrase "coming out" to describe their conversion to Republican partisanship. However, this should not be mistaken for any sympathy toward issues that gays and lesbians might face. Most, if not all, of the participants would bristle at the comparison.

3. Derrick also illustrates his own sense of racial identification when he compares "our relationship with God" to "my being black." Slipping from "our" to "my" in the same sentence shows just how closely Derrick's personal identity is linked to African Americans as a collective.

4. Mendelberg (2001); Gillens (1999).

5. The white racial frame is a meaning system that encompasses racialized knowledge and understandings. The frame shapes behavior in a range of ways. The white racial frame is primarily attributed to whites across social location, but Feagin (2010) allows for acceptance of it among non-whites as well.

6. Race-conscious African American Republicans also report feeling constrained by their racial identity. However, for them, this constraint is a function of white Republicans' attitudes and behaviors. This is discussed in detail in the next chapter.

7. See http://articles.latimes.com/2005/jan/18/nation/na-faith18.

8. Carter (1991).

9. Although this is a common critique of affirmative action programs, there is no convincing empirical evidence to support this point. See Thomas (2007); Carter (1991).

10. See Thomas (2007, pp. 74–75). Thomas's opposition to affirmative action is, perhaps, more complex than it seems on its face. Thomas has supported affirmative action in the past. The authors of *Supreme*

Discomfort (Merida and Fletcher 2007) suggest that his resistance to the policy is, in part, driven by personal insecurities.

CHAPTER FOUR. BLACK POWER THROUGH CONSERVATIVE PRINCIPLES

1. Pager (2003).

2. I draw a distinction between "racial uplift" and "race consciousness." Racial-uplift politics are aimed at lifting up black people. All African American Republicans I spoke with would describe themselves as engaged in racial-uplift politics. Color-blind African American Republicans just think that the best thing for blacks is to not focus on race. Race consciousness is distinct from racial uplift. For race-conscious Republicans, race is central to the program of the politics, not just about uplifting black people.

3. Over the course of my fieldwork, only one African American Republican who could be classified as being racially oriented grew up with Republican parents. He was also one of the older respondents in the study, so he grew up well before blacks migration to the Democratic Party was fully cemented. But he was certainly the exception to the general trend among race-conscious African American Republicans.

4. Dawson points out that "Black nationalists' theoretical vision of black liberation continues to be based on the contention that understanding the plight of blacks and achieving black salvation must be based on taking race and racial oppression as the central feature of modern world history" (2001, p. 86).

5. Other research has found similar differences among conservative blacks. Simpson (1998) found that young black conservatives often invoked a "pro-black" framing to support their conservative politics. Lewis (2013) also found important variations among black conservatives. Bracey (2008) also highlighted distinctions between "organic" and "inorganic" black conservatives.

6. Sellers et al. (1998, p. 28).

7. Moore (2010).

8. Reed (1999).

9. Griswold (1987, 2008).

10. Griswold (2008, p. 12).

11. This move to treat race as a cultural object is primarily an analytic one. Certainly, among my respondents, there is little self-awareness of their invoking of narratives about black people. The African American Republicans I observed and spoke with would never categorize their behavior as a product of constructing a symbolic representation of blackness. In fact, many would find such a claim laughable and indicative of precisely the sort of race-based formulations they like to think they are opposing. For them, their claims about black people represent objective statements of the reality of black life. However, Griswold notes that "the status of the cultural object results from an analytic decision that we make as observers; it is not built into the object itself" (Griswold 2008, p. 12).

12. Bonilla-Silva (1997, 1999).

13. Loveman (1999); Lamont (2002).

14. DiMaggio (1997); Sewell (1992); Zerubavel (1999).

CHAPTER FIVE. LIKE CRABS IN A BARREL

1. Ghaziani (2008); Armstrong (2002).

2. Rigueur (2015); Simpson (1998).

3. Bracey (2008).

4. It is worth considering how African American Republicans compare to another constituency engaged in unexpected politics, LGBT Republicans. Gay and lesbian Republicans have long had a national organization, the Log Cabin Republicans. The group formed in 1977 in response to a proposed California initiative that would have prevented gays and lesbians (along with anyone supporting gay and lesbian rights) from working in California public schools. Now it is a national organization with local chapters in nearly half the states. No organization can claim to represent *all* LGBT Republicans, but the Log Cabin group has long been recognized as the leading organizational home for politically conservative gays and lesbians.

5. This is historically bound. At different points in the GOP's history, black groups were better able to influence internal policy deci-

sions, and they might have had a seat at the table of black politics. Rigueur (2015) provides a thorough examination of this history. But in the current political climate, black Republican groups have little or no impact on "black politics" writ large. As we'll see, their impact on internal GOP politics is more complicated, but still relatively marginal.

6. Fauntroy (2007).

7. There is very little evidence to suggest that King was a Republican. Indeed, to the extent that King spoke of partisanship, it was with a skeptical eye cast on both parties. In an interview at Bennett College, he is quoted as saying, "I'm not here to tell you how to vote. That isn't my concern. I'm not a politician. I have no political ambitions. I don't think the Republican Party is a party full of the almighty God nor is the Democratic Party. They both have weaknesses. And I'm not inextricably bound to either party." Certainly, the Republican Party of today would only be recognizable to the extent that it reflects the Goldwater tradition he explicitly rejected. In his autobiography, King wrote that "The Republican Party geared its appeal and program to racism, reaction, and extremism. All people of goodwill viewed with alarm and concern the frenzied wedding at the Cow Palace of the KKK with the radical right. The 'best man' at this ceremony was a senator whose voting record, philosophy, and program were anathema to all the hard-won achievements of the past decade." In response to this controversy in Florida, King's son responded unequivocally, "It is disingenuous to imply that my father was a Republican. He never endorsed any presidential candidate, and there is certainly no evidence that he ever even voted for a Republican. It is even more outrageous to suggest that he would support the Republican Party of today, which has spent so much time and effort trying to suppress African American votes in Florida and many other states."

8. An "AstroTurf" organization is a fake grassroots group. Indeed, the Tea Party, with which the NBRA has aligned itself, has been accused of not really being fronted by "people" but rather supported by moneyed interests (Skocpol and Williamson 2012; Rosenthal and Trost 2012).

9. I read Derrick's use of the term "Negro" as a colloquial way of bonding with another black person. Indeed, it's an example of code switching: he talked one way with me and another way in front of white audiences. Though he would go on to have pitched battles with other members of the Black Republican Alliance, this code switching was something I observed among all the former members of the organization that I spoke with.

10. Ghaziani (2008).

CHAPTER SIX. WHITHER THE REPUBLICAN PARTY

1. See www.deseretnews.com/article/705396842/Love-would-take-apart-Congressional-Black-Caucus-if-elected-in-Utahs-4th-District.html?pg = all.

2. See http://atr.rollcall.com/mia-love-congressional-black-caucus/.

3. See www.washingtonpost.com/news/the-fix/wp/2014/11/05/mia-love-i-wasnt-elected-because-of-the-color-of-my-skin/.

4. See https://gop.com/new-year-new-congress-new-faces/.

5. See http://video.foxnews.com/v/3877721433001/tim-scott-we-should-focus-on-tomorrow-not-yesterday/?#sp = show-clips.

6. See www.msnbc.com/morning-joe/watch/tim-scott-makes-history-in-south-carolina-354316355773.

7. This is probably because his seat is much less secure. Also, there are a lot of Latino voters in his district.

8. See www.texastribune.org/2015/03/05/hurd-defies-odds-us-house-republicans/.

9. See http://republicanracism.blogspot.com; http://republicans areracists.com.

10. Skocpol and Williamson (2012); Rosenthal and Trost (2012).

11. Richie is referring to a 2002 incident. Trent Lott was pushed out of the GOP leadership after he said, while speaking to a group at Senator Strom Thurmond's birthday party, that the United States would have avoided "all these problems" if Thurmond's 1948 segregationist presidential bid had succeeded.

12. See www.washingtonpost.com/wp-dyn/content/article/2005/07/13/AR2005071302342.html.

13. Seehttp://mediamatters.org/video/2005/07/14/limbaugh-blasted-mehlmans-renunciation-of-gop-r/133493.

14. Seehttp://talkingpointsmemo.com/muckraker/touchy-subject-steele-slammed-for-criticizing-gop-s-southern-strategy; http://voices.washingtonpost.com/right-now/2010/04/steeles_biggest_gaffe_so_far.html.

15. See www.washingtonpost.com/news/post-politics/wp/2015/02/11/priebus-vows-gop-will-make-gains-with-black-voters-in-2016/.

16. See www.washingtonpost.com/news/post-politics/wp/2015/02/11/priebus-vows-gop-will-make-gains-with-black-voters-in-2016/.

17. See https://gop.com/rnc-launches-committedtocommunity-engage-empower-uplift/.

18. See www.gop.com/chairman-reince-priebus-explain-why-its-important-to-engage-with-all-comm/. These sorts of proclamations are not new. Even at its origins, the Republican Party was looking to get black votes. Statements calling for increased outreach have continued into the contemporary era. As recently as 1992, the GOP could talk with a straight face about getting 20 percent of the black vote. Lee Atwater was one party elite who thought the GOP could lure black voters back to the party. But the irony of Atwater, the man behind the Willie Horton ads, calling for more inclusion of minority entrepreneurs proved too much for black voters to bear, and George H. W. Bush won only 11 percent of the black vote.

19. Frymer (1999).

CONCLUSION

1. See www.politico.com/magazine/story/2016/02/donald-trumps-sizzling-sister-act-213659; www.slate.com/blogs/browbeat/2016/03/22/black_trump_supporters_on_the_nightly_show_further_emphasize_how_terrifying.html.

2. Brooks and Manza (1997); Manza and Brooks (1999).

3. Walsh (2004, p. 28).

4. Brubaker and Cooper (2000, p. 8).

5. Here the role of intersectionality is important to consider (Crenshaw 1991; McCall 2005; Shields 2008). With its emphasis on the "multiple dimensions and modalities of social relations," an intersectional approach operates under the assumption that individuals belong to multiple social categories (McCall 2005). The relationship between those categories is an empirical fact to be determined. Hancock (2007) offers important insights into how one should incorporate intersectionality into a political research program.

6. The complaints on the left and the right look the same. Interestingly, while they complain about identity politics, often what they are really complaining about is the identity that is prioritized. Class is what should matter, not race. Or religious and national identity are legitimate, but sexuality and gender are not.

7. Simpson (1998); Dawson (2001); Harris-Lacewell (2004); Lewis (2013).

8. Price (2009, p. 7).

9. Reed (1999); Cohen (1999).

10. Anderson (1990); Watkins (2009); Lacy (2007); Boyd (2008); Cohen (1999); Pattillo-McCoy (1999); Pattillo (2007); Smith and More (2000); Robinson (2014).

11. Jiménez et al. (2015).

12. Levi-Martin and Yeung (2003); Saperstein (2006).

13. Berezin (1997); Abdelal et al. (2006); Smith (2004); Chong and Rogers (2005).

14. Hunter (2013).

15. Research consistently shows the difficulty of trying to constitute a singular and unifying "black agenda." In a study of black representation in Congress, Swain (2006) categorizes black interests as either objective or subjective. Objective interests are "observable" indicators like income, health, employment status, and education level. Objective interests are material, and more is generally assumed to be better. Subjective interests, by contrast, are related to the "feelings, emotions, and temperaments of the people involved" (Swain 2006, p. 6). For blacks, these subjective interests are often unobservable and conceived as related to the perception of the group by non-

blacks, and to the need for African American representation in all aspects of society. However, for African Americans, or any group for that matter, framing issues as collective obscures internal group differences. Swain acknowledges this but still finds the similarities among African Americans more salient in structuring group interests.

Reed's (1999) work is characteristic of approaches that question the empirical reality of a collective, racially based set of interests that unite African Americans. Reed is particularly suspicious of the analytic power of "black interests" in scholarly analysis. For Reed, black interests are not objective and observable things to be taken for granted. Rather, they are the culmination of a set of social and political processes, often framed in ways that favor the interests of middle- and upper-class blacks and align with a broader "mainstream" agenda. In response to Swain's (2006) notion of objective interests, he argues that while the characterization of objective interests is "reasonable enough … it implies a condition of racial parity as the goal of black aspiration and standard of equity, and that is a questionably modest ideal of egalitarianism or social justice…. In addition, linking the determination of black interests to cross-racial comparison perpetuates the practice of defining black interests in terms of an exclusively racial agenda" (Reed 1999, p. 42). As for subjective interests, Reed argues that reliance on the way "most" black people think serves as a poor proxy for black interests. On both the empirical-measurement and theoretical foundations, Reed is dismissive about the scholarly treatment of black interests. Although he is primarily concerned with the ways scholarship is complicit in obscuring class divisions in black communities, he calls for attention to the processes through which politicians and organizational leaders within black communities are successful at constructing corporate racial interests.

16. Though, to be fair, they would not say that they are using whites as the measure and that "blacks don't measure up to whites." They would argue that the things they criticize blacks for lacking are not "black" or "white" values. Rather, they are "correct" values.

17. Higginbotham (1994).

18. Criticism of the politics of respectability focus on how such a political approach limits who can be included in the "us" of blackness. Cohen (1999) has argued that such an approach to politics can constrain

the responses of black political leaders. Both groups of African American Republicans illustrate why the idea of a bounded set of "black interests" grounded in respectability politics must be constantly contested. The diversity of the African American population complicates any formulation of unified policy preferences. Are the interests of an affluent African American attorney in New York City the same as those of a working-class oil-rig worker in New Orleans? Even within any single community, do the interests of the religious element always align with business interests? And across a number of political arenas, there are competing ideas about what "counts" as black interests and who the appropriate beneficiaries of black politics should be. In relying on narrow definitions of black people and their problems, both the color-blind and race-conscious approaches to black Republicanism proffer an incredibly circumscribed view of black interests.

19. Daynes and Lee (2008, p. 151; emphasis in original).

20. See Lacy (2007) and Anderson (1990) for instances where different ideas about black people structure interclass division among African Americans. Wilkins (2012a, 2012b) examines how ideas about blacks as a collective inform individual-level social-psychological processes.

21. Cohen (1999, p. 71).

22. Hughey (2012); McDermott (2006).

23. Chavez (2008).

24. The move to treat race as ideas is consistent with efforts to examine the role of cultural influences in the political arena (Anderson 2008; Steesland 2006; Campbell 2002; Berman 1998; Dobbin 1994; Hall 1993). In this most recent resurgence, much of the focus has been on illuminating the process through which policy making is structured by ideas. Research illuminates how some ideas "win" in political debates while others "lose." Such approaches, while undoubtedly moving the needle forward in our understanding of how culture informs politics, are bound by a relatively narrow focus on one political process, policy outcomes. Ideas inform a range of political behaviors, including organizing and alliance building.

25. Tarman and Sears (2005, p. 733).

26. Sears et al. (2000).

27. Bobo and Johnson (2004).

28. See Johnson (2003) for a discussion of the ways in which blackness is a perfomative achievement.

29. Berrey (2015).

30. Binder and Wood (2013).

31. See McAdam (1999), Koopmans and Olzak (2004), and McCammon et al. (2007) for discussions of political and discursive opportunity structure.

32. Bobo and Dawson (2009); Harris (2012); Gillespie (2010); Alim and Smitherman (2012); Hunter (2013).

33. Danigelis (1977, 1978). Also see Walton (1972, 1985) for a discussion of the importance of embedding black political behavior in a broader political context.

34. McAdam (1988); Polletta (2002); Espeland (1998); Armstrong (2002).

METHODOLOGICAL APPENDIX

1. Glaser and Strauss (1967).

REFERENCES

Abdelal, Rawi, Yoshiko M. Herrrera, Alastair Iain Johnston, and Rose McDermott. 2006. "Identity as a Variable." *Perspectives on Politics* 4(4): 695–711.

Alim, H. Samy, and Geneva Smitherman. 2012. *Articulate While Black: Barack Obama, Language, and Race in the U.S.* New York, NY: Oxford University Press.

Anderson, Elijah. 1990. *Streetwise: Race, Class, and Change in an Urban Community.* Chicago, IL: University of Chicago Press.

Anderson, Elisabeth. 2008. "Experts, Ideas, and Policy Change: The Russell Sage Foundation and Small Loan Reform." *Theory and Society* 37(3): 271–310.

Armstrong, Elizabeth A. 2002. *Forging Gay Identities: Organizing Sexuality in San Francisco, 1950–1994.* Chicago, IL: University of Chicago Press.

Berezin, Mabel. 1997. "Politics and Culture: A Less Fissured Terrain." *Annual Review of Sociology* 23: 361–383.

Berger, Joseph, Bernard P. Cohen, and Morris Zelditch, Jr. 1972. "Status Characteristics and Social Interaction." *American Journal of Sociology* 37(3): 214–255.

Berlin, Ira, Barbara J. Fields, Steven F. Miller, Joseph P. Reidy, and Leslie S. Rowland, eds. 1992. *Free at Last: A Documentary History of Slavery, Freedom, and the Civil War.* New York, NY: New Press.

Berman, Sheri. 1998. *The Social Democratic Moment: Ideas and Politics in the Making of Interwar Europe.* Cambridge, MA: Harvard University Press.

Berrey, Ellen. 2015. *The Enigma of Diversity: The Language of Race and the Limits of Racial Justice.* Chicago, IL: University of Chicago Press.

Binder, Amy J., and Kate Wood. 2013. *Becoming Right: How Campuses Shape Young Conservatives.* Princeton, NJ: Princeton University Press.

Bobo, Lawrence D., and Michael C. Dawson. 2009. "A Change Has Come: Race, Politics, and the Path to the Obama Presidency." *Du Bois Review* 6(1): 1–14.

Bobo, Lawrence D., and Devon Johnson. 2004. "A Taste for Punishment: Black and White Americans' Views on the Death Penalty and the War on Drugs." *Du Bois Review* 1(1): 151–180.

Bolce, Louis, Gerald De Maio, and Douglas Muzzio. 1993. "The 1992 Republican 'Tent': No Blacks Walked In." *Political Science Quarterly* 108(2): 255–270.

Bonacich, Edna. 1973. "A Theory of Middleman Minorities." *American Sociological Review* 38(5): 583–594.

Bonilla-Silva, Eduardo. 1997. "Rethinking Racism: Toward a Structural Interpretation." *American Sociological Review* 62(3): 465–480.

———. 1999. "The Essential Social Fact of Race." *American Sociological Review* 64(6): 899–906.

———. 2010. *Racism without Racists: Color-Blind Racism & Racial Inequality in Contemporary America.* Lanham, MD: Rowan & Littlefield.

Boyd, Michelle. 2008. *Jim Crow Nostalgia: Reconstructing Race in Bronzeville.* Minneapolis, MN: University of Minnesota Press.

Bracey, Christopher A. 2008. *Saviors or Sellouts: The Promise and Peril of Black Conservatism from Booker T. Washington to Condoleezza Rice.* Boston, MA: Beacon Press.

Brooke, Edward W. 2007. *Bridging the Divide: My Life.* New Brunswick, NJ: Rutgers University Press.

Brooks, Clem, and Jeff Manza. 1997. "Social Cleavages and Political Alignments: US Presidential Elections, 1960 to 1992." *American Sociological Review* 62(6): 937–946.

Brubaker, Rogers, and Frederick Cooper. 2000. "Beyond 'Identity.'" *Theory and Society* 29(1): 1–47.

Cain, Herman. 2005. *They Think You're Stupid: Why Democrats Lost Your Vote and What Republicans Must Do to Keep It.* Macon, GA: Stroud and Hall.

Campbell, John L. 2002. "Ideas, Politics, and Public Policy." *Annual Review of Sociology* 28: 21–38.

Carter, Stephen L. 1991. *Reflections of an Affirmative Action Baby.* New York, NY: Basic Books.

Chavez, Leo R. 2008. *The Latino Threat Narrative: Constructing Immigrants, Citizens, and the Nation.* Stanford, CA: Stanford University Press.

Chong, Dennis, and Reuel Rogers. 2005. "Racial Solidarity and Political Participation." *Political Behavior* 27(4): 347–374.

Cohen, Cathy. 1999. *The Boundaries of Blackness: AIDS and the Breakdown of Black Politics.* Chicago, IL: University of Chicago Press.

Conover, Pamela. 1984. "The Influence of Group Identification on Political Participation and Evaluation." *Journal of Politics* 46(3): 760–785.

Correll, Shelley J., and Cecilia Ridgeway. 2003. "Expectation States Theory." Pages 29–52 in *The Handbook of Social Psychology,* edited by J. Delamater. New York, NY: Kluwer Academic/Plenum.

Crenshaw, Kimberle. 1991. "Mapping the Margins: Intersectionality, Identity Politics, and Violence against Women of Color." *Stanford Law Review* 43(6): 1241–1299.

Danigelis, Nicholas L. 1977. "A Theory of Black Political Participation in the United States." *Social Forces* 56(1): 31–47.

———. 1978. "Black Political Participation in the United States: Some Recent Evidence." *American Sociological Review* 43(5): 756–771.

Dawson, Michael C. 1994. *Behind the Mule: Race and Class in American Politics.* Princeton, NJ: Princeton University Press.

———. 2001. *Black Visions: The Roots of Contemporary African-American Political Ideologies.* Chicago, IL: University of Chicago Press.

Daynes, Sarah, and Orville Lee. 2008. *Desire for Race.* New York, NY: Cambridge University Press.

Dillard, Angela D. 2001. *Guess Who's Coming to Dinner Now? Multicultural Conservatism in America.* New York, NY: New York University Press.

DiMaggio, Paul. 1997. "Culture and Cognition." *Annual Review of Sociology* 23: 263–287.

Dobbin, Frank. 1994. *Forging Industrial Policy: The United States, Britain, and France in the Railway Age.* New York, NY: Cambridge University Press.

Elder, Larry. 2008. *What's Race Got to Do with It? Why It's Time to Stop the Stupidist Argument in America.* New York, NY: St. Martin's Griffin.

Espeland, Wendy Nelson. 1998. *The Struggle for Water: Politics, Rationality, and Identity in the American Southwest.* Chicago, IL: University of Chicago Press.

Faryna, Stan, Brad Stetson, and Joseph G. Conti, eds. 1997. *Black and Right: The Bold New Voice of Black Conservatives in America.* Wesport, CT: Praeger.

Fauntroy, Michael. 2007. *Republicans and the Black Vote.* Boulder, CO: Lynne Rienner.

Feagin, Joe R. 2010. *The White Racial Frame: Centuries of Racial Framing and Counter-Framing.* New York, NY: Routledge.

Fields, Corey D. 2014. "Not Your Grandma's Knitting: The Role of Identity Processes in the Transformation of Cultural Practices." *Social Psychology Quarterly* 77(2): 150–165.

Frymer, Paul. 1999. *Uneasy Alliances: Race and Party Competition in America.* Princeton, NJ: Princeton University Press.

Gay, Claudine, and Katherine Tate. 1998. "Doubly Bound: The Impact of Gender and Race on the Politics of Black Women." *Political Psychology* 19(1): 169–184.

Ghaziani, Amin. 2008. *The Dividends of Dissent: How Conflict and Culture Work in Lesbian and Gay Marches on Washington.* Chicago, IL: University of Chicago Press.

Gilens, Martin. 1999. *Why Americans Hate Welfare: Race, Media, and the Politics of Antipoverty Policy.* Chicago, IL: University of Chicago Press.

Gillespie, Andra, ed. 2010. *Whose Black Politics? Cases in Post-racial Black Leadership.* New York, NY: Routledge.

Glaeser, Andreas. 2000. *Divided in Unity: Identity, Germany, and The Berlin Police.* Chicago, IL: University of Chicago Press.

Glaser, Barney, and Anselm Strauss. 1967. *The Discovery of Grounded Theory: Strategies for Qualitative Research.* New York, NY: Aldine Transaction.

Goldstein, Richard. 2003. *Homocons: The Rise of the Gay Right.* New York, NY: Verso.

Golland, David Hamilton. 2011. *Constructing Affirmative Action: The Struggle for Equal Employment Opportunity.* Lexington, KY: University of Kentucky Press.

Griswold, Wendy. 1987. "A Methodological Framework for the Sociology of Culture." *Sociological Methodology* 17: 1–35.

———. 2008. *Culture and Societies in a Changing World.* Newbury Park, CA: Pine Forge Press.

Gurin, Patricia, Shirley Hatchett, and James S. Jackson. 1989. *Hope & Independence: Blacks' Response to Electoral and Party Politics.* New York, NY: Russell Sage Foundation.

Hall, Peter. 1993. "Policy Paradigms, Social Learning, and the State: The Case of Economic Policy Making in Britain." *Comparative Politics* 25(3): 275–296.

Hancock, Ange-Marie. 2007. "When Multiplication Doesn't Equal Quick Addition: Examining Intersectionality as a Research Paradigm." *Perspectives on Politics* 5(1): 63–79.

Harris, Fredrick C. 2012. *The Price of the Ticket: Barack Obama and the Rise and Decline of Black Politics.* New York, NY: Oxford University Press.

Harris-Lacewell, Melissa Victoria. 2004. *Bibles, Barbershops, and BET: Everyday Talk and Black Political Thought.* Princeton, NJ: Princeton University Press.

Higginbotham, Evelyn. 1994. *Righteous Discontent: The Women's Movement in the Black Baptist Church, 1880–1920.* Cambridge, MA: Harvard University Press.

Hogg, Michael, Deborah J. Terry, and Katherine M. White. 1995. "A Tale of Two Theories: A Critical Comparison of Identity Theory with Social Identity Theory." *Social Psychology Quarterly* 58(4): 255–269.

Hughey, Matthew W. 2012. *White Bound: Nationalists, Antiracists, and the Shared Meanings of Race.* Stanford, CA: Stanford University Press.

Hunter, Marcus Anthony. 2013. *Black Citymakers: How The Philadelphia Negro Changed Urban America.* New York, NY: Oxford University Press.

Jiménez, Tomás R., Corey D. Fields, and Ariela Schachter. 2015. "How Ethnoraciality Matters: The View Inside Ethnoracial 'Groups.'" *Social Currents* 2(2): 107–115.

Johnson, E. Patrick. 2003. *Appropriating Blackness: Performance and the Politics of Authenticity.* Durham, NC: Duke University Press.

Kabaservice, Geoffrey. 2012. *Rule and Ruin: The Downfall of Moderation and the Destruction of the Republican Party, from Eisenhower to the Tea Party.* New York, NY: Oxford University Press.

Kanter, Rosabeth Moss. 1993. *Men and Women of the Corporation.* New York, NY: Basic Books.

Kennedy, Randall. 2008. *Sellout: The Politics of Racial Betrayal.* New York, NY: Pantheon Books.

Key, V.O. 1949. *Southern Politics in State and Nation.* New York, NY: Vintage Books.

King, Desmond S., and Rogers M. Smith. 2011. *Still a House Divided: Race and Politics in Obama's America.* Princeton, NJ: Princeton University Press.

Kirkpatrick, David D. 2004. "Black Pastors Backing Bush Are Rarities, but Not Alone." *The New York Times,* October 5.

Koopmans, Ruud, and Susan Olzak. 2004. "Discursive Opportunities and the Evolution of Right-Wing Violence in Germany." *American Journal of Sociology* 110(1): 198–230.

Lacy, Karyn R. 2007. *Blue-Chip Black: Race, Class, and Status in the New Black Middle Class.* Berkeley, CA: University of California Press.

Lamont, Michèle. 2002. *The Dignity of Working Men: Morality and the Boundaries of Race, Class, and Immigration.* Cambridge, MA: Harvard University Press.

Lemann, Nicholas. 1992. *The Promised Land: The Great Black Migration and How It Changed America.* New York, NY: Vintage Books.

Levi-Martin, John, and King-To Yeung. 2003. "The Use of the Conceptual Category of Race in American Sociology 1937–99." *Sociological Forum* 18(4): 521–543.

Lewis, Angela K. 2013. *Conservatism in the Black Community: To the Right and Misunderstood.* New York, NY: Routledge.

Loevy, Robert D. 1997. *The Civil Rights Act of 1964: The Passage of the Law That Ended Racial Segregation.* Albany, NY: State University of New York Press.

Loveman, Mara. 1999. "Is 'Race' Essential?" *American Sociological Review* 64(6): 891–898.

Manza, Jeff, and Clem Brooks. 1999. *Social Cleavages and Political Change: Voter Alignment and U.S. Party Coalitions.* New York, NY: Oxford University Press.

McAdam, Doug. 1988. *Freedom Summer.* New York, NY: Oxford University Press.

———. 1999. *Political Process and the Development of Black Insurgency, 1930–1970.* Chicago, IL: University of Chicago Press.

McCall, Leslie. 2005. "The Complexity of Intersectionality." *Signs* 30(3): 1771–1800.

McCammon, Holly J., Courtney Sanders Muse, Harmony D. Newman, and Teresa M. Terrell. 2007. "Movement Framing and Discursive Opportunity Structures: The Political Successes of the US Women's Jury Movements." *American Sociological Review* 72(5): 725–749.

McDermott, Monica. 2006. *Working-Class White: The Making and Unmaking of Race Relations.* Berkeley, CA: University of California Press.

McGlowan, Angela. 2007. *Bamboozled: How Americans Are Being Exploited by the Lies of the Liberal Media.* Nashville, TN: Thomas Nelson.

Mendelberg, Tali. 2001. *The Race Card: Campaign Strategy, Implicit Messages, and the Norm of Equality.* Princeton, NJ: Princeton University Press.

Merida, Kevin and Michael Fletcher. 2007. *Supreme Discomfort: The Divided Soul of Clarence Thomas.* New York, NY: Broadway Books.

Moore, Mignon R. 2010. "Articulating a Politics of (Multiple) Identities: LGBT Sexuality and Inclusion in Black Community Life." *Du Bois Review* 7(2): 315–334.

Morris, Aldon. 1986. *Origins of the Civil Right Movement.* New York, NY: Free Press.

Olsen, Marvin. 1970. "Social and Political Participation of Blacks." *American Sociological Review* 35(2): 682–697.

O'Reilly, Kenneth. 1995. *Nixon's Piano: Presidents and Racial Politics from Washington to Clinton.* New York, NY: Free Press.

Orum, Anthony. 1966. "A Reappraisal of the Social and Political Participation of Negroes." *American Journal of Sociology* 72(1): 32–46.

Pager, Devah. 2003. "The Mark of a Criminal Record." *American Journal of Sociology* 108(5): 937–975.

Parker, Star. 1997. *Pimps, Whores, and Welfare Brats: From Welfare Cheat to Conservative Messenger.* New York, NY: Pocket Books.

Pattillo, Mary. 2007. *Black on the Block: The Politics of Race and Class in the City.* Chicago, IL: University of Chicago Press.

Pattillo-McCoy, Mary. 1999. *Black Picket Fences: Privilege and Peril among the Black Middle Class.* Chicago, IL: University of Chicago Press.

Pearlman, Joel, and Mary C. Waters. 2005. *The New Race Question: How the Census Counts Multiracial Individuals.* New York, NY: Russell Sage Foundation.

Philpot, Tasha S. 2007. *Race, Republicans, and the Return of the Party of Lincoln.* Ann Arbor, MI: University of Michigan Press.

Polletta, Francesca. 2002. *Freedom Is an Endless Meeting: Democracy in American Social Movements.* Chicago, IL: University of Chicago Press.

Price, Melanye. 2009. *Dreaming Blackness: Black Nationalism and African American Public Opinion.* New York, NY: New York University Press.

Reed, Adolph. 1997. "The Descent of Black Conservatism." *Progressive* 61(10): 18–20.

———. 1999. *Stirrings in the Jug: Black Politics in the Post-Segregation Era.* Minneapolis, MN: University of Minnesota Press.

Ridgeway, Cecilia L. 2011. *Framed by Gender: How Gender Inequality Persists in the Modern World.* New York, NY: Oxford University Press.

Rigueur, Leah Wright. 2015. *The Loneliness of the Black Republican: Pragmatic Politics and the Pursuit of Power.* Princeton, NJ: Princeton University Press.

Robinson, Paul. 2005. *Queer Wars: The New Gay Right and Its Critics.* Chicago, IL: University of Chicago Press.

Robinson, Zandria. 2014. *This Ain't Chicago: Race, Class, and Regional Identity in the Post-Soul South.* Chapel Hill, NC: University of North Carolina Press.

Rogers, Reuel R. 2006. *Afro-Caribbean Immigrants and the Politics of Incorporation: Ethnicity, Exception, or Exit.* New York, NY: Cambridge University Press.

Rosenthal, Lawrence, and Christine Trost. 2012. *Steep: The Precipitous Rise of the Tea Party.* Berkeley, CA: University of California Press.

Roth, Wendy. 2012. *Race Migrations: Latinos and the Cultural Transformations of Race.* Palo Alto, CA: Stanford University Press.

Saperstein, Aliya. 2006. "Double-Checking the Race Box: Examining Inconsistency between Survey Measures of Observed Race and Self-Reported Race." *Social Forces* 85(1): 57–74.

Schreiber, Ronnee. 2008. *Righting Feminism: Conservative Women & American Politics.* New York, NY: Oxford University Press.

Sears, David O., John J. Hetts, Jim Sidanius, and Lawrence Bobo. 2000. "Race in American Politics: Framing the Debates." Pages 1–43 in *Racialized Politics: The Debate about Racism in America,* edited by David O. Sears, Jim Sidanius, and Lawrence Bobo. Chicago, IL: University of Chicago Press.

Sellers, Robert M., Mia A. Smith, Stephanie A.J. Rowley, and Tabbye M. Chavous. 1998. "Multidimensional Model of Racial Identity: A Reconceptualization of African American Racial Identity." *Personality and Social Psychology Review* 2(1): 18–39.

Sewell, William H., Jr. 1992. "A Theory of Structure: Duality, Agency, and Transformation." *American Journal of Sociology* 98(1): 1–29.

Shields, Stephanie A. 2008. "Gender: An Intersectional Perspective." *Sex Roles* 59(5): 301–311.

Sheridan, Earl. 1996. "The New Accomodationists." *Journal of Black Studies* 27(2): 152–171.

Simien, Evelyn M. 2005. "Race, Gender, and Linked Fate." *Journal of Black Studies* 35(5): 529–550.

Simpson, Angela. 1998. *The Tie That Binds: Identity and Political Attitudes in the Post–Civil Rights Generation.* New York, NY: New York University Press.

Skocpol, Theda, and Vanessa Williamson. 2012. *The Tea Party and the Remaking of Republican Conservatism.* New York, NY: Oxford University Press.

Smith, Candis Watts. 2014. *Black Mosaic: The Politics of Black Pan-Ethnic Diversity*. New York, NY: New York University Press.

Smith, Rogers M. 2004. "Identities, Interests, and the Future of Political Science." *Perspectives on Politics* 2(2): 301–312.

Smith, Rogers M., and Desmond S. King. 2009. "Barak Obama and the Future of American Racial Politics." *Du Bois Review* 61(1): 25–35.

Smith, Sandra S., and Mignon R. Moore. 2000. "Intraracial Diversity and Relations among African-Americans: Closeness among Black Students at a Predominantly White University." *American Journal of Sociology* 106(1): 1–39.

Sowell, Thomas, ed. 1980. *The Fairmont Papers: Black Alternatives Conference*. Piscataway, NJ: Transaction.

Steesland, Brian. 2006. "Cultural Categories and the American Welfare State: The Case of Guaranteed Income Policy." *American Journal of Sociology* 111(5): 1273–1326.

Steinhauer, Jennifer. 2010. "Black and Republican and Back in Congress." *The New York Times*, November 5.

Stikoff, Harvard. 2008. *The Struggle for Black Equality*. New York, NY: Hill and Wang.

Stryker, Sheldon. 1980. *Symbolic Interactionism: A Social Structural Version*. Menlo Park, CA: Benjamin Cummings.

Stryker, Sheldon, and Peter J. Burke. 2000. "The Past, Present, and Future of Identity Theory." *Social Psychology Quarterly* 63(4): 284–297.

Swain, Carol M. 2006. *Black Faces, Black Interests: The Representation of African Americans in Congress*. New York, NY: University Press of America.

Tajfel, Henri. 1981. *Human Groups and Social Categories: Studies in Social Psychology*. New York, NY: Cambridge University Press.

Tarman, Christopher, and David O. Sears. 2005. "The Conceptualization and Measurement of Symbolic Racism." *Journal of Politics* 67(3): 731–761.

Tate, Katherine. 1998. National Black Election Study, 1996 [computer file]. ICPSR version. Columbus, OH: Ohio State University [producer], 1997. Ann Arbor, MI: Inter-University Consortium for Political and Social Research [distributor].

———. 2003. "Black Opinion on the Legitimacy of Racial Redistricting and Minority-Majority Districts." *American Political Science Review* 97(1): 45–56.

Thomas, Clarence. 2007. *My Grandfather's Son*. New York, NY: Harper Collins.

Thurber, Timothy N. 2013. *Republicans and Race: The GOP's Frayed Relationship with African Americans, 1945–1974*. Lawrence, KS: University of Kansas Press.

Turner, John C. 1987. *Rediscovering the Social Group: A Self-Categorization Theory*. Oxford, UK: Basil Blackwell.

Verba, Sidney, and Norman Nie. 1972. *Participation in America*. New York, NY: Harper.

Walsh, Katherine Cramer. 2004. *Talking about Politics: Informal Groups and Social Identity in American Life*. Chicago, IL: University of Chicago Press.

Walton, Hanes, Jr. 1972. *Black Politics: A Theoretical and Structural Analysis*. Philadelphia, PA: Lippincott.

———. 1975. *Black Republicans: The Politics of the Black and Tans*. Metuchen, NJ: Scarecrow Press.

———. 1985. *Invisible Politics: Black Political Behavior*. Albany, NY: State University of New York Press.

Waters, Mary. 1999. *Black Identities: West Indian Immigrant Dreams and American Realities*. New York, NY: Russell Sage Foundation.

Watkins, Celeste. 2009. *The New Welfare Bureaucrats: Entanglements of Race, Class, and Policy Reform*. Chicago, IL: University of Chicago Press.

Watson, Elwood. 1998. "Guess What Came to American Politics?—Contemporary Black Conservatism." *Journal of Black Studies* 29(1): 73–92.

Watts, J.C., Jr., and Chriss Winston. 2003. *What Color Is a Conservative? My Life and My Politics*. New York, NY: Perennial Press.

Weakliem, David L. 1997. "Race versus Class? Racial Composition and Class Voting, 1936–1992." *Social Forces* 75(3): 939–956.

Weaver, C. Mason. 1998. *It's OK to Leave the Plantation: The New Underground Railroad*. Fallbrook, CA: Reeder.

Weiss, Nancy J. 1983. *Farewell to the Party of Lincoln: Black Politics in the Age of FDR*. Princeton, NJ: Princeton University Press.

Wilkins, Amy C. 2012a. "Becoming Black Women: Intimate Stories and Intersectional Identities." *Social Psychology Quarterly* 75(2): 173–196.

————. 2012b. "'Not Out to Start a Revolution': Race, Gender, and Emotional Restraint among Black University Men." *Journal of Contemporary Ethnography* 41(1): 34–65.

Youill, Kevin. 2006. *Richard Nixon and the Rise of Affirmative Action: The Pursuit of Racial Equality in an Era of Limits.* New York, NY: Rowman & Littlefield.

Young, Alford A. 2004. *The Minds of Marginalized Black Men: Making Sense of Mobility, Opportunity, and Future Life Chances.* Princeton, NJ: Princeton University Press.

Zerubavel, Eviatar. 1999. *Social Mindscapes: An Invitation to Cognitive Sociology.* Cambridge, MA: Harvard University Press.

INDEX

abolitionism, 27, 36–37, 38, 55
abortion, 67, 121, 146, 185, 195,
  240–41n17
ACASI (Audio Computer-Assisted
  Self Interviewing), 223
affirmative action, 75–76, 80, 87,
  111–14, 240n16, 242–43n10
Affordable Care Act (ACA), 176–77,
  190–91
African Americans. *See* black
  identity
American Conservative Union, 155
American National Election Study
  (ANES), 16–17, 81, 223, 224,
  225*table*
anonymity, respondents, 219–21,
  232n8
armed forces desegregation
  (Executive Order 9981), 45
"artifacts," from fieldwork events,
  222
assassination: Kennedy, 47;
  Lincoln, 37
Atwater, Lee, 247n18

Behind the Mule (Dawson),
  234–35n19
Black Alternatives Conference
  (1980), Fairmont Hotel, 50–51
Black and Right, 80
Black and Tans, 39–40
black churches, 17; civil rights
  movement formed within,
  234n18; color blindness and,
  94–95, 110–11, 112, 134; and
  faith-based initiatives, 110–11,
  112, 134; hypocritical religiosity,
  195–96; Republican Party
  conservative overtures to,
  233n14
Black Family Values Summit,
  194–96
black identity, 7–10, 25–30, 61–115,
  117–18, 137, 231n3; black Republican alienation from, 146;
  centrality of, 24, 82, 118, 205–6,
  241n21, 243nn2,4; color-blind
  view of, 7, 88–89, 91–96, 104–5,
  148, 174; and conservatism, 8,

165, 168–69; and black Republican relations with white Republicans, 191–94, 212–13; black Republicans as models for political conservatives generally, 73; centrist, 13, 53; color-blind, 1–6, 106–15, 144, 165, 192–93, 207; "compassionate conservatism," 52–53, 110–11; Conservative Political Action Conference (CPAC), 1, 155, 156–57; "core conservative principles," 163; Democrats shifting to, 47–48, 49; "existential predicament," 80; Goldwater campaign sparking, 47; "inorganic" black, 49–50, 147–48, 243n5; multiple expressions of, 207; "new" black, 49–55; New Connections conference, 85–88, 116–17; "organic" black, 49–50, 63, 147, 243n5; policy framing, 106–15, 130, 177, 190–91; race-conscious, 116–40, 144, 197, 207, 243–44; racial, 6, 51, 213; of "regular" black persons, 11–13; religious, 3; Republican partisanship distinguished from, 13, 62–63; as Republican Party attraction, 11–13, 17, 47–48, 67, 90; social, 121, 233n14
convenience sampling, 217–18
Cooper, Frederick, 203
courage, African American, 73, 80, 100
crime: color blindness and, 109; criminal justice, 5, 45, 109, 191; prison reform, 117; race consciousness and, 126, 131; tough-on-crime stance, 52, 189. *See also* police

Cruz, Ted, 239n5
cultural objects, 138–39, 244n11
"culture of poverty," 97–98

Danigelis, Nicholas, 214
Dash, Stacy, 201
Dawson, Michael, 19–20, 234–35n19, 243n4
Daynes, Sarah, 209
death penalty, blacks' attitudes toward, 211
Democrat blacks, 26–27, 33–34, 54, 188, 201; church-going, 233n14; demographics, 16–18, 224–26; Great Depression, 42–44; Hurricane Katrina, 152; hypocritical religiosity, 195–96; leaving for Republican Party, 89–91, 118–20; majority, 19; migration from Republican Party, 44–48, 53–54, 243n3; New Deal and, 41, 43–44, 231n16; "plantation politics," 70; "poverty pimps," 70–71; presidential elections (1930s), 27; RBE and, 159; Republican blacks criticizing, 70–71, 91; Republican black similarities with, 16–18; "skeptical embrace" of Republican blacks and, 74–75; and unexpectedness of black Republican partisanship, 59–60. *See also* Obama, Barack
Democratic Party: and black churches, 111; and civil rights, 46–49, 155, 157, 237n29; Civil War, 38; and governing coalitions, 76; Hurricane Katrina, 152; Ku Klux Klan, 38, 142, 157; liberals, 19–20, 50; migration of blacks to, 44–48, 53–54, 243n3; NBRA and, 152,

elections: American National
Election Study (ANES), 16–17,
81, 223, 224, 225*table*; demographics, 18, 223–26, 225*table*; NBRA
and, 154–55, 174; Republican
Party lack of assistance to
minority candidates, 186–89;
state and local, 48–49, 52, 189.
See also congressional elections;
presidential elections; voters
"electoral capture," 54
employment. *See* jobs
entrepreneurship: race consciousness and, 133; structural issue, 117
equality: redlining and, 131. *See also*
civil rights; racial equality
ethnography, 222–23
Executive Order 9981, armed
forces desegregation, 45
"existential predicament," 80
"expectation states theory,"
232–33n12
expected politics, 15–16, 34, 88

Fair Housing Act (1968), 47
Fairmont Conference (1980), 50–51
faith-based initiatives, 110–11, 112, 134
family values: Republican black, 11,
65–66, 68, 194–96. *See also*
marriage
famous black Republicans, 9, 12, 15;
King, 155, 161, 245n7; Powell, 3,
73–74, 76, 177; Condoleezza
Rice, 3, 76, 177; Thomas, 4, 113,
242–43n10. *See also* Carson, Ben
Fauntroy, Michael, 42, 51, 237n31
Feagin, Joe, 103, 242n5
field notes, 222
fieldwork, 222–23, 227–29
Frederick Douglass' Paper, 36–37
French, David, 6
Frymer, Paul, 47, 54, 121

Gallup polling, 232n10
gays. *See* LGBT identities
gender: black public opinion by, 17.
See also LGBT identities
German unification, and identity,
230n10
Ghaziani, Amin, 170
Glaeser, Andreas, 239n10
Goldwater, Barry, 47, 48, 49, 178,
179, 245n7
GOP. *See* Republican Party
government: antidiscrimination
duties, 131; dependence on, 51,
101, 120, 125, 136, 143, 184;
intrusion of, 135; small/limited,
120, 121, 135–36, 163, 237n31; social
welfare programs, 67, 101–2,
119–21, 133; spending slashes,
190–91. *See also* elections;
laws
Great Depression, 42–44
Griswold, Wendy, 138, 244n11
Growth and Opportunity Project,
180–82
The Guardian, 2

Hancock, Ange-Marie, 248n5
health: Affordable Care Act (ACA),
176–77, 190–91; disparities
between blacks and whites, 109;
HIV/AIDS, 196, 210; system
reforms, 176–77
Higginbotham, Evelyn, 208
historically black colleges and
universities (HBCUs), 181
history: black voters, 34–46, 53–55;
Democrat blacks, 71; discrimination, 86–87, 94, 116, 126–27; in
identification process, 240n10;
NBRA and, 155–57; race and
racial oppression as central in
modern world history, 243n4;

Nationalists, Black, 136, 243n4
National Politics Study (NPS),
    223, 224, 225*table*, 233n13
National Prayer Breakfast, Carson,
    2–3
The National Review, 6
NBRA. *See* National Black
    Republican Association
Nelson, Adam, 86–87, 88, 116, 117
neoconservatives, black, 49–55
networking, RBE and, 159–61
"new accommodationists," 61
"new" black conservatives, 49–55
New Connections conference,
    85–88, 116–17
New Deal, 41, 43–44, 47, 231n16,
    237n22
New Orleans, Hurricane Katrina,
    151–53
New York City, mayoral election
    (1965), 49
New York State, governor race
    (1966), 49
The Nightly Show, 200
Nixon, Richard, 48, 86, 87, 178,
    240n16
No Child Left Behind, 110
North: civil rights support, 47;
    Democratic Party, 41–44,
    46–47; Republican blacks,
    41–42; white, 47

Obama, Barack, 4, 52–53, 60, 125;
    Carson and, 3, 21–22; elections,
    21, 52–53, 73–74; health-care
    reform, 176–77; Powell's
    endorsement of, 73–74;
    Republican racism vs., 176–77
"Obamacare," 176–77
Office of Faith-Based and
    Community Initiatives
    (renamed Office of Faith-Based

and Neighborhood Partner-
    ships), 110–11
"organic" black conservatives,
    49–50, 63, 147, 243n5
organizations, black Republican,
    29–30, 49–55, 68–69, 145–50;
    AstroTurf, 157–58, 245n8; Black
    Family Values Summit, 194–96;
    Black Republican Alliance,
    162–71, 246n9; divisions, 29–30,
    148–54, 163–71; "fronts" for white
    activists, 147–48; "inorganic,"
    49–50, 147–48; names, 232n8;
    NBRA, 141–42, 144, 150–62, 168,
    174, 191, 245n8; "organic," 49–50,
    63, 147; and politically liberal
    black organizations, 175; RBE,
    142–44, 158–62, 195; respondents
    in, 219; tension between color
    blindness and race conscious-
    ness, 146–47, 165–66, 168, 170,
    212
organizing behavior, 29–30, 145–54,
    162, 163–71
Orum, Anthony, 234n18
outsider status, 3, 32, 104

Pager, Devah, 117
partisan choice, 217; historical
    contexts, 35, 36, 53; racial
    identity and, 21, 66, 83, 117;
    unconventional/"unique"/
    unexpected, 15, 59, 64. *See also*
    Democratic Party; Republican
    Party
pathology, black, 96–105, 117–18, 125,
    193–98, 240n14
patronage (whites supporting
    blacks), 51, 84, 191, 213–14, 241n23;
    Democrat, 43; liberal areas, 77;
    South, 40–41, 237n24
Pew Research Center, 232n10

"sellout critique," *(continued)*
authenticity questioned, 28,
61–72, 79, 87–88, 165–66; Uncle
Tom label, 56, 64, 70, 80, 165
"semi-elites," 219
Senate, Republican blacks, 3, 49,
173, 238n33
sexual identities. *See* LGBT
identities
similarities among blacks, 10, 16–18;
assumed and projected, 227; and
"black interests," 249n15;
color-blind and race-conscious,
115; concern for responsibility
and respectability, 129; and
difficulty getting along and
organizing, 169; feelings of
isolation and misunderstanding,
57, 70, 146, 234n18; identification
based on, 235n19; narratives of
conversion, 26–27, 50, 89–90,
118–19, 242n2; school choices, 95.
See also black identity; black
voters; differences among blacks
Simpson, Angela, 243n5
"situatedness," fieldwork, 227
"skeptical embrace" of blacks, by
white Republicans, 28, 58–61,
72–79, 83, 87
slavery, 35–36; abolitionism, 27,
36–37, 38, 55
snowball sampling, 218
social conservatism, Republican,
121, 233n14
social identities, 18, 31. *See also* class;
gender; identity; race
social media: Black Lives Matter,
5; "#CommittedToCommunity:
Engage, Empower, Uplift," 180
social policy. *See* policy framing
social values: black pathological,
96–105, 117–18, 125, 193–98,

240n14; election wins based on,
173; family, 11, 65–66, 68, 194–96;
"traditional"/"mainstream," 50,
97, 125–26, 129. *See also* work
ethic, black people
social welfare programs, 67, 101–2,
119–21, 133
"sociological" approach, to
political behavior, 202–5
Sons of Confederate Soldiers, 186
South: Democratic Party, 39, 41, 43,
46–48, 237nn24,29; Republican
Party, 39–41, 47–48, 51, 178–79,
237nn24,31; urban unemployed
blacks, 42
"Southern Strategy," 47–48, 51,
178–79, 237n31
state and local elections: black
candidates, 189; black support
for Republican candidates,
48–49, 52
"states' rights," 51
status beliefs, 232–33n12. *See also*
class; identity
Steele, Michael, 3, 63, 178–79,
183–84, 189
Steele, Shelby, 201
stereotyping, 103–5, 114, 176–77, 211
structural issues, 117
survey data, 16–18, 81, 223–26,
225*table*, 232n10, 233n13
Swain, Carol M., 248–49n15
symbolic racism, 210–11

Tarman, Christopher, 210
Tate, Katherine, 20
taxes, 51–52, 106–9, 133, 146, 190–91
teachers, and vouchers, 131
Tea Party, 53, 176–77, 245n8
theoretical sampling, 218
Thomas, Clarence, 4, 113,
242–43n10